# CROFT'S CROSSING

## A North Yorkshire parish in the mid-twentieth century

Kathryn Streatfield

*Crofts Crossing*

Published by Country Books
*an imprint of*
Spiral Publishing Ltd

Country Books
38 Pulla Hill Drive,
Storrington, West Sussex, RH20 3LS

email: jonathan@spiralpublishing.com
paul@spiralpublishing.com

www.spiral-books.com

ISBN 9781739530389

© 2024 Kathryn Streatfield

The rights of Kathryn Streatfield for this edition have been asserted in accordance with the Copyright, Designs and Patents Act 1993.

All rights reserved. No part of this publication may be reproduced, stored in a retrieval system, or transmitted, in any way or form, or by any means, electronic, mechanical, photocopying, or otherwise, without the prior permission of the author and publisher.

British Library Cataloguing in Publication Data.
A catalogue record for this book is available from the British Library.

Printed and bound in England by
4edge Limited, 22 Eldon Way Industrial Estate, Hockley, Essex SS5 4AD

Cover design by Genevieve Lloyd

*Dedication*

*I've decided to dedicate the book to Charlie Headon,
an indomitable shaper of life in Croft, and my first interviewee.
A first class purveyor of Community Glue.*

*To Charlie Headon
(1932 – 2020)*

# CONTENTS

**5**
Introduction

**9**
Prologue: The village in 1930

**17**
Chapter 1: What is 'Croft'?

**27**
Chapter 2: A Croft Childhood

**61**
Chapter 3: The Impact of World War II

**107**
Chapter 4: Bust and Boom

**149**
Chapter 5: Living on the Land

**195**
Chapter 6: Community Glue

**213**
Epilogue

**215**
Appendix A: Croft Voices

**219**
Appendix B: Maps and Aerial Photographs

**231**
Bibliography

**234**
Index

# Introduction

**T**his project started with Charlie Headon and his scrapbooks.

We had moved to The Moorings in summer 2016, and we'd been told by Peter Young, the previous owner, that we were the fifth owners since the house was built in 1911. Peter and his wife had bought the house from Charlie. Once all the labours of getting the house and garden straight were done, I started to research the other two owners (Mr Chambers, who built it, and Dr & Mrs Tindall). In due course Charlie was invited for lunch.

He arrived with three groaning carrier bags full of scrapbooks; scrapbooks containing his own photographs, newspaper clippings and various leaflets about events in Croft during his lifetime, mostly. That piqued my interest – a lot. I'd been interested in the history of Croft for a while so I decided to interview Charlie after another lunch. His was the first interview – on 4 March 2018. He was quite frail by this point so the interview didn't last that long but it was fascinating. I decided to do more interviews and started making a list of people to talk to.

My original intention was to publish a book full of interviews but, being interminably curious, I also started to do research about things people were talking about. Consequently this book is a blend of memories and stories from the people who have been interviewed (some by me, some by Georgie) alongside my own research. However the interviews have led my research, so that is why I have focussed on the period 1930 to 1990. The oldest interviewees could just about remember the early thirties and 1990 seemed a suitably recent end point. The ' Croft Millennium Book', produced by the Parish Council in 2000, exists to describe the last years of the twentieth century.[1]

Covering this period has given me some challenges, notably because of data privacy. Dead people do not have data privacy rights, but the living do, so I have had to make editorial decisions about revealing personal information and publishing photographs, seeking explicit permission wherever I can. Also, because of data privacy and the '100 year rule' some information in official records has not been available to me.

I've written the book primarily for someone who is interested in Croft, rather than necessarily someone who knows Croft. However, I haven't explained every reference in the interviews, there are far too many of them. Instead, I have added several maps (Appendix B) and made a lot of use of footnotes. I also hope that there is enough colour and detail for the contents to interest anyone who is curious about Yorkshire or Britain during this mid-twentieth century period. It was a period of great national change. The period 1914 to 1991 has been described by the historian Eric Hobsbawm as 'The Age of Extremes' as it encompasses some of the most dramatic changes in the modern period. Two world wars, numerous revolutions, the cold war and countless other struggles, the nuclear bomb, globalisation, a revolution in social customs and behaviour, men on the moon, unheard of wealth and technological advance, but also population explosion and horrifying famine. Such upheavals caused faint tremors in places like Croft, but even these had their effect.

This book is not a complete history of Croft and it does not cover every topic of interest. It's a bit lacy: has threads and patterns but also lots of holes. Where other books or articles cover material in depth I refer to them rather than repeat what they say. For example, I say relatively little about the operations on the Aerodrome because it is covered copiously in Alan Todd's book[2] and now a new book by Bob Middleton[3]. However, I do talk about the impact of building and having the Aerodrome in the parish and I hope I add something to the material in both of those books.

I'd like to think that the book will stimulate others to fill up the holes with new memories and new research.

Also, there are two things that I am not: (1) I am not a proper historian and I don't have a detailed grasp of national history in this period. I've tried to put Croft events in context, but am very aware that really understanding that context needs a lot more knowledge than I possess. If I've learned anything about myself in writing this, it's that I know too little about practically everything. I just hope I know enough to have written an enjoyable book! (2) I am not a local person. I'm not even from the North of England, so I'm looking in as an outsider. That could be an advantage in seeing the whole picture and certainly, I may, at times, point out things that don't fit with local viewpoints.

I owe a great deal to a range of people.
- The people interviewed of course who are listed in Appendix A. I hope they feel their input has been given just attention and due respect.
- Special thanks to staff at North Yorkshire Record Office and Darlington Local Studies, but also the National Archives, Historic England and several other archives who I have pestered with queries. Also the British Library. Archivists/librarians are invariably helpful and too often unsung.
- All those who gave advice on the mechanics of publishing and copyright,
- Thanks to several people who helped identify the car and date for the picture in the Prologue page 12: notably Stuart Skilbeck and Jeremy Pattison of Tennents Auctioneers.
- Chris Lloyd has been a big help in sourcing newspaper picture has responded to numerous queries from me with laudable patience
- Kerry Craddock Of Business Friend has been a big help with interview transcription but I acknowledge the part played by otter.ai in transcribing the nearly 100 hours of audio I collected from the interviews
- The many people who reviewed the first draft and gave me honest feedback. Notably my great friend Kate Berkeley, Juliet Hill, Ian Dougill, Gillian Sulley and Ana Richards.
- Special thanks to Paul Lawrence and Jonathan Taylor for all their help in guiding this work through production, and to Joanna Luke for proofreading and indexing.

I should also note that I have a vast amount information, including the full interviews, that hasn't made

## Introduction

it into the book. I'm considering how to make that available to those who are interested.

Last but by no means least, gargantuan thanks to my partner Georgie, for putting up with my absences and absent-mindedness, for listening to me droning on, for doing a big swathe of interviews and for enticing people to lunch with her superlative cooking! Couldn't be done without you, I owe you, I hope it was worth it.

I'd like pay special tribute to departed friends. All those notable Croft people who spent time talking to me and who have since passed on. I'm lucky to have heard them, their voices are precious and live on in the pages that follow:

*Mary Andrew,*
*Doris Cameron,*
*Bill Chaytor,*
*Charlie Headon,*
*Peter Metcalfe,*
*Bob Middleton,*
*Bert Walker,*
*Mike Wood*

---

**Endnotes**
1 Published by Croft Parish Council. Various people in the village have copies.
2 Alan A Todd, *Pilgrimages of Grace: A History of Croft Aerodrome*, Alan Todd Associates, 1993
3 Robert J. Middleton and Daniel R Middleton, *Luck is 33 Eggs: Memories and Photographs of an RCAF Navigator*, 2021. Available by print on demand via Amazon.

## LIST OF ABBREVIATIONS

**Ancestry**: www.ancestry.co.uk
**Croft PC**: Croft Parish Council (Civil Parish)
**CSLG**: Croft School Headteachers Logbook
**CSMM**: Croft School Management Committee Minutes
**CWAEC**: County War Agricultural Executive Committee
**D&S**: Darlington & Stockton Times
**KellyNEY**: Kelly's Directory North and East Ridings of Yorkshire
**MAF**: Ministry of Agriculture and Food
**MoH**: Ministry of Health
**NE**: The Northern Echo
**NRCC**: North Riding Division, Yorkshire County Council
**NRRD**: North Riding Register of Deeds
**NYCC**: North Yorkshire County Council
**NYRO**: North Yorkshire Record Office
**OS**: Ordnance Survey
**PCC**: Parochial Church Council
**RCAF**: Royal Canadian Air Force
**RDC**: Rural District Council
**RDC RB**: Rural District Council Rate Book
**Richmondshire DC**: Richmondshire District Council
**RoP**: Croft RDC Register of Plans
**TNA**: The National Archives
**W(R)VS**: Women's (Royal( Voluntary Service
**WI**: Women's Institure
**YP**: The Yorkshire Post

*Prologue: The village in 1930*

# PROLOGUE: THE VILLAGE IN 1930

To begin at the beginning. It is early morning on the 8th of March 1930 and a thin grey light is spreading across the pitch dark village. The fields are white with recent snowfall, the roads white and brown from footsteps and passing traffic, which is sparse. Frost and snow makes footsteps sound like crumpled cellophane. The houses are beginning to wake and yellow shafts of light fall from windows onto the surrounding trees and gardens. Smoke goes straight up from the rows of chimneys. There is a low fog in the damp air. The river exhales, and its breath hangs heavy over the water.

Farmers are preparing to milk and feed. Others are getting ready to cycle or bus to work. There's a hum from the Turnbull & James bus garage, opposite the Rectory garden, behind the hotel, as buses are warmed up for the early run into Darlington. They will run all day until the last bus from Darlington at 10.45 in the evening. And children are rising too, ready for a long walk to school in some cases, although some only needed to walk across the road.

In the Croft Spa Hotel, spread along the road north, watching and waiting by Croft's historic bridge, Mr Ernest Hinde is also getting ready for his day. Ernest's life had been in brewing, in Darlington, but in 1928 he'd bought the Croft Spa Hotel as a retirement project. The outgoing owners – Mr Loris Dingle and his wife Mary – had bought the hotel in 1921 from Sir Edmund Chaytor, fifth baronet of Croft and Witton Castle. It was hard work to make the hotel pay and the Dingles decided to sell. Ernest was approaching retirement from the brewery so he bought the hotel in 1928. He had put in a manager who left a few months ago. He'd just advertised for a new manager, and had appointed one. Mr DuGay was due in a weeks time, so Ernest was taking some time to reside in the hotel and really understand what needed to be done to make it viable. In March 1930 the hotel was not busy because the weather that year had been exceptionally cold and wet. In January there had been a big flood, just after New Year. As usual, it was the Durham side of the river that had suffered most, with only the tops of the riverside railings visible above the flood water, but passage on the Northallerton to Darlington road was impossible for several days due the flooding of the Spa Beck and all low-lying farm land by the river had been awash.[1] However, the hotel had persisted with their schedule of dances and events as far as possible and there were often visitors from County Durham – Sunderland and Hartlepool particularly – who arrived by train. The trains could always get through and the route from the station, just about a quarter of a mile, was usually passable. The petrol pump at the front of the hotel – close to where the carriages used to be parked in earlier times – might be in use today but there would be few private cars. Since the New Year,

A postcard image of the New Spa bath-house when it was still in operation.. Undated, but clothes indicate early 1930s.

business had been slack, and the last few weeks had been one long snowfall.

The Spa Hotel had always been an established part of local life in the past. People used to come and stay in order to hunt, or to 'take the waters' at the baths. All major local events – social occasions, auctions, weddings and funerals – would be at the Croft Spa. But things were changing. The spa trade was much diminished, especially since the tragic death of Mr Riseborough a couple of years back.[2] Even local organisations were going elsewhere. Only a couple of months ago the Croft Farmers had their 36th annual ball in *Richmond*. At the Kings Head Hotel in fact. The paper was full of how good a ball it had been. '*... was attended with the utmost success. Dancing commenced at 8 p.m. and was continued until 3.30 this morning, music being provided by Trumpet-Major Parkin's band.*'[3] Pah, thought Ernest. And what was wrong with the magnificent ballroom at the Croft Spa Hotel? Ernest made a note to contact Mr SG Simpson, chair of the Croft Farmer's committee and farmer at Old Spa Farm. The 37th ball was certainly *not* going to be in Richmond.

There were more and more cars on the road now but only well-off people, or people who needed them, like doctors and vets, had them. The new Austin Seven which was about to be launched cost £140, while the average take-home wage was around £1 10/- for a 50 hour week. In Croft itself, the Rector had a car and so did Captain Parlour at Monkend Hall. Dr Tindall had a car but he lived in Hurworth, at Chatwin House. The Chaytors – Alfred and his wife Dorothy, and their son Christopher (always known as Kit) – out at Clervaux Castle would have cars.  Lady Wilson-Todd at Halnaby Hall would definitely have one. Buses yes. Trucks maybe. But ordinary people could not think of owning a car. Most farm work was still done by horses.

Ernest was very aware that a hot topic in the local papers was the Government decision to raise the

## Prologue: The village in 1930

minimum wage for farm labourers. For example, to 32/- for a 50 hour week if you were a horseman and a householder, or 43/- if you were a stockman or shepherd. Casual workers were to be paid 6d an hour.[4] The Agricultural Wages Board now set minimum wages for farm labourers and the farmers were hopping. 'How can we raise wages when prices are flat or falling? I'll have to lay men off' they'd say. Ernest had heard them getting hot under the collar in the bar at the back of the hotel. They would come in for NFU meetings or maybe after the Darlington market on Tuesday on their way home. The farm labourers were equally mad that they were being denied a living wage while some farmers, they said, kept cars to drive to market in. Some of the letters in the Darlington & Stockton Times had got quite nasty. In one exchange, a farm worker hit back at a farmer noting '... if the farmer's wife reaps no reward for her work, what does the hind's wife reap?[5] Nothing but worry as to how to make the most of a small wage, and a breakdown in health through living in houses not fit for animals.'[6] It would be interesting to know what Captain Dugdale thought. Captain Dugdale was the local MP. A Conservative, he was currently campaigning on the theme of 'Empire, Employment, Economy' for re-election[7] but Ernest hadn't heard what he thought about farm wages.

Anyway, Ernest thought, it's all about motor transport now. The Great North Road was no longer the main road north, the A1 had been built to the west of Croft and that was taking the traffic away from the road through Croft. "We need to get into the Automobile Association Hotel Guide, then we will be on the map!" he said to himself. He wondered why he was keeping on the large stable at the back of the hotel, a remnant from coaching days. There weren't many horses in it. Maybe he should let the stables out. Or build something else there.[8] Not to mention the garden on the south side... why did a hotel need it's own garden when there were three market gardens already in the village? Surely they could provide all the hotel needed.

One blessing of the cold was that Mr Thornton at Strawberry Cottage, just along from The Limes, would have his cows in the yard and there wouldn't be a hold-up while he drove them, at leisurely pace, from the field across the Northallerton Road to his milking parlour. That permanent trail of mud and cow dung across the road was not the best introduction to Croft or the hotel. The modern guest would expect better. What people wanted was a bit of glamour, something to take them away from the humdrum. They wanted dancing, music, cars, golf, swimming! Ernest frowned. Yes, this hotel really did need a bit of updating.

The morning light is stronger now and the village is stirring. Lawrence Headon, who had recently moved in at number 2 South Parade, was taking his bicycle out of the back gate into the lane. There was a layer of frozen mud under his feet which crunched at his every step, the bare trees were glistening white, birdsong was starting. That always cheered up these early morning starts, the first sound of birdsong, or maybe a woodpecker in the woods around Monkend Hall. But it was so cold, and he had a longish ride to his job at Black Banks Chemical Works. He'd had a good breakfast. His wife Ada always left eggs and bacon out for him to cook. He never saw the boys – Jim and Jack – much in the morning although they too had to get up for work as they'd both left school, Jim last year after he turned 14 and Jack before that.

Further out from the hotel, beyond the bus garage, was The School and the Schoolmaster's House.

A scene outside Croft Rectory in the early Thirties. Experts tell me the car is an AC Royal from about 1930/31. If the clergyman in the picture is the Rector of Croft, it would be Harry Tompkins at this date.

In the Schoolmaster's house, George Fell, the headmaster, had just started breakfast. His wife Jean was waking their two daughters, who could afford to get up a little late as they only had 20 yards to walk to school! George had just been out to the privy at the back and noted the cold. Another icy walk for all the farm children, they'd need their heavy overcoats and knitted gloves and hats. Thankfully the school's coke boiler was strong and the School House stayed warm – the janitor would have been up early to stoke it. This was more than could be said about the toilets which were cold and, too often, especially in freezing conditions, blocked. A Victorian National School house had had no accommodation for toilets – buckets were thought perfectly adequate – so the addition of toilets, in a block attached at the back, was not entirely successful. They were now a problem. The drains couldn't cope. He would have to approach Reverend Tompkins about it and get something done. Perhaps Reverend Tompkins could speak to Captain Parlour, who was on Croft Rural District Council as well as being a Churchwarden and who had a lot of clout. The council might be thinking of sending the Sanitary Inspector round, and that wasn't to be welcomed. Also there might have to be planning permission if alterations were to be made. The church would have to pay of course.

He looked out his back window across the field on the south side of South Parade. He could see lights on at Inness's market garden although they would not have so much to do today given the weather. A large orchard of apples, plums and pears needed work for sure but it was too cold to start spring pruning. The vegetable and fruit garden on the other side of the road, which used to be Robert Beswick's, would be facing a similar day.

The Schoolmaster's house was almost opposite the Smith family at 1 South Parade and they also had a very large garden, on the East side. Then there was The Rectory, which had a huge one with a large

*Prologue: The village in 1930*

T-shaped glasshouse put in by one of the Victorian rectors. The rector was now Harry Tompkins who'd come a few years back. George himself had come to Croft School as Headmaster in 1925, and Reverend Tompkins came in 1927. Just as well the latter had David Fyfe, his gardener, installed at Rectory Cottages. What with parish duties and being head of the School Management Committee, there wasn't much time for Rev Tompkins to do gardening.

Mr Fell took a look a little further up South Parade to Mr Chambers house[9] and The Gable. Mr Chambers was a very elderly man now, although his wife was younger and they had one servant. But George just liked to see they were up and about. And Mrs Zelasko too at The Gable, because she too was elderly and lived on her own now both her daughters were married. These, with Headons at number 2 were his immediate neighbours. George knew almost everybody in the village centre, around two hundred of them, and those farming families that had children at his school, which wasn't all by any means.

From the village you cannot see the spread of Croft's farmland – over 4000 acres of it. The soft undulation of hills tumbles outward, offering patches of woodland dense enough to make the wanderer feel hidden and alone The whisper and dapple of leaves in the breeze, the sudden crack of a twig, stumbling over roots, stumps and creature holes, but also small oases of grass and, yes, springs. The woods around Croft have those famous springs, becks and sometimes pools. The springs have names, Sweet Well, Canny Well, Iron Well. Then there is Old Spa Beck formerly the Sunnebeck, The Stell and Clow Beck. And here and there, farmhouses and byres, cottages and barns tucked into the land folds by rough lanes.

Out near Halnaby Hall, Captain Frederick Scarth Beadon was preparing for a busy couple of weeks.

**This Croft School class photo allegedly contains Jim Headon somewhere. Jim was born in 1923 so the photo is probably 1929-30. The class are seated in the school yard, with The Moorings and The Gable behind them.**

It was March, coming up to Lady Day, when farm rents would be due, and the time when his job, as Land Agent for the Halnaby Estate, was to take stock of returns on land and consider whether there should be rent rises. He needed a meeting with her Ladyship because it was a difficult time for farmers. He couldn't see how they could risk rent rises when some were struggling to survive. Lady Wilson-Todd tended to be indulgent with tenants but this wasn't the time to recommend she put her foot down. Agriculture was depressed and everyone felt it.

**A pre-WW2 picture of the front of Halnaby Hall.**

The Captain had his family home in Winston, but inevitably found himself staying over at Halnaby from time to time because Winston was about 14 miles away. He had the most marvellous room, one of 14 principal bedrooms (there were another 10 smaller ones), overlooking the mature woods and gentle rise of farmland all around, white and lit by a pale sun this wintry morning. Above the trees, some geese rose from the lake. It was perfectly peaceful and magnificent.

Even though it was 12 years since the end of the war he still woke up sometimes with the sound of guns in his head. He'd been back there in his dream. He'd been lucky, he'd avoided France until 1916. He'd been awarded the Military Cross, but sometimes wondered why. And why he was alive to enjoy this morning while others were not.[10]

He pushed the thoughts away. You know, it had to be said that Lady Wilson-Todd was excellent at choosing pictures and furniture and such things. The decorative quality of the Hall could not be faulted. This was not his forte but he could appreciate the talent. Only a coal fire in a grate though, so chilly on this cold morning. The Hall seemed lonely since the death of her ladyship's husband, Captain William Pierrepont Wilson-Todd, in 1925. And all of that on top of the death of her only child, James, in 1919. He felt sorry for her, alone in the Hall with just her servants for company. A woman of her class could never really be friends with servants. It was said she had a good relationship with her chauffeur, Mr Lindboe.[11] He lived in North Lodge and she would phone through for him. He was the only person on the estate with a phone, other than the Hall. As a member of the landed classes her ladyship was invited to a lot of do's – weddings, christenings. funerals. Johan Lindboe would drive her in her Rolls-Royce as he would drive her to Croft Church on a Sunday. She liked to go to church because it was usually full and she liked to make an appearance and sit in the Milbank pew. That was the only time her ladyship went to Croft, unless it was to attend an event. She did invite the girl guides up for a day in the summer, and she'd go to the church fete. She liked to help the school. But she didn't go down to the village much. The Hall still hosted shooting parties and there were occasionally point-to-point races but not so many events these days. It wasn't what she liked. She sometimes talked about her childhood in Edinburgh. They'd lived in Moray Place and there was a dance or a dinner every week. It wasn't much fun being a ladyship, unless there were other ladyships around to talk to.

Beadon made his plan for the day. Farmers would likely be around the farmstead, because of the weather. He'd perhaps catch them and find out, from the horse's mouth, how things were going. He'd pick up his favourite horse from the stables, ride over and have a chat, none of the farms were that far from the Hall. The tenants could be a little guarded with him, but he had a way of getting the information he needed. It was important to understand them. How else could he give good advice to his employer? And at the end of the day, these local people were the heart of England, the war had taught him that. King and country needed them to prosper.

It is now almost 8 o'clock. Darkness is gone and an ethereal light shines from the snow on the field in front of The Terrace sloping down to South Parade outside George Fell's house. The many terraced houses on South Parade, The Terrace and Monkend Terrace are coming to life as people step out, shovels and brooms in hand, to clear steps and paths. Children's voices echo as they arrive for school. The staccato chatter of neighbours exchanging greetings can be heard, and then some horses' hooves and a rattle of cartwheels. Farmers bringing grain by cart down to the Mill for the Wilson family to grind into flour. Despite the cold, the mill dam would still be flowing from Clow Beck. The dark and mighty presence of the River Tees, swollen by union with the Skerne, roars on under the seven ancient arches of Croft Bridge. The river is still high from January's big flood. You could get close to the surge and the noise by standing at one of the parapets of the bridge. It was thrilling staring down an the tumult, full of torn branches and twisted threads of water. But if this snow melted quickly the waters would soon disgorge across the roads and the nearby fields. Spring flood was familiar.

So here it is then, the stage is set, and our sixty year story of Croft is about to begin.

---

**Endnotes**
1. D&S Times, 4 January 1930
2. Arthur Riseborough was the manager of the New Spa bath-house, situated on Northallerton Road, on the right as you leave Croft. It's not there any more (see my chapter 'Erasing the Past'). On 8 August 1928 he was killed while cycling just outside the entrance to the Spa. He was a good example of a community 'good egg' and I've included his obituary in the D&S Times at the end of this chapter.
3. D&S Times, 11 January 1930
4. Rates announced in the D&S Times 1 March 1930 and payable from 14 May that year.
5. 'Hind' is a north country term for a hired labourer.
6. D&S Times, 11 January 1930
7. In March 1930 the Labour Party were in power, having narrowly formed their second ever government in June 1929. However, they did not have an overall majority, were dependent on the Liberal Party for voting through legislation. and were faltering. The view was that they could fall soon. In fact, they lasted until August 1931, and a General Election was held in October that year. Captain Thomas Dugdale (C), having beaten a Liberal candidate in 1929, was re-elected for Richmond (Yorks) unopposed in 1931. In 1935 he was elected again against Liberal opposition with 77% of the vote. He remained MP for this constituency until 1959, when he was replaced by Timothy Kitson (C).
8. The stables were advertised to let in the Yorkshire Post in May 1930. And then in 1936 the garden was replaced by the outdoor swimming pool (see Chapter 8: 'Good Times'). At some point around this time the stables were greatly reduced in size and a garage business set up to the rear of the hotel.
9. Now The Moorings
10. Frederick Scarth Beadon joined up in 1914 when he was 30. He belonged to the 18th Battalion Durham Light Infantry and was stationed in Egypt until late 1915.
11. Johan Lindboe was a Norwegian man who had married a woman from Lancashire, Emma Binks. He came to Halnaby in the late 1920s and stayed on after the estate sale. He was employed as a chauffeur and handyman. After the estate sale his daughter Margarete Smith lived in North Lodge, and he'd had a cottage built for himself at the back. Lady Wilson-Todd left Lindboe £500 in her will.

*Chapter 1 – What is 'Croft'?*

# CHAPTER 1

# WHAT IS 'CROFT'?

The village of Croft-on-Tees (Croft, Yorkshire not Cheshire or Leicestershire or any where else where there is a Croft) is pressed hard against the boundary between the county of North Yorkshire and County Durham. This boundary runs invisibly down the middle of the River Tees and has always separated Yorkshire and Durham. The impressive Croft Bridge which crosses the Tees is half in one county, and half in the other. There has been a bridge here since at least the early fourteenth century and the site was probably a crossing place even before the bridge. A sign in its middle says 'Welcome to North Yorkshire', and on the other side 'Welcome to County Durham – Land of the Prince Bishops'.

Whenever there is a new Bishop of Durham a medieval ceremony is performed on the bridge. It occurs when the new Bishop, following his consecration by the Archbishop of York at York Minster,

**The year is 1986 and David Jenkins has just been consecrated Bishop of Durham. According to ancient tradition, here he receives the Conyers Falchion from the Mayor of Darlington as he enters County Durham on Croft Bridge.**

travels north on the old Great North Road (now the A167) to the very edge of Yorkshire on Croft Bridge. Here he is met by a dignitary representing the County of Durham and is presented with an ancient and powerful sword – the Conyers Falchion, which dates from the 13th century – in acceptance of the Bishop as overlord and protector. These words are then recited:

> *My Lord Bishop, I hereby present you with the falchion wherewith the champion Conyers slew the worm, dragon or fiery serpent which destroyed man, woman and child; in memory of which the king then reigning gave him the manor of Sockburn, to hold by this tenure, that upon first entrance of every bishop into the county the falchion should be presented*

There's a lot to be said about this ceremony, and the Conyers Falchion, and the legend of the Sockburn Worm, referenced in the ceremonial speech, not least because the falchion and the worm are believed to have informed Lewis Carroll's poem *Jabberwocky* ( Lewis Carroll's family (his real name was Charles Lutwidge Dodgson) lived in Croft from 1843 until 1868 because his father was Rector of Croft). I'm mentioning it because it is an illustration of the importance of Croft Bridge, and indeed Croft, as a boundary and crossing place. It's possibly Croft's crossing that resulted in it having an early church, a Saxon church, from the 800s. There are references to a bridge in Croft needing repair in the 1300s and the stone river bed may have made it a crossing place long before that.

When crossing Croft Bridge in medieval times you were not only crossing from one county to another but from one jurisdiction to another. The 'Prince Bishops' of Durham were effectively rulers of the county, the Palatinate of Durham, granted by licence from the king in 1075. Durham was a quasi-independent 'buffer state' between the King of England's lands and those of Scotland. So crossing Croft Bridge was a big deal. And Croft was a significant place, in the medieval period, even if it was not necessarily a populous one, because of its boundary position.

But boundaries, while clearly defined, are often challenged by the ebb and flow of human activity.

It seems that the name 'Croft' is a bone of contention. I did not expect this. But listen to some of the Croft voices and it seems that the boundary of 'Croft' is a matter for discussion. Heated discussion in my experience. Some of the interviewees for this book felt strongly that there was 'one community' in their lifetime straddling both sides of the river.

**Ian Calvert** was born in Hurworth Place and lived there most of his life:

"*I was born at number three Banks Terrace* [in 1940] *which are the large houses standing at the top of the bank, the area now known as Hurworth Place. But when I was born it was all referred to as Croft, known as Croft.*"

**Molly Ingham** started her life locally on the Durham side and then moved to Oakwood in Croft in the 1960s:

"*... Croft was up the road then* [1940s] *over as far as before they altered it, you know. It went up the hill as far as the Grange and Rockcliffe. And that was all Croft. And when they changed all the boundaries, then we got Hurworth Place. It used to be, it was all Croft.*"

## Chapter 1 – What is 'Croft'?

**Margaret Horseman** lived all her life on the Durham side of the river, on Tees View:

*"But no, there was a very strong community spirit, very strong village spirit. When I was younger, you know, we, that side and this side joined together for a lot of things. And we called ourselves Croft over here. We did. I mean, I've still got notepaper with 'Croft' on it. And that's Croft post office stuff. And then they said that this is Durham, and this is technically Hurworth Place. And, you know, we must put Hurworth Place on our postal addresses and yada yada. And people still say Croft which I do because it's shorter than Hurworth Place. But what really annoys me is when people refer to this as Hurworth, and it's not. Hurworth starts at the Grange. Once you get past the Grange, then you're in Hurworth, we're in Hurworth parish. But it is not Hurworth its Hurworth Place. [...] So it just annoys us a little bit well, it annoys me, how people referred to us. We've been told not to use our identity as Croft use Hurworth Place."*

**Margaret Chapman**, who was born and lived on the Yorkshire side, remembers everything being Croft Spa:

*"Now, you see, Croft was always Croft Spa. All the time I was at school and even when I went to technical college, it was always 2 South Parade, Croft Spa. Croft Spa Station, Croft Spa Post Office, everything Croft Spa. Because I always remember Bob Nettlefriend, he said, 'I got the shock of my life when I was demobbed'. 'Cos he was away during the war and came back home and saw Hurworth* [laughs]. *'Where has 'Croft' gone to'?"*

**Ian Dougill**, born in Croft in 1933, has also been quite adamant that Croft was both sides of the river, not just what is called 'Croft-on-Tees' now:

*"The other thing in Croft, which is very pronounced, was the strange mystic barrier of the River Tees between one Croft and the other. They were so utterly different, you could say the Durham Croft was chapel, working-class, and a bit dour.* [Laughs] *The Yorkshire Croft was snobby, aristocratic, and a bit offhand. I'm now speaking as a child, but you do pick this up very quickly. Children are much better pieces of blotting paper than people sometimes realise. They don't necessarily say anything, but my God, they pick it up."* [1]

If you go back to the Domesday Book, Croft is mentioned only as 'wasted' and part of the lands of the Breton lord Enisan Musard, vassal of Alan Rufus. On John Speed's map of the North Riding dated 1610 it marks only 'Croft Bridge'. Croft was never documented as a significant settlement in those early times although it's clear from various early documents that there was a settlement of some kind. It did not have a tie to a big single estate like, for example, Coxwold, or Sledmere or Coneysthorpe, that shaped it's development for its own purposes. It did not have a tie to a big industry such as a colliery or factory mill. Nor did it develop over hundreds of years as a place to support agriculture and settlement, where labourers and skilled farm workers and tradesmen gathered together around a common green. Croft grew slowly until the nineteenth century, and the ecclesiastical parish of Croft – an ecclesiastical parish being everywhere that paid tithes to the minister of the parish, and received ministrations like mass, justice and poor relief in return – took in several administrative areas called 'townships'. These were

Croft, Halnaby, Walmire, Dalton, Stapleton, Jolby and Monkend.

During the nineteenth century a community arose and took on a shape something like the village called Croft in 1930, which is the starting point for this book, and which then became Croft-on-Tees in 1971. The pages that follow chart 60 years of development and change in the twentieth-century history of Croft, describing the lives of people certainly but also the geography, in its widest sense, and architecture of the village.

There isn't a complete history of Croft I can point the reader to. So, just as background, Croft's story after the medieval period goes a bit like this:

From 1086, the date of the Domesday survey, to the mid 1100s the lands identified as Croft – the manor of Croft – were owned by the descendants of Alan Rufus, Count Alan of Brittany who had been gifted the Honour of Richmond (roughly equivalent to Richmondshire today) by William of Normandy in 1069. Enisan Musard was lord of the 14 carucates[2] of land. In 1131 Enisan gifted 4 carucates to St Mary's Abbey in York, followed by the gift of the church which already existed. This land included the township of Monkend. Later, another Norman called Roald gave a similar amount of land to St Agatha's Abbey at Easby. This was likely to have included much of Stapleton. The land left passed into the control of the Scrope family of Bolton Castle in the mid 1200s but by this time a Robert Clervaux was resident in the district. In 1465, Robert's descendent Richard Clervaux did a land swap with the Scropes and took control of their lands in Croft, which he carefully augmented over his lifetime. He did not, however, own the township of Halnaby which was in the possession of the Place family. In the sixteenth century the Clervaux family were in want of a male heir and so their lands went to the son of a daughter – Anthony Chaytor – in 1590. And the estate, with some variances, has remained with the Chaytor family until this day when it is known as the Croft Estate.[3]

Fast forward to the late sixteen hundreds when spa waters were discovered at Croft. The Chaytor family were keen to develop the potential of the spas which were on their land. We know that spa water was being bottled and sent to London in the mid seventeen hundreds. Croft started to become a place of interest. Some cottages – Woodbine, the Limes – appeared along the Great North Road and travellers had to pay a toll to cross the bridge. The Old Spa bathhouse – close to where Old Spa Farm is today was erected in the late eighteenth century and allowed visitors to take a dip in the water as well as drink it. The water was drawn from the Canny Well, which rises in the woods behind the Old Spa Farm and the Sweet Well which rises next to the Spa Beck.

Enter Sir William Chaytor, 1st Baronet of Croft and Witton Castle (1771-1847). Sir William's vision for making Croft a kind of Spa Mini-Town set the shape of the village centre as we now know it. Over a period of 30 years (1817-1847), Sir William built the New Spa, the extended Croft Spa Hotel with Ballroom, The Terrace and South Terrace in Croft. And of course he was a significant influence on the decision to bring a passenger railway to Croft in 1836. And to call the railway station Croft Spa, even though it wasn't in Croft, or even Yorkshire. It was 'over the bridge', and the county boundary, in Hurworth Place.

What Sir William did not build was Monkend Terrace or South Parade. Because his land was bounded

## Chapter 1 – What is 'Croft'?

by the Croft to Stapleton Road, and everything north of that road and south of the Croft Mill dam/race was Monkend, with the exception of the river border and the mill itself. The two terraces certainly augmented Sir William's idea for a Spa Mini-Town but they arose from the desire of other individuals to tag along with the idea. From 1865, terraced houses of the kind you'd see in Harrogate started to be built along the Croft to Stapleton road, and the renaming of South Parade[4] cemented the impression. Monkend Terrace developed in a similar timescale. These houses were either bought or rented by genteel people or used as lodging houses for the spa trade, just as The Terrace and South Terrace were. However, the land they were built on had ultimately been bought from the Monkend estate. In the second half of the nineteenth century George Allison and Robert Bamlett had previously bought large parcels of the Monkend estate and Allison particularly was behind the building of Monkend Terrace and South Parade. The western end of South Parade was developed for market gardens, then gradually sold for housing. Monkend Hall, which probably dates from the seventeenth century and was extended in the eighteenth, was in the hands of the Bowes family up to 1925 when it was bought by the Parlours.

Furthermore, historically, Monkend was not in the Parish of Croft, due to its derivation from the former lands of St Mary's Abbey, York. It wasn't until the suppression of St Mary's in 1539 that the current Church lands became part of the Church of England and the rest of Monkend went to secular landowners. But shortly after that time, when St Marys was dissolved, what was then known as Monkend seems to have been bought by Christopher Place of Halnaby. The estate remained part of the Parish of Great Smeaton (because St.Mary's had organised it thus). It wasn't until the Local Government Act of 1894, which gave us local councils and civil parishes pretty much like we know them now that this awkward arrangement was rationalised. At that point Monkend, Halnaby, and Jolby became part of a new *Civil* Parish called Croft, and governed by Croft Rural District Council, which also governed the civil parishes of Dalton, Barton, Stapleton, Eryholme, Over Dinsdale, Manfield, Cliffe and Cleasby, and reported in to the North Riding County Council[5]. It's a bit more complicated than that, but that is pretty much the arrangement for the period covered in this book, except for the tweaks from another Local Government Act in 1974, which we'll hear about shortly.

But let's go back to the business of 'Croft Spa' and Croft being both sides of the bridge, and the accusation that 'Croft-on-Tees' is a modern invention.

Anyone who has picked up some of the many postcards of 'Croft Spa' from the early twentieth century (e.g. p22) will see that that name is used for both sides of the river. 'Croft Spa' is the Hotel, South Parade, the Spa Woods and Bath-house on the Yorkshire side. But 'Croft Spa' is also the Station Hotel, Belgrave and Banks Terraces 'over the bridge'. The post mark is 'Croft Spa'. And this is often 'Near Darlington'.

If you then look at early twentieth century Directories such as Kelly's, the same language is used. People are listed under Croft Spa, or maybe just Croft, and they are in two groups, one for the Durham end of the bridge, the other for the Yorkshire side. A Part 1 and a Part 2. Or, in the case of the Darlington Year Book for 1930[6], there was Croft (which equated to modern Hurworth Place) and then 'The other side of the bridge' (which was the Yorkshire side).

**And here we have a postcard giving greetings from Croft on Tees. Looks as though it would be mid Fifties to early Sixties. Have you spotted the anomaly? Every one of the five views shows a scene in Hurworth Place. How confusing.**

The organisation of the postal system seems to have added to this debate. In the early part of our period, letters to recipients in the civil parish of Croft could come via Croft Spa (Hurworth Place in effect), Darlington, Barton or Middleton Tyas. Some of the addresses on the Halnaby estate said 'Barton' or 'Middleton Tyas' even though the places were within the parish boundary. 'Croft Spa' was a ubiquitous address for both sides of the river during the Edwardian era when postcards were a standard form of communication and many of the postcards said 'Croft Spa' on them, referring to either the Yorkshire or the Durham side. This habit seems to have continued into the mid twentieth century. However, in the 1960s, automation and rationalisation started to reform how the postal system was organised, post started to come primarily through Darlington and more local delivery services were discontinued. In the mid 1970s postcodes were being rolled out nationally. And it was important that people addressed things correctly, otherwise automation would fail and the cost of sending a letter would rise. So there was a push to be clear about addresses at that point.

Up to the 1960s at least, people from Croft parish did much of their shopping in 'Croft Spa', although there was only ever one shop in Croft parish – Richard Raw's shop at number 3 Richmond Terrace and that seems to have disappeared by 1930. For a while 'Croft Village Hall' was what is currently the Christadelphian Hall in Hurworth Place.[7] Similarly there was never a medical or dental practice in Croft parish. The Doctor always came out from Hurworth, the nearest place that had one. However, 'Croft Spa' did not appear on any Ordnance Survey maps, not even the early Victorian ones. It was always 'Croft' and 'Hurworth Place'.

So, as far as administration, education, apportionment of monies and public accountabilities were concerned, Croft was in Yorkshire and 'the other side' was Hurworth Place in County Durham. That was always the case.

As **Margaret Horseman** notes about her early school days (Late 40s, early 50s):
*"Oh, you see, I couldn't go to school over the bridge because it was Yorkshire. We had to stay on this side of the bridge. Now they can go over there. We couldn't. So I had to go to Blackwell School, which isn't there anymore. You know where Evans Halshaw is? That boundary that they've got that that garage on is the exact same boundary where the school was, and the McCormick international tractor outlet. That was on that corner. And it's exactly the same boundary. And that's where it was, there. And the children from Blackwell village [...] went there and the children from this side of the bridge went there as well."* [8]

This whole debate came to a head in the 1970's, ahead of that 1974 reorganisation which I've just mentioned. There were two things to understand:

First, Croft Parish Council applied, in 1969 I believe, to the North Riding Council for a change of name for the Parish. There's always been a little bit of ambiguity about 'Croft' as there is a village called Croft outside Warrington, one outside Skegness and another one outside Leicester. At least. There was a wait to resolve this request, possibly because of the local government changes happening at the same time, and it wasn't until June 1971 that a change of name was granted. It was announced in the *Darlington and Stockton Times* for 12 June 1971, that 'Croft' was now 'Croft-on-Tees'. The press story said this:

### CROFT IS NOW CROFT-ON-TEES [9]

*The village of Croft has won a two-year fight for a positive identity and from this week the official address will be Croft-on-Tees.*

*The parish council felt the river name should be incorporated the village name and two years ago it asked the North Riding County Council to back the idea. This week official notices of the name change have been distributed.*

*Mr Herbert Coates, the man behind the battle to have the name changed said the new official name would save confusion. Croft mail used to come direct from Darlington, while Hurworth mail for Croft went to Hurworth Place for delivery by hand. Now mail for Croft-on-Tees will come direct to the village.*

*Mr Coates also feels the official name will prevent people thinking that Croft on Tees is in Durham.*

It should be said at this stage that the name 'Croft-on-Tees' was not new. It was in current use in Edwardian times at least. I have seen numerous pre-World War 1 advertisements in the press for the Croft Spa Hotel where the address was given as 'Croft-on-Tees'.

The second, more complicated, issue was that, during the passage of new Local Government legislation in 1971, when new counties like Cleveland, Tyne&Wear and Cumbria were created and Yorkshire had its boundaries nibbled from all directions, Croft-on-Tees so nearly ended up in County Durham.

During the twentieth century there had been several revisions to the local boundaries determined in the 1894 Local Government Act. However, none of these changed much in the North Riding and Croft RDC continued largely untroubled for some 75 years. It wasn't until 1970, when Peter Walker became the Minister for Housing and Local Government, that big changes started to be discussed. Walker was of the opinion that small communities, rural communities, were best grouped into local government units with cities or towns that could give provide modern amenities. And that conurbations were best governed as units, not across historical county boundaries. So that was the thinking that gave us Cleveland, Humberside, Tyne and Wear, Avon and other new groupings. As discussions went on, people came to expect a big shake up but when Mr Walker published his white paper in February 1971 no-one in Croft was expecting to see a proposal that the area covered by Croft Rural District Council should be part of County Durham.

There was some logic in this given the area's proximity to Darlington, transport routes and other links. The Croft Rural District Council had offices in the same building at 51 Coniscliffe Road (to 1951) and then Uplands Road up as the Darlington Rural District Council (this would have contained villages such as Hurworth, Neasham and Middleton St George amongst others).

In **Ian Dougill's** assessment of his young life in the area:

*"Darlington was always the town for Croft, Richmond was – you couldn't get to, well, you could get to Richmond, but it was a long weary journey. Everybody went to Darlington automatically. Few people went to Northallerton, people only went to Northallerton when they started getting cars. In those days, it was a bore to go to Northallerton, you just went into Darlington."*

However, the news of Croft's planned exit from the North Riding received a very firm rebuff from the RDC itself. The minuted response was that they would make it clear that they did not see any argument for this action. The council minutes note:

*Members were forthright in protestation that Croft should be included in* [North Yorkshire] *on the grounds that the district has greater affinity both historically and socially with the North Riding of Yorkshire.*[10]

They were ready to fight, resolving to write directly to the government and enlist the support of Timothy Kitson (Richmond Yorks MP), County Councillor Bill Chaytor, Alderman Parlour and other Rural District Councils in the North Riding such as Richmond (this contained villages, e.g.

Middleton Tyas and Skeeby, not the town which was a separate Town Council). This last was a good move, because in May County Durham put in a case for taking in part of Richmond Rural District as well. However, Croft RDC councillors also agreed to meet with Darlington Rural District and Darlington Borough, to discuss how these areas would come together, if their campaign did not win through.

The whole issue of the erosion of Yorkshire's boundaries rumbled on in the *Darlington and Stockton Times* for months, with Croft, along with Stokesley (who were bound for Cleveland), as the *causes célèbre*.

It was reported that the North Riding Council did not accept the case for Croft to remain with them.[11] It was reported that the Ministry of Housing and Local Government didn't either.

On 29 May the D&S came off the editorial fence and supported rural areas in:

*the belief that once merged with big towns these less thickly populated rural areas would soon lose their identity. [...] These beliefs and fears are justified [...] Judging by what has usually happened, local feeling will count rather less than administrative convenience or the theory that country and town should not be separated from each other. The rural areas are going to have to fight very hard to remain rural...*[12]

However, on the 1st of November, 3 days before the Local Government Bill was due to be put to parliament for approval, having had declarations of public declarations of support from Richmond, Bedale, North Riding and Mr Kitson, Croft still did not know where it would sit in the new arrangements.

On 4 November 1971, Peter Walker presented the final decisions in the House of Commons and everyone knew where they stood. Croft would go to North Yorkshire. The reactions to the changes were headline news and not everyone was pleased with the fact that across the North East region, the shire counties had won out on several key arguments. 'This is a victory for the hacking jacket and the Purdey gun' said one council leader from Newcastle, who was less than happy.[13]

The reaction from Croft was clear:

*At Croft, the chairman, Percy Alderson was delighted with the news that Croft Rural [District] will stay in North Yorkshire. He said:*
*This is the end of a long and involved campaign to keep our northern boundary along the River Tees. Durham wanted Croft and parts of Richmond but I am delighted they have been unsuccessful. We are all very happy about it...*[14]

Identity is a powerful thing, perhaps the most powerful in terms of human behaviour. These two episodes in 1971 tell us something about what 'Croft', at least on the Yorkshire side, then thought it was, how it viewed itself. As we go through this book we may reflect whether that sense of identity was consistent across the whole period. Was Croft always 'hacking jacket and Purdey gun'? Does it belong in North Yorkshire? Has it changed? And we will understand better that the few streets near the bridge and the river are actually a small bit of Croft parish, which has some 4500 acres, the vast majority of which are for agricultural use.

Let me declare that, in order to set a clear boundary for this book, I have taken the civil parish of Croft, as established in 1894, and renamed Croft-on-Tees in 1971, as the unit of examination. I do talk about Hurworth Place, Dalton and occasionally Barton, because there is such a close connection, but I have had to draw a line somewhere. So Croft parish it is, and the whole parish. Not only the village centre but also the majority of the parish acreage which is made up of agricultural land, estates and farms.

**Endnotes**
1. Ian Dougill's first interview @ 41.00
2. A carucate is an obsolete measure of acreage common in medieval documents. It's equivalent to about 120 acres.
3. For a rundown of the medieval land exchanges in Croft see *A History of the County of York North Riding*, published by the Victoria County History, 1914, Vol 1, pp192-71.
   The definitive account of the development of Richard Clervaux's lands is A.J. Pollard, *Richard Clervaux of Croft: A North Riding Squire in the Fifteenth Century* in *Yorkshire Archaeological Journal*, Vol 50 (1978) pp151-170. An online version is available via the Internet Archive.
4. I'm unsure of the date but postcards have 'Monkend' up until the 1900s.
5. The history of Monkend before the period covered by this book (1930-1980) is interesting and intricate. It will be the subject of another study.
6. Published by *North of England Newspapers*.
7. This is discussed in detail in Chapter 6 'Community Glue'.
8. Margaret Horseman @ 01.32
9. D&S, 12 June 1971
10. RDC minutes March 1971
11. D&S, 08/05/1971 – North Riding said they accepted the government's proposals.
12. D&S 29/05/1971 p12.
13. *Northern Echo*, 05/11/1971, p2.
14. D&S, 06/11/197, p26

# Chapter 2

# A Croft Childhood

In the 1930s the rising star of children's literature was Enid Blyton. Blyton was in turn lauded, loved and lambasted, the last most rigorously in the late twentieth century. Blyton's child heroes were independent, adventurous and fun. They adventured to islands, valleys and mountains, they knew how to sail and make camp, they outsmarted adult crooks and enjoyed an outdoor life of dens, bike rides and picnics, undoubtedly with 'lashings of ginger beer'.

At age 10 (1964), I confess that my favourite book was *The Island of Adventure* by Enid Blyton. I longed for a world of independence and daring just like the adventurous four.

But in 1982 Blyton was mercilessly lampooned by the Comic Strip's *Five Go Mad in Dorset*. A more modern adventurous four – Dawn French, Ade Edmondson, Jennifer Saunders and Peter Richardson – made their name by poking fun at their parents' heroes. Blyton was now old-fashioned, reactionary, steeped in class and racial prejudice, sexist, unrealistic and a bad influence.

My point here is that ideas of what makes a good model for childhood change, and they changed during the period being discussed in this book. But whether they changed so much, particularly in Croft, you can decide for yourself.

The story our Croft voices tell varies, depending on when they were children, whether they were farm children or in the village centre, but there is a consistent sense at all stages of a safe place rooted in the pleasures of the countryside. A place where children were relatively free and part of a community that looked out for them. Where they could have fun, make friends, learn, feel part of the landscape, be useful, but also sometimes be exposed to the divisions, challenges and injustices of the grown-up world.

This chapter explores all of those aspects through the memories of those who lived here, our Croft voices. Let's hear what they have to say.

**Doris Cameron**:

*"I was born on the 14th July 1927. The only thing I'm wondering, I can't think I was born here, but I probably was, at Vince Moor West. But I know my sister, who was six years older than me, she went down to Croft to Tees View to be born at her aunt's house.[1] I don't think I was. But, I think a doctor trailing up five fields, opening and closing five gates to get here might have found it difficult. And the doctor came from Hurworth-on-Tees. But I've lived here all my life."*

**Margaret Chapman**:

*"Charlie* [Headon] *and I were born in 1932 and '34. I was born in the bedroom at the front*

of No.2 South Parade.² And Dr Tindall was the old doctor at that time. Dr Tindall was in Hurworth. I think it's Chatwin House, the big house. The big black and white one. [...] My parents would move to Croft from I believe either Hurworth or Barton. It was all rented accommodation in those days, and they moved to Croft, where Charlie and I were born. But my two elder brothers [Jack and Jim] would also move there when they would be about six or eight, before we were born. So, they would move as two schoolboys and then we were born there. Jack was the eldest."

**Peter Metcalfe**:
"I was born at Pepperfield Farm on the 4th of November 1930. I went to school, at Croft, at five year old and left the same school at fourteen."

Up until the late 1940s it was the norm for children to be born at home, with the attendance of a midwife and maybe a doctor. Before the creation of the National Health Service in 1948, doctors and midwives had to be paid by the people calling for them. Some people could pay directly, others used different subscription schemes or poor law unions to find the money. But from 1902, the law said that a qualified midwife should attend a birth. In 1947 the rate was 1/6 for a midwife while attendance by a doctor would have cost a lot more, depending on what he had to do. From 1911, manual workers could access some health care throughout the 'stamp' – National Insurance. But this did not cover wives and children. It was possible also to get a nurse through a provident scheme run by the local Nursing Association, but it's not known whether Croft had access to one of these. Doris Cameron's sister Gladys could have been born at her aunt's house, because her Aunt Ada Bramley was a nurse.

The only doctor mentioned by our voices in this pre-NHS period is Dr Tindall. His practice was based at Chatwin House in Hurworth and he served the area from 1919 until he retired with ill-health in 1946. On retirement he came to live at The Moorings on South Parade. There has never been a medical service in Croft village – access has always been through Hurworth. Dr King succeeded Dr Tindall, and then Drs Mark and Eva Robson in 1968. Dr Ian Bagshaw arrived in 1983.³

Mary Andrew was born at Waterloo Farm, Brian Walker at Birch Springs, Alan Kirk at Bullmire. Along with Julie Clacher and Janet McKenzie these are all people who have been born in the Parish of Croft and have lived here all their lives.

Some people were born here and moved away for ever, such as Ian Dougill and David Kellie-Smith.

**Ian Dougill**:
"I was born in 1933. So I think [my parents] had moved in at the end of '32 or the beginning of 1933 [to 5 South Parade]. It was their first home as a family with a child. And if you ask me where they were living prior to this, you know what it is with parents, you know everything about them, and you know nothing about them. I don't know."

**David Kellie-Smith**:
"So I was born in Croft. Where my goddaughter Kate now lives – at the Hall [Croft Hall]. In 1940, Dunkirk days to be precise."

## Chapter 2 – A Croft Childhood

Some were born here, went away, and came back – Sandra Veerman and Alison Kennedy, for example.

**Sandra Veerman**:

*"I was born in Croft. At Monkend Hall. Actually I was born in the maternity hospital in Northallerton. So I'm true North Yorkshire! That was in 1949. And brought up like John* [Green, her brother] *at Monkend Hall."*

**Alison Kennedy**:

*"I was born here in this house* [Sundern] *in 1974. Well, I was actually born in Northallerton. But we were living in this house."*

Others were not born here, but can account for their first early acquaintance with the village.

**John Hennessy**:

*"My father was a career military soldier. He was stationed at Catterick and my dad left the army when I was one year of age* [1964], *and he bought a house in Croft. And I don't remember this but I'm told that my introduction to Croft was being hung up on the fence* [outside 8 South Parade] *in the baby harness. I watched the removals people walk backwards and forwards and that kept me quite happily entertained for several hours."*

**Ann Reed (Carnelly)**:

*"I was born in York. And when the station was bombed* [29 April 1942] *I was 18 months old. We were evacuated* [...] *When we first moved to Croft it was in a wooden gypsy caravan my father found parked on Stairmand's market garden*[4] [...] *They had a caravan and my father bought this wooden one and Maureen* [sister] *and I slept in that."*

Whatever the means of coming to Croft it is clear from all interviewees that a childhood in Croft was one of considerable freedom and simple pleasures. There was much running around, climbing trees, playing games, dabbling in water, being inquisitive and getting in adult's hair. And this is true right across the whole period covered by this book. From Doris in the thirties and forties right up to Alison in the seventies and eighties.

**Doris Cameron**:

*"I had an absolutely wonderful life. I was the best wanderer there was in the district. And my mother used to nearly go purple. Audrey Biglin lived on the next farm,*[5] *which has disappeared, pulled down*[6] *and we used to go off together down the streams, and it was called The Stell, over there. I mean it's still there. And we used to wander. And if we got wet we used to hang our clothes out on the fence and then put them on to come home.* [...] *And the mothers, I think, used to go mad. But we used to have ponies as well. We used to go riding. We had dogs. So we always had dogs. But we used to wander around here. But one wonderful time, I was a bit older, I think I was actually, I might have been fourteen, fifteen,* [...] *I decided, I always had two dogs with me, I walked over to Clervaux* [Castle], *private land, and thought I'd get in through the window. And I got in. This is before they pulled it down. And I got in, and I think I had a friend outside who pushed me*

*and helped me. And I got the dogs in, in this most beautiful ballroom. I've never seen anything so beautiful. And a staircase. So I was just ready to go up the staircase because I was so interested in Clervaux Castle[7] and then a voice shouted through the window, 'What are you doing?' So I said, 'I'm going home.' He says, 'Right, I will see you home.' And it was a policeman."*

Both Doris and Mary Andrew talked about the free access to places on the Halnaby Estate before it was sold.

**Mary Andrew (40s and 50s)**:
*"It was just, you know, a childhood, I had a sister and a brother and we just ran wild. I don't have another word. Really, you know, we used to just run around the farms. Because then before the estate was broken up, anybody could go just anywhere and went anywhere because the roads were just free for all, very different to what it is now."*

It's important to understand that people did not a travel a great deal, there weren't always opportunities to, particularly if you were in a farming family.

*"No, we didn't leave the farm very often. I had a relative. Well, she wasn't a relative, but we always called her auntie, and uncle, you know, and they took us for a week's holiday in the summer, somewhere where you went and took your own food and you went to a lodging house. You know, that was it. We never never had a holiday as a family. No. But when I got older and was able to do more on the farm, then mum and dad did have little holidays on their own. But we were old enough to stay at home. No, never had a holiday with them. We had a biggish extended family. Dad was one of one of eight and Waterloo Farm was the home, that was where they all came to. We saw family but we didn't go very far."*

The distinctiveness of later childhood for farm children is illustrated by the activities of the Croft Young Farmers' Club. The club was open to anyone under the age of 21 but younger teenagers participated. The Croft YFC was started in 1932 and the breeding, care and sale of livestock was integral to its activities, as well as organising social events for members. They had an annual show which was always held in the back field at Monkend Hall. It was reported that in the early years they had 70 members but it was reported in 1939 that this had dropped to 30. At this point, Captain Parlour was the president and Lawrence Arnett the club leader, with Peter Parlour of Dalton the chairman.[8]

Another farm child was Brian Walker, born at Greenbank Maternity Hospital in Darlington in 1954, but he has lived at Birch Springs all his life. He recalled a similar childhood to Doris and Mary, roaming freely and having mostly his own sister Ann and his cousins David and John at Portobello Farm as companions. Or having running races with Ian Cameron on the old aerodrome tracks. Childhood on the farms often came with privations as well as freedoms. Before the 1960s farms in the parish did not have piped water or electricity. Heating was sporadic.

**Peter Metcalfe** remembers Pepperfield Farm in the 1930s:
*"Electricity? We had nothing. We had a lamp in the middle of the table. An oil lamp. We had to*

## Chapter 2 – A Croft Childhood

From the early 1930s the Croft Young Farmers had an annual show hosted by Monkend Hall. This 1936 picture shows a young Ruth Thurlbeck of Paradise Frm proudly holding her prize-winning calf.

*go to Dalton to the pub and they had a container with paraffin in. Get a gallon the paraffin and took it back to Pepperfield for the stable lamp to go and milk. And I used to go with me father to milk, as I remember, but I had two brothers. And when we come back into the house, the lamp was in the table. And that was sat there all night."*

**Ann Reed** lived in the village centre but also remembers how basic things could be in the 1940s: *"Where the old baths were,⁹ that was three cottages. And we had the one nearest – we moved from the caravan to the old cottage. The nearest one to the woods. And Chaytors owned the other two. We had running water but no electricity. We used to have to walk from there to the Spa Hotel, where there was the Garage. And we'd have to walk there with the accumulators to get them charged up for the radio. And of course, oil lamps. And not just a tin bath, a hip bath.*

*And eat your hearts out kids, to be able to go upstairs to the loo. We had to go across the back. And there were three dry toilets that were shared between the three. Most of the waste went down into the beck, because they were built out over the beck, and then into the river."*

However, life in the village centre held choices for companions and things to do.

**John Hennessy** (mid 60s to 70s):

*"We roamed far and wide. I'd be one of the older kids. We were very keen on racing around on bikes, as I mentioned before. The back woods were obviously fantastic facility. That's the woods behind South Parade. So the woods immediately behind my house, number eight, that was great for climbing trees. As a young lad, I remember mum coming down the back lane to telling me that my lunch was ready. And she was shouting my name. And I heard her shouting. So I called back to her. And she said 'where are you?' looking around for me at ground level, and I was up one of the trees at quite a considerable height. And when she spotted me, she said to me 'you just take your time coming down'. [...]"*

**Sally Still** has a memory of playing with friends around Monkend Hall:

*"They used to stook the hay in the back field. And one afternoon, at Sunday tea, we were playing Block 123 in the field, round the haystacks You had to run across past the old kennels. And the stone is still there, the corner is still there. And that was the block you had to get to, you know, Block 123 and you've won or whatever. I made the fatal mistake of hiding inside one of the hay stooks. And eventually, whoever else was there – Sandra [Veerman, nee Green] was there, Trevor [Green] was there – we all decided to do the same. Well we made such a mess of the hayricks. Were we in trouble. I don't know what punishment Trevor and Sandra got, I think I might have gotten away with it quite nicely. I think it was bread and butter and a glass of water and sent to bed. But God it was fun."*

**Sally Lilley's** childhood memories are of the 1970s:

*"[Croft was] very friendly, child friendly. You could go out and play out and nobody would worry, you know, you didn't. I used to go out on my bike up the village and or, even when I was a little kid, I used to take my little fishing rod, fishing net and go up to the Clow Beck farm and walk through the pig farm because that's where there was pig sties on either side. And I used to go through where they've they got the bridge, but then there's like that little walking bit. I used to sit on there and catch minnows and ball heads. Yeah, put them in my little bucket and then throw them back in before I went home, but I used to do that quite a lot."*

The role of the river, and the beck, was significant. Fishing was a frequent pastime and swimming was also a joy (presumably in summer!). And this was true on both sides of the bridge.

**Margaret Horseman** (born 1948):

*"I used to join in with my brother. We used to go up the river an awful lot. In those days, we used to go and swim in the river because it was a bit cleaner than it is now. And he'd go fishing and I'd probably go with him. It was a lot cleaner then though but we went above the Skerne. Don't go below the Skerne, you go above the Skerne."*

John Hennessy also remembers this. **Alison Kennedy** has extensive memories of playing in and around the river:

*"We went to the river when the weather was nice. And there was always a bit of a danger. And we*

used to go to the pig farm[10] as well and used to be down that end of the river and we would jump from the bridge onto that pathway – doesn't seem that big a distance now – and the water used to drop into a drain. [...]

I'll tell you what else was nice when we were younger. We used to have sports days. We had rafts. We'd all build a raft. So it used to be Croft, Eryholme, Dalton. And it would be a competition with village against village and you'd build a raft and race it down. But at the same time there were other races, so egg and spoon race, that kind of thing, at the same time. [...] I'm thinking it was near the wedding you know, Charles and Diana's wedding, in that age.[11]

My brother used to canoe. They used to go and take a car and leave it further up, down river, And then they used to canoe. But we just used to paddle with just the fishing stick and the net? That kind of thing.

But at one point the water was quite bad. So I think when we were young, I think a few of us got ill, but I didn't. The water pollution was bad. And that must be sort of middle eighties."

**Ian Calvert** (born 1946) had specific memories of summer by the Clow Beck:

"I think Croft was more open in those days. I mean, one thing was, it was a fantastic playground. In the summer all the children from both sides of the river would go to Monkend and your parents would go with you. You'd have a picnic. Get the blankets out. You'd have a picnic and lemonade and sandwiches. And then if it was warm enough, you'd jump in the beck and back. Then fish for pool heads sticklebacks, and go looking for different birds. You could find a kingfisher's nest up there."

**Julie Clacher** had a specific memory of 'helping' with the re-routing of the Tees in 1977, with her friend Lisa Wood:[12]

"Well, obviously we used to go in the river a lot when I was a bit bigger, we would take ourselves off. If you go along the footpath out of the church, along the footpath more or less where the sign is now, that says it's a permissive footpath, on the other side [of that]. It was a nice deep swimming bit there with a Tarzan across, that the older kids had put up. So we used to spend a lot of time there. And we also used to spend a lot of time because obviously the river changed. I remember the day they did that actually, that was, well, five days with all the work that went into it. And then finally the river changed direction. And I remember me and Lisa Wood paddling in the mud for an afternoon. Getting fish out there that were going to be trapped and die, and throwing these fish back in the river."

For teenagers, these simpler joys were not quite enough, and sometimes activity and friendship was found within an organisation.

**John Henessey** remembers:

"So, Croft was was fortunate enough to have cubs and scouts. I tried the cubs as soon as I was old enough to be able to do so. And the cubs and scouts was run by a gentleman called Ron Fletcher, who everybody knew as Skip. He lived in a little standalone house, which is on the Middleton Tyas Road. Okay, so you go past the Croft Spa woods, and then there's like a, like an S bend. Yeah. On the right hand side of those bends was the house that Ronald Fletcher lived in.[13] I think Ron

**Scouts and Cubs parade past Croft church. Date unknown but maybe early sixties.**

*worked for Bill Chaytor. But he was a very, very good Scoutmaster. exceptionally good Scoutmaster. And, I would say I probably learned as many life skills by being a member of the Cubs and the Scouts as I did actually through a formal education.*

*We used to go to Marske in Swaledale. And there was a place where we were allowed to camp. And that was great fun, we were allowed to build an aerial runway. So basically, a zip line. There was a tree at the top of quite a steep bank, and we would tie a rope around this huge, huge tree. And then we'd make an A frame. And then on this we would sling a rope with a pulley on it between the tree and the A frame. And with another piece of rope hanging off the pulley. We used to hurtle down this thing at huge speed. And when we got down to the bottom and we approached the A frame, it was essential that you dropped your head because you'd go flying through the centre of the A frame. Almost go vertical and then swing back through again, remembering to duck your head otherwise you would have taken quite a serious blow. Quite dangerous looking back on it, but super super fun."*

**Nick Kirkwood** was also a keen scout and remembers 'Skip' as a man who had:

*"knowledge of the ground and his practical abilities. He was really a guy who was in very close contact with the land and the soil and the trees and their sort of immediate environment. We did all those things, you know: fire lighting, a bit of open-air cooking, knots. But a lot of being out and about, a lot of wide games where we were roaming through the woods in groups trying to try to work our way through to avoid the other group and find your way to a destination point or move things through to a destination point. Just lots of practical things, memory games... I think we did a bit of code writing. A bit of sort of trying to hide communications that that would pass between you and all of those sort of fairly traditional scouting skills that that came from the the Baden-Powell*

## Chapter 2 – A Croft Childhood

*thinking that were almost slightly pre militaristic. It was 'What are the things that little boys would find fun, but actually have some practical value in a semi-military environment'?"*

And, of course, having the Scouts in Croft resulted in the building of the Scout Hut, which was a substantial building and served as a meeting place for the whole village from when it was built in 1967, on land leased by the Croft Estate. There was an early hut before that which I believe Ron and Bill Chaytor put up, but the later Scout Hut was the real deal. Although a prefabricated building it lasted 20 years nearly up until the new Village Hall was erected in 1986. (See Chapter 6 for this story.)

Ron 'Skip' Fletcher and scout.

**Paul Fletcher** has these memories of his father Ron 'Skip' Fletcher and the Scout meetings:

*"I'm not exactly sure but I think Mr Charlesworth, the Vicar, was running the original scout troop in Croft. When he had to move to take up a new position he made enquiries trying to find someone to take over. He discovered that Ron had been in the Scouts as a boy in Washington and eventually persuaded him to take over. Initially Ron was just scout master and Barbara Gibbon was cub mistress. At that time there was a shortage of cubs so younger boys aged 6 were allowed to enrol. That was when myself and a few lads of the same age joined* [approx. 1958]. *Not long after that Barbara Gibbon moved and no new cub leader could be found. Ron agreed to do both the scouts and cubs, and did so for the next thirty or more years, as a result of which he was commonly known as 'Skip' by any boys, and the parents who had sons in the scouts.*

*Scouting activities and various indoor games were carried out in the scout hut. Football and cricket on Captain Parlour's field. Best of all were the activities in the various woods and streams on the estate, making rope ladders, bridges, rafts, climbing trees and playing 'Wide Games' (the scout version of Hide & Seek)*

*If I remember correctly it was cubs on a Monday evening and Scouts on Friday evenings. When I was too young for the Scouts Mum and I would often walk cycle/down to the village with Dad and while he was being Skip, Mum and I would go round to Sandra Green's parents' house and watch things like Rawhide and Wagon Train on the TV which was a real treat as we didn't have a TV set in those days.*

*Dad had two weeks holiday every year. One week was spent taking the boys to Camp, the other week was spent working for John & Tom Parlour on Jolby Farm."*

There was a brownie pack in Croft run by Sue Dent, but I'm not sure that wasn't later than the period covered by this book. In the later 1980s there was also a Girl Guide troop. Margaret Horseman was involved in this and became District Commissioner for Richmond and then an Area Commissioner. The

Guides met in the new Primary School.

The Tennis Club, which started in the early Fifties (and which I discuss in Chapter 6), had a junior section, and this created new opportunities. The Tennis Courts were situated on the large green in front of the New Spa Bath-house, on Northallerton Road. Margaret Chapman, Margaret Horseman and Janet McKenzie were all members of the junior section.

Lastly, there was the Sunday school. A lot of children in Croft went to Sunday school. Ann Reed remembers attending in the Forties. Janet McKenzie, Sally Lilley, Margaret Horseman and John Hennessy all went. It was part of life for many Croft children and helped to cement a strong relationship between the church and the village, even though any child who went to Croft School attended church services regularly, and was regularly in contact with the Rector.

After the war the Sunday school was, I believe, run by Clare Kellie-Smith and her sister Betty Chaytor. During the 1970s Alison Kennedy and her brother were regular attendees:

**Alison Kennedy**:
*"Mrs. Dent did the brownies. She also did the Sunday school. So once a month on family service, I'd go. I don't know if we went every Sunday but I think it was definitely once a month we would go to Sunday school in the primary school. The [current] primary school. And then from there would walk down to the church and then either the parents would be at the church service or they would pick us up from the church service but I really enjoyed that it was just a Sunday morning thing. Sunday school started about 9 to 9.30 and lasted until the main Sunday church service at 11. A lot of it was just sort of colouring sort of stuff and fundraising. I remember this L shape money box that you put money and it was sealed, but it was for the lepers ... you put your money in, your pocket money or something like that. And then I guess Mrs. Dent just sent it off."*

Neighbours, school mates and friends from clubs were the main sorts of pal. But sometimes it was advantageous to pick your friends:

**Margaret Chapman**:
*"At the very top of South Parade I used to play with a little girl there, Heather Reynolds. And they lived in The Anchorage.*[14] *And because I was a nice little girl I was allowed to play with Heather. She went to Polam Hall.*[15] *She was a lovely girl. And she used to walk down with me and we'd go to church on a Sunday morning at half past ten – we'd be about seven or eight – and sit in the back row with Mrs Tompkins, who was the rector's wife.*
*On the other hand, there were some children on South Parade she wasn't allowed to play with. I wasn't supposed to play with them because they always had nits. The nit nurse used to set to work with them all. It wasn't the kids' fault how they were, really'."*

And sometimes friends were picked for you, either by circumstance, or by who your parents associated with. Sally Still was brought up in Hurworth up until she went to boarding school. But she came to her aunt and uncle's (Captain and Mrs Parlour's) in Croft frequently.

**Sally Still** remembers:

*"My bedroom [at Monkend Hall] overlooked, in those days, the yard. I had a very wobbly tooth. And it fell out in the night because you know how as a child you pull away and pull away. It fell into the guttering at the back.. Mr. Green, Sandra [Veerman]'s father, was gardener and Mrs. Green the housekeeper. And they lived in one end of the house. Now I had to ask Mr. Green, 'could you find my tooth?'. Because it's very precious when you're six. That was about my first, one of my first real memories. But we went down [to Monkend Hall] every Sunday for tea. Afternoon tea. And if I was very good, I was allowed to go and play with Sandra. That was my joy. Yes, because you were actually sitting with some quite old people."*

**Margaret Horseman**:

*"Going over the bridge really was a little bit verboten. We didn't mix. Our mothers were in the young wives. A lot of our mothers in the area were in the young wives which was attached to the church.[16] [...] But a lot of the ladies on that side of the bridge, were in the young wives and my mother was, so we tended to mix with the families of the children of those people. Because we were part of the church over there. We're not actually in the parish because we're in the Hurworth parish. But we went to church there. A lot of people still do."*

# Croft School

Not every child in Croft parish went to Croft School. Children from Hurworth Place or beyond were not allowed to attend Croft School until 1988.[17] Croft School served Croft parish, and then, later, Dalton, Eryholme and Girsby. Although some children from Croft parish were nearer to Barton village than Croft, and these were children on the furthermost farms like Bullmire and Waterloo. They went to Barton School. Other children attended independent schools. Furthermore, there was more than one school in Croft in the twentieth century. So 'school' in Croft is a slightly more complicated topic than you might at first think.

We'll begin with Croft Church of England Primary School. The history of the school is reasonably well charted as having been founded by Reverend Dodgson in 1845. The founding of the school, and the initial arguments about staffing, curriculum and funding is another topic, not for this book.[18] However, it is important to know that it was founded as a National School and it stayed a National School until it became a school voluntarily controlled by the North Riding Education Committee on 25/01/1949. This was following the implementation of the 1944 Education Act, a radical act that gave Education Committees the major supervisory role for all schools, although in the case of Croft, as a CofE school under voluntary control, this was in association with a School Management Committee on which the church still had a major role.

A 'National School' was one founded according to the principles of The National Society for Promoting Religious Education. This was a Church of England body in England and Wales for the promotion of church schools and Christian education founded in 1811. At that point in history the

Church of England, as the established state religion, was worried about the growth of non-conformism amongst the poor, and also a resurgence of Roman Catholicism, and the accompanying lack of standardisation in education. So the National Society was founded in order to 'to instruct and educate the Poor in suitable learning, works of industry and the principles of the Christian Religion according to the Established Church.' From the mid nineteenth century National Schools were partly funded by the state, partly by the church and 'subscribers'. It's important to understand that these National Schools were different to the Board Schools that were set up under the 1870 Education Act which came under Local Authority control much earlier, in 1902.[19]

For some of our older voices, Croft School was the only School they attended. The 1918 Education Act mandated attendance at school from 5 to 14. The leaving age was raised to 15 after 1944 and again to 16 in 1972.

The exception to these leaving ages was for children who passed the 11-Plus exam. If you passed the 11-plus you would go to Grammar School, if you were a boy, or High School, if you were a girl. And you would leave school at 16 having taken the School Certificate, or 18 if you stayed on to do Higher School Certificate. This system operated up until after the 1944 Act which not only raised the school leaving age but also created the Secondary Modern and County Secondary schools and, in 1951, replaced the School Certificates with O levels and A levels. So then, the 11-plus still selected the children for Grammar or High School, but all children over 11 went to a designated Secondary School. At this point, Croft School became a Primary School, educating 5-11 year olds.

**Doris** (at School 1933 to 1945):

*"I was a very good girl, very honest. 'Cos I used to go to Croft School. And we used to walk across the fields. And you know Paradise Farm? [...] you used to walk across the fields to Paradise, put our wellies behind their gate, put our shoes on and walk to school. And we walked back. But I'll tell you this story. The Thurlbecks – 'cos they used to live there – one night we came home from school and walking, and they'd filled our wellies with water. I think, you know, they probably thought 'this will do them good'. So when I got back up to the road to change me shoes there were me wellies full of water. But that was getting to school. Then we used to cycle. And there's no Mrs Minns to talk to is there? Well she was the angel of Croft. And she lived in The Limes, 'Cos there were two lime trees there, which have gone. And it was not big now, it was just sort of a little sloping roof at the back. And she had a shed at the back and a nice big garden. And all the people of Halnaby would never have been able to get the bus to Darlington if it hadn't been for Mrs Minns. She let us all, and you talk to people, take our bikes round the side of her house and put them in the shed, this shed, and then go over the bridge and get the bus. What would we have done if we hadn't got Mrs Minns? And her shed used to be full, and she never got a penny or anything.*

*[...]*

*And I went to Croft School. I was in the small class, which was at the far end near where the house is. It was the infant class. 'Cos the class where the yard is that was the top class. But the head* teacher was Gaffer Fell. Mr Fell. But I started school when I was five. Now I don't know whether I walked down 'cos my sister would have been at Croft School. But I only stayed a short time in infant class 'cos I thought at five I was too young, so I left and started when I was six. Well, I wasn't going to school down there when I was five and trailing down there because there's no transport and things. So I made my decision. So I started when I was five and left, and went back when I was six, [...] and then I stayed at Croft School 'til – 'cos then they stayed at Croft School 'til they were fourteen, didn't they. That's right. So I stayed 'til I was eleven. And then I went to Darlington. Darlington High School. But my sister, I think she was a bit cleverer than me, she went to Richmond High School. Well latterly I used to walk, and then I had bicycles. And then when I went to Darlington School, bless Mrs Minns, I used to leave my bike at Mrs Minns, go over the bridge, get the bus. And then walk to the High School. Without Mrs Minns we wouldn't have managed."

**Peter Metcalfe** (at school 1935 to 1945):
"The teacher was Miss Brittain for the small children. Miss Berry from Darlington in the middle class. And George Fell who lived in the schoolhouse with his wife and two daughters.

There was the school and the toilets and the cloakrooms in the middle. And it was heated by a big coke boiler in the middle class. Which you used to fill up with coke and the big pipes around the school. And there was a gardens at the back of the toilets and locker room in the field and then the behind that field was the football field. They played football in that field that sweeps up to them Chaytor's houses at the top.[20] And there was the Turnbull family in the farm there that farmed that."[21]

**Margaret Chapman** (at School 1939 to 1949):
"We had at least twenty in a class. Yes. I can remember my first day going to school, and Charlie took me, and of course he was ready to move up into the next class, and sort of I was clinging on to his hand and pushed myself on his seat, next to himself and Eric Ibbotson, another boy there. And he says, you sit here, you know. Then of course I was put in a little chair, 'cos the little ones had tables and chairs. And I can remember having little tins with plasticine in and counters. I can always remember the coloured counters there at school. Yes, there'd be about sixty I would think, because they came from Dalton, and then Eryholme.[22] One of Abbott's little buses brought them to school. And then when Girsby School closed a Neasham bus, a Neasham company, I can't remember them – they brought children from Girsby. And that would be, yes, that would be when I was about eleven, twelve, they came from there. So, it was a full school. [...]

We only ever had three teachers in all the ten years we were there, because there was no secondary modern if you didn't pass to go to the Grammar School or the High School, and that covered the whole area of all the villages. I'd never seen an exam paper 'til you got it pushed in front of you. And I wasn't aware that you could do your working – I can always remember I couldn't do everything mentally and I wasn't aware that you could work things out, you know, in margins or anything. It was a complete foreign language to me, getting this pushed in front of me.

*So, we had the infants' teacher. I can't remember my first one there. Miss Berry was for years in the middle class. And always Mr Fell, seniors. So, we only ever had three teachers. And the middle teacher – Mrs Fell used to take over as well sometimes. We were taught needlework, dressmaking and needlework and knitting and things like that. Two days a week we had that. And the boys did gardening, and I don't know what else they did. Woodwork? I don't know. They were all good gardeners 'cos there was plenty of them to work at it. [...] We had all the usual, reading, writing, arithmetic, history, geography. Poetry was very popular. We knew all the poems.*[23]

*We used to write – we used to put it on the blackboard to start with, you see, and then go through it and we used to have to write it out. First lesson was – we used to line up in the schoolyard – boys, girls, boys and girls, the top two classes. And Mabel* [Crisp, a senior pupil] *used to play the piano and we would all march in and to our seats. And then we'd have the hymn probably and a prayer. And then next lesson was the Bible. We had Bible reading. Then we had maths, which would probably take us up to break, half time. And then we had history or geography after that, then went home. And afternoon would be English. I loved the lessons. Yes."*

**Peter Metcalfe** also remembered the gardening:

*"Where the block of houses is, Carroll Place, that was all garden. Yeah, there was blackcurrant bushes. Redcurrant bushes. There was digging area for planting. And Charlie Headon was working in there as well as me and I used to like to get under a bush and eat blackcurrants. I liked blackcurrants. Charlie Headon wasn't really a farm worker – rough. He was more polite. Yeah, he had a business. He stuck the garden rake through his foot one day.*

*It was a big thing with Boss Fell, he was a big farming man and so we had so many days gardening. And Boss Fell was a big beekeeper. He used to get all his gear on and take us in to see the bees. 'Just don't do anything. Don't get excited. Then we'll be alright'."*

**John Green,** as a fourteen year old, started to find it a bit tedious:

*"The last six months I was at school Mr. Fell the headmaster said to me, he says, I think it's a waste of time to try and get you to do anything else. He says, go and spend the rest of the time in the garden. So the last six months I was in the garden."*

It's worth knowing that gardening in schools was very much something that was recommended. There was a Schools Gardening Movement that was international and dated back to the early nineteenth century. It began in Germany and Austria, had many adherents in the USA and originated from the concern that industrialisation meant that many children were not connected to nature and that they did not understand the process of growing and food production. It was an idea that persisted and became particularly strong in England in the first half of the twentieth century. The idea was that 'reading, writing and arithmetic', the basic education that all children were to have, should be supplemented with 'special subjects'. In July 1921, a school inspector took Croft School to task for not exploiting the potential of a school garden:

## Chapter 2 – A Croft Childhood

*The Head Master, who was appointed a year ago,[24] does not realise the educational possibilities of Gardening; this is largely the result of inexperience.*

*The class consists of thirteen boys, of whom four are in the 3rd year, and six in the 2nd year. It is unfortunate that much of the garden is not cultivated by the boys. There are now seven dual plots, each 36 square yards in area, and, as only six varieties of vegetables have been grown, the practical work provided is inadequate.*

*Attention is directed to the need for progressive work for the older boys and for the systematic planning of winter lessons, the necessity for keeping gardening records and for taking better care of the tools.[25]*

George Fell was appointed Headmaster in October 1925. He continued with gardening and in 1930 was able to increase the amount of land available for this use. A letter tells the Ministry of Education:

*the land used for the teaching of school gardening is no longer available, but a new plot measuring 850 square yards, adjoining the playground is now being rented for use instead.[26]*

I believe this is land referred to by Peter Metcalfe above, and that it was to the east side of the school, probably where Lewis Close is now, rather than as far as Carroll Place. To support this, I read that when the bungalows were built in Lewis Close, under the auspices of Richmondshire District Council, it was they who chose the name Lewis Close. The Croft parish councillors wanted to call it School Gardens but decided it to let it lie.[27]

In 1922, the inspectors said that the teaching of gardening had improved, although better notes should be kept, and that it had been linked with Nature Study. In 1924, the inspectors were unhappy about the progress of the older children in the school. The first report after Mr Fell's arrival, 1928, noted that his 'influence is evident in terms of improved behaviour' but that 'educational aspects of gardening still need more attention'. However progress was 'satisfactory'. In 1931 and 1934, progress was 'satisfactory' again but a 'weakness of speech and oral expression' was noted in the latter year, not for the first time.

Gardening at Croft School was for boys. Girls did not do gardening, they did needlework. Girls might be allowed into the garden to pick flowers or maybe do some nature lessons, but they did not labour or learn the practical craft. As Margaret Chapman notes, the older girls, those who had not passed the eleven-plus and continued in the senior class at Croft until the leaving age of 14 or 15, had two days a week of needlework, so we can assume the same was true of gardening for the boys.

However, what was a notable feature of education for girls was the Cookery Van. According to the school log books this was in use from 1921 at least, as there is an entry for Friday 25 November that year: ' ... Cookery Van 1 (Teacher Miss G Sharp) arrived this morning from Barton'. On 28 November it was logged that 'Cookery and Housewifery classes commenced today, 18 girls in attendance'. It seems to have been phased out after the war.

**Peter Metcalfe**:

*"...once a year used to come the girls cookery lessons. And they brought an old roly thing, like a caravan, and it was all built on wooden wheels, I think it was. I don't know what towed it there, they towed it from somewhere. Put it in the schoolyard and then the girls used to go out into this thing and somebody trained them how to cook."*

**Margaret Chapman**:

*"It came for a fortnight. And it was a great big wooden thing on massive wood, metal, wheels, and windows, not on all sides, and steps up. I remember the steps up, and I was as miffed as hell because they stopped doing it the year I was going to go. They used to cook dinners, I think as well because I can remember them coming into the school and saying did anyone want dinners that they'd cooked? And I thought oh, I'm dying to get in there.*

*I think you went in the cookery van when you got into Mr. Fell's class you see. But they stopped it. The year I was going to be going into it, it was no more and I was never so miffed in all my life. It must have come in in quite icy weather as well sometimes, because I can remember Mr. Fell saying that 'You'd better scrape the ice off the steps'. And it was quite good because when it was in the schoolyard, we could play hide and seek and you could get hid. You could hide underneath the big wheel."*

No-one who was interviewed knew what happened to the produce grown on the school garden, but Julie Clacher remembered that at least some of it was used in the preparation of school meals. Julie started at Croft School in the mid 1970s. The school kitchen was added to the school in 1945, as a separate building at the back.[28] Another entry in the School Management Committee book for 1960 mentions sale of produce, maybe to parents or at the school gate. Whatever the case, gardening lasted far longer than the cookery van, and after 1950 girls didn't get cookery lessons at Croft School.

I'm not clear when gardening ceased to be a school subject. I found an inspection report from 1960, the first after Miss Allen's appointment as Head. It was also the first inspection after the opening of the Richmond County Modern School in 1959, when Croft School became an Infant and Junior School. It's largely complimentary but contains the following paragraph...

*Needlework for the girls is based on a progressive scheme and some attractive articles are being made. Gardening is undertaken by the boys and it was felt that the large vegetable and fruit garden they attend takes up a disproportionate amount of time and effort relative to its educational value. Perhaps its conversion to lawn should be considered.*

It never did become a lawn. It became Lewis Close instead, some 22 years later.

What is also also clear from our village voices is that corporal punishment was a feature of life at Croft School from the the thirties up to the opening of the new school in 1974. And it was the head teachers who administered it.

## Chapter 2 – A Croft Childhood

As already noted, Mr George Fell became head of Croft School in 1925 and he retired in 1955. He was respected in the village and participated in village life for example as a member of the church choir and a cricketer. He also took on extra roles during the war. A portrait of George Fell and his wife Jean is at the end of this chapter. They lived in the Schoolhouse, to the west of the school, the entire time he was head. Jean also helped in the school as the middle class teacher when this was needed, and occasionally for the infants.

**George Fell was the headmaster at Croft School from 1929 up to his retirement in 1955. Here he is presented with a television set as a retirement gift. His wife Jean is beside him.**

Charlie Headon was at school from 1937 to 1947 and remembered Mr Fell well, not least because the Schoolhouse was across the road from where he lived at No.2 South Parade. The Fells' only son John died in February 1935, at the Schoolhouse. John was 7 years old. After this, Charlie felt that Mr Fell 'adopted' him as a bit of substitute son:

**Charlie Headon**:
*"… he had a son that would have been three or four years older than me, he died … And so, he sort of adopted me as a son. He used to take me all over just for company.*
*When they'd retired we took him and his wife, they lived at Bowes, we took them to The Spa Hotel about twice a year for lunch, on a Sunday, about sixteen or seventeen of us, that used to go to his school that lived in the village. And this particular time I was sitting next to him […] and I said, 'Do you know,' I said, 'I thought you were so two-faced.' 'What was the matter Charlie?' he said, 'Well – you caned me at school for doing something naughty and then at night you'd come and take me out like a father,' and I said, 'I used to think you were so two-faced.' 'Oh,' he said, 'I'm sorry about that.' He said, 'You were rather a naughty boy at times'."*

The particular thing that Charlie remembers being caned for was this…

*"the headmaster used to go out for a walk, walk in the garden, and leave us with work to do, and he'd come back and he'd walk past one window and look into our big room, and invariably he saw me dashing back to me desk."*

**Peter Metcalfe** told this story of getting a lad who was not liked into trouble with Mr Fell:
*"In school there was five to a desk. I was one of the five. There was twins, Albert and Alan Pearson. There was Stan Hardy from Dalton. And me. [And the lad they didn't like.] And Boss Fell, he was a hard man. Boss Fell was writing on the board right in front of us. We sat there and he stepped back towards where we were sat. So this lad he had a long pencil. And when Boss Fell stepped back,*

*He was grinning at us thus making a pencil imitate poking out of his backside as he stepped back. Anyway, job went wrong somehow. He must have been looking at us, and the pencil made contact with his [Mr Fell's] backside. He whipped round. 'Who did that?' Nobody spoke for a while. Then Alan said 'It was him sir'. Just like that. He took him outside and I'm pretty sure he chucked him up in the air. He howled ... howled. Because he brayed hell out of him. That was school teaching then."*

Miss Allen was also an administrator of corporal punishment, and some other things as well.
**John Henessey** remembers from the 1960s:
"She ruled with a rod of iron. She was a very, very old-school teacher. I think it was very rare that she actually had to sort of punish anybody. But she was very, very quick to jump on anybody stepping out of the line. She was a tough teacher in that respect. But she was also fair. And she was actually a very, very good teacher. I suspect I'm not the only one who left Croft primary school and found that the quality of their spelling actually deteriorated in later life."
**Sandra Veerman** (at Croft School 1954 to 1960):
"I went to Croft school until I went to Richmond School. Mr. Fell was still headmaster, when John and Trevor, two years older than me, were there. It was actually a lovely school until Miss Allen came and became headmistress and she was strict with all of us. We got the slipper or stick, or anything she could hit you with."
**Sally Lilley** had a particularly tough time with Miss Allen towards the end of the latter's career (early 1970s):
"It wasn't a good memory of Miss Allen because she was the headmistress of Croft School. You ask anybody my age and they'll tell you what she was like. She put the fear of God into every child, the fear of God. And if your face fitted you were alright. But if you were somebody like me, who was a bit quiet and sheepish sort of thing when I was little, she picked on you. She wasn't very nice. She wouldn't get away with it now. She'd be struck off. She sort of scarred me as a kid. Because I was frightened. I wasn't very good with maths [...] she would embarrass you in front of all the other kids. And it was horrible."
**Molly Ingham** had grandchildren at Croft School:
"Miss Allen, she was a character. Everybody knows her. She was the head teacher for so long. They didn't have a man teacher. So Doris used to take the place of the man teacher to take the cricket and all the activities that boys do. She was good at that. Miss Allen was a good Headmistress. But the kids said they were shivering, shivering in their shoes when she shouted. She had a lot of discipline, and it paid off in the end. [...] She wouldn't stand for any nonsense."

Alison Kennedy also came across Miss Allen and recalls a big furore when her brother Tim was hit by her. This was when his mother (Tessa Matthews) was away with Alison (who was preschool at the time). Alison recalls that her mother's view was that if he deserved it, he deserved it.

## Chapter 2 – A Croft Childhood

**Alison Kennedy**:

*"Mum was a teacher anyway. She knew Miss Allen. So she knew it must have been deserved, although mum never hit us. But I think she must have just wanted to stick up for the teacher, you know, because the other parents were complaining".*

**Julie Clacher** could see the positives in Miss Allen's approach:

*"I have very happy memories of Croft School. I mean, granted, I was absolutely terrified of Edith Allen. Although she ended up a very good friend of my mum's in the end. And when I got older, I could understand why she was like she was. She was very old school. She was very, very old school. And as a result, I would say 90% of the people who grew up in that school came out instilled with a massive respect for other people. Incredible morals, and really good work ethic as well. Which was fine."*

Corporal punishment was abolished in state schools in England and Wales in 1986, and in private schools in 1999.

Between Mr Fell's retirement at Easter 1955 and Miss Allen's arrival in 1959 there was Mr Harold Wigley. Janet McKenzie remembers him as 'lovely'. When Mr Fell retired the school was still waiting for the Richmond County Modern school to open. With the rise in school leaving age coming into effect in 1947, it was becoming crowded. Rev Charlesworth wrote to the Education Committee in February 1955 with scarcely disguised despair about when the school might be ready:[29]

> *"Would you kindly furnish me with details as to when the new secondary modern school in Richmond is to be ready for use ? [...] The Managers are most anxious about the immediate present, and if three or four years lapse before the new school is built, they would wish for the temporary arrangements suggested in my letter of 28 January be implemented. It is obvious that Croft School will be very crowded during the next three to four years."*

What the School Management Committee wanted was a temporary headteacher to tide them over until the new school was available, at which point Croft School would become Infants and Juniors only. Then they would appoint a person permanently as head of a primary school. Interviews were held in March 1955 and Mr Wigley was offered the job. He was coming from the Methodist School in Pickering. He had some reservations about coming to Croft, and a lot of them were to do with the state of the Schoolhouse.

On 23 April 1955 Mr Wigley wrote to Rev. Charlesworth noting that he had now had an opportunity to look round the Schoolhouse and that he had some suggestions:[30]

> *"I don't know what the managers are prepared to do but may I suggest that two things seem essential to improve the amenities. First there is no privacy for toilet and bathing and I wondered if it were possible to remove the bath from the scullery and convert the small lobby on the stairs to a bathroom.* ▶

*Secondly, gas lighting is very inconvenient considering that electricity is already on the premises and it would be very much appreciated if these were replaced with electric fittings. I understand the gas cooker is on hire and this could be taken away at the same time. We prefer an electric cooker. Further I should like permission to remove the Yorkist Range from the living room and replace it with a modern fireplace."*

And, having set out his stall, he offered to meet the school managers and added that his wife and he were looking forward to residing in Croft. With just a few weeks to go until Mr Fell's retirement, the school was not in a strong position to argue. At the next School Management Meeting in May 1955 Herbert Coates (who lived at 3, The Terrace) proposed that the county architect's estimate of £525 for completion of a range of improvements, to include Mr Wigley's requests and redecoration, be accepted and they write to the North Riding Education Committee asking them to invite tenders for the work We can only assume that Mr and Mrs Wigley had to bath in the scullery while the process was completed.

Miss Allen was born in Rotherham in 1914 and she still lived in Rotherham when the 1939 Register was taken. She was in her first teaching job and living at home. She'd done her teacher training in Sheffield. Her father was a lorry driver and she had two older brothers. She retired from teaching in July 1979, 4 years after the new Croft Primary School had opened in September 1975. I'm led to believe she remained in the Schoolhouse, which then belonged to the Dodgson Trust, a charity formed specifically to manage the property after closure of the old school and distribute the rental money for the benefit of both the church and the school. Miss Allen died in Darlington in 1997.

When Miss Allen was appointed Head in January 1959 (she took up her duties on the 6th of that month) the school managers were against having a woman as head teacher. They seemed to feel that a woman would not keep control and remonstrated strongly with the local authority. On 2 January 1959, the School Managers – Captain Parlour (chair), Kit Chaytor, Herbert Coates, Robert Whitworth and Thomas Wilson (the Rector was absent) met at Monkend Hall, which was the custom. They resolved *"... That the North Riding Education Committee be informed the the managers object strongly to the appointment of a peripatetic woman teacher as Head"*.[31] Also that the local authority be informed that *'an atmosphere of respect for authority'* existed in the school and they did not want to lose this,. Therefore they requested the appointment of a temporary male head. Captain Parlour and Kit Chaytor were mandated to meet with the Head of Education, Mr Barraclough. Their fear seemed to be that, until the senior class (which was always taken by the Head) transferred to the County Modern school, a woman Head would not be able to cope.

At the next meeting in February, which was chaired by Reverend Charlesworth, Captain Parlour and Kit Chaytor reported on their meeting with Mr Barraclough. The latter had explained that no male head teacher was available for the post, and that, given its likely small size when it became Infants and Juniors only, the school could not afford a male head in any case. After this report "Miss Allen was introduced to the meeting and warmly welcomed". There is nothing to suggest that the school managers were hostile to her, but she might have felt she had to prove herself in the circumstances.

By this time, it was not just the Schoolhouse that was in need of modernisation. The School building itself was over a hundred years old. It was designed for children who came from houses with no electricity or running water, and probably not much heating. Ideas about what children should be doing in a classroom had changed from the rote learning done in Victorian times to a broader engagement of both body and mind. Following the raising of the school leaving age which took effect in 1947 the school was overcrowded for 12 years while Richmond County Modern was built, and by the 1960s the infants were being taught in a pre-fabricated building behind the main school. It was time for something new. It was reported in the press as early as 1947…

> *CHAOTIC CONDITIONS IN VILLAGE SCHOOLS FEARED*
> *A clear indication that the effect of raising the school leaving age to 15 when the building of new school premises is virtually at a standstill will result in chaotic conditions, particularly in village schools, was given at the North Riding Education Committee…*

An inspection report from 1960 started to highlight how restrictive the school building was and that this was noticeably preventing the best teaching: "though the room itself is large, actual conditions of working are not easy as part of the room has to be used for the mid-day meal each day and this greatly restricts the space urgently needed for display of work". It wasn't until the early 1970s that serious work on getting a new site for new school came into play. Again the church was a key player since the field to the west side of the old school was glebe land and the Church Commissioners had the power to assign it for use by the new school. The existing school and grounds now belonged to the education authority. Land north of the old school was used as a football pitch, and this was also earmarked as part of the new school field. This particular land was part of the Croft Estate, and my understanding is that it was agreed it would be sold to the North Riding County Council for a minimal sum. Consequently, the site was easy to identify and all that was needed was to secure funding from the Minister of Education and agree suitable design. Outline planning permission was agreed by the Parish Council on 14 February 1973.[32]

The design was made to a set of criteria unimaginable to the school designers of the National School in 1845. There was to be a separate assembly/dining hall and a large school kitchen next to it. The school playing field would enable football, cricket and athletics. There would be indoor toilets, separated for pupils and staff. There would be a staff room and parking for staff cars. Each class would have its own large room and reading area. The caretaker and ground staff would have their own rooms with a separate store for PE equipment.

However, the next bit, getting the detailed design agreed, was not so easy. The council wanted the whole building raised further up the site due to the risk of flooding. The last major floods had been 1965/66 but the stipulation was that the floors had to be 18 inches above the highest recorded flood level. However, the hardest bit was overcoming objections from the residents of South Parade about access to the site. There was a complaint that they had not been consulted, by the Parish or the County Council. A

Mrs A J Tomalin-Reeves, 4, South Parade, wrote on behalf of the Croft Residents Association on 17 July 1974 (more about this body on page 145). They wanted access to the school to run behind Carroll Place. If not that then an entrance road should be constructed from the Barton or Middleton Tyas roads. The council said this would be 'costly and tortuous' to achieve. The Residents Association said:

> *Mr Bigland, 10, South Parade, has already written to you pointing out the concerns of the residents in South Parade of the dangers to the children in the area that the increased traffic flow that the school will bring.*

Herbert Coates, then Chair of the Parish Council notes that the 'South Parade lobby' had been invited to all Parish Council meetings and had seen all plans. But what is clear is that their concerns did not result in any change to the school access. It was to be exactly where it is today, from the middle of South Parade.

The new school opened on 14 September 1975 as a Church of England Voluntary Controlled Primary School, under the jurisdiction of the new North Yorkshire County Council. Miss Allen was the first Head and she was succeeded by Mrs E.M. Day, on 1 September 1979.

Following the opening of the new school, discussions began on what to do with the old school building. The church wanted to build a new rectory on the site. All this is discussed in Chapter 6. It took some time, but on 6 June 1979, the Department of Education and Science informed the County Council that the whole of the sale proceeds from the old school would be theirs: £18,167.07. My understanding is that it was sold to A W Scott-Harden estate agents and was used as an additional office to their registered address at Monkend Hall.

## Other schools, other lives

However, not every child in Croft parish went to Croft School. Those who didn't roughly fell into two groups: first, children who lived on farms so distant from the village centre that they were in the catchment areas for Barton or Middleton Tyas and, in Peter Percival's case, North Cowton, and secondly the children who went to independent or boarding schools.

And then of course, Croft Church of England School wasn't the only school in Croft. There is the whole story of Oakwood and Oakwood School, which I will finish this chapter with.

Mary Andrew and Alan Kirk went to Barton School, from Waterloo and Bullmire Farms respectively, because they were more than two miles from Croft and a bit nearer to Barton. It was always a faff for farm children to get to school in the 30s and 40s and Mary remembers the trip to Barton every day on her bicycle. The Head Gardener on the Halnaby Estate was called Arthur Flowers and the Flowers lived at West Lodge. *And the mother Mrs. Flowers, her daughter, elder daughter* [Margaret], *was just a bit older than me and she used to take us to school on our bikes. Come and get us.* Even when she went to the High School in Richmond, Mary still had to cycle to Barton and then get a bus.

Mary's three sons started at Barton school and were then sent to board at Barnard Castle and this was also what the Banner family did. Mary's sons came home at the weekend. It meant more freedom for the children and the ability to join in with after-school activity, because farm families didn't always have time for a 'school run' even if they had a car.

However, Brian Walker and his sister went to Croft from Birch Springs: as he was three miles away he qualified for a taxi which was provided by Gibbon's garage at the rear of the Croft Spa Hotel.

Some Cockleberry[33] children went to Croft, but it was a long walk for them and some were placed at North Cowton. The Reverend Charlesworth wrote to the North Riding Education Committee in October 1950 noting that children as young as 5 were being asked to walk almost 4 miles a day to North Cowton school because they did not qualify for a place on one the school buses. He noted specifically that very young children were being asked to cross a railway line (probably at Dalton Gates) and walk along the main Scorton Road and that its was dangerous. (In addition, his letter indicates that there was a school bus from Eryholme to Croft School that also picked up pupils from Dalton, and that some Cockleberry children could make use of that).

Peter Percival was born at Cockleberry in 1951, at number 23, Halifax Site. He went to North Cowton school and his first day was a big shock.

**Peter Percival**:

*"I just remember going on my first day. My mum took me and that and I just happened to look up and thought 'I don't like you' I just saw this teacher dragon. [...] So I went to the door and, being a kid, the door handles were where you stretch up to, they seemed a lot higher. And I went out the door I and I ran off up the road and I remember shouting my mouth off. My mum had just dropped me off. And she said 'No, go back'. [...] And I'm thinking Oh, my mum doesn't want me and then I've got this dragon chasing me. I laid down in the road and I just cried. Well they took me back and me sister Sheila had to come from the biggest class and come to sit with me all day apparently. But I did go after that."*

For Peter, it was tricky to get to school and, as a Cockleberry kid, he felt unwelcome. He met an old class mate later, as an adult, and he remembers she said 'Well, I remember your lot and we were told not to have anything to do with you.' Peter is puzzled by this: 'But we never went short, we were always fed, and we weren't going round in rags or anything.' When he was 9, Peter's family was re-housed at Barton and he finished school there. Unfortunately his segregation as a 'squatter' did not finish. There's more about this in Chapter 4.

Ian Dougill, who was an only child, went to an independent prep school and then Darlington Grammar, and he felt awkward in the village.

**Ian Dougill**:

*"My earliest memories are dictated by the circumstances of my family. My father was on a salary, which was very unusual in those days. My mother was a very highly qualified nurse. And she particularly was aspirational. So my early memories do not involve for example going to the local*

*school. I was sent to a private school in Darlington. And this was, as it were, alienation from my friends, play friends in the village, continued upwards. I didn't go to the local school, so I was to some extent separate. And when it came to the Eleven Plus, I sat my Eleven Plus at Richmond. So in normal circumstances I'd have gone to Richmond Grammar School, which was a very good grammar school, actually. But my parents had already paid for me to attend the junior school at Darlington Grammar School. And when I passed the eleven plus, they petitioned the Grammar School that I continue my education there. So instead of going every day to Richmond in the morning, as the other grammar school boys did in Croft, I went to Darlington. So there was always this sense of separation, not being quite the same thing, which would sometimes end in mild scale bullying. Sometimes people would lie in wait for me, as I came over the bridge from the bus from Darlington. And lie in wait for me near the church gates. Low scale stuff, but it did happen. There was always this sense of resentment and not animosity, but it marked me, which it wouldn't have done of course, if I'd gone to the local school and gone to the Richmond Grammar School. It seems absurd, but these things do happen, they always have. It's no good people protesting they didn't, 'cos*

**A teenage Ian Dougill stands next to his mother Betty and Ada Headon, at the back gate to 2 South Parade. Date around 1950.**

*they do, and they did. It all petered out eventually, but I do remember once my father drove to a local farm, and read the riot act to the family, because their son was one of the ringleaders. And I was an immature child for my age, I was edgy and jumpy and so a very likely victim. And these memories persist, they do persist. [...]*

*I unintentionally became a bit of a loner. Although I played with the local children, because I didn't attend the same school and mix with them all the time, I tended to move off into my own world. And so, from a very early age, I would become very familiar with the landscapes and nature in the village. By the time I was seven or eight, I could take you for a walk and describe all the flowers and the butterflies and birds to you, without a doubt. And in those days at least, nature was not a specific subject of interest for most people. They lived amongst it."*

Ian left Croft to go to university, and he did not return except to visit his parents who lived at 5 South Parade into the the 1970s.

David Kellie-Smith, a wartime baby [born 1940], also had a different experience of the village, surrounded by his Chaytor family, and then away from Croft at boarding school.

**David Kellie-Smith**:

*"They were living in the Hall. I think by that time it probably technically belong to Kit. He was away, I guess he was away at the war probably. Anyway, Granny was the matriarch. There was a whole gang of us all through the war all these armies of my cousins, me, my mother. My mother was the cook. My granny ran the place. My Aunt Betty[34] was an engineer with the Bristol aircraft company so she wasn't there that often. There were a hoard of us, mostly children, in the Hall throughout the war and then at the end of the war initially my mum and I moved out we went to Woodbine Cottage which is just opposite the hotel.*

*I don't remember mixing very much at all [in the village]. I'm guessing there was kind of social apartheid to some extent when I was a child, a single only child from the big house. I probably didn't mix much anyway. There wasn't really any communal mixing that I can think of. And that's partly why when my mother died, we spent part of her estate building the village hall.[35]*

*Fell was the proprietor of the village school, quite a formidable sort of man as far as I remember. But I didn't go there, I went to a lovely lady in Low Middleton. She was the widow of a school inspector, I think, as far as I remember. And then I went down south to a boarding school when I was seven. You just went home for weekends and, and sometimes to shoot. And that was about it really. I think I used to go home for my holidays probably.*

*But you know, I became a Londoner, quite a comfortable Londoner. Because in those days, it was quite a trek getting up. [...] Like many people from the North I fled to London when I was 18. And never came back again. So to some extent now I feel more of a tourist in Croft. In a weird way I think I feel slightly more comfortable in the North as a tourist than as a young man growing up, though. [...] London was tremendously exciting and felt very different to the North, it felt very different. So did the North of England."*

# Oakwood School

The other school in Croft was not one that people in Croft could attend. It was Oakwood School.

Of the people I spoke to, no one was quite sure what Oakwood School was. Many knew nothing and a few had an idea about it. They knew there were a number of children there, and that there were small children, but other than that, opinions varied.

**Ian Dougill**:

*"... there was always a bit of mystery about Oakwood, let's put it that way. It wasn't of direct interest to me as a boy. But I do know that there was a Sunderland connection, a Wearside connection, and that it was girls, not boys. I'll suggest it might very well have been orphaned girls or girls from problem families that would be the direct responsibility of Sunderland Council. And this is quite common in those days. They'd have a place some councils around farms, and then they took the kids to the farms. Anything to get out for the back streets of Sunderland. Yeah, because they'd have never escaped that on their own, they needed help to do so."*

**Margaret Chapman**:

*"They used to have two girls who used to walk* [the small children] *along the road. When you think, would you cross the road with twenty kids without having anyone to stop the traffic? Yes, and they were from Sunderland or wherever they came from, the girls that were nursery nurses. There were a couple of them. But* [the children] *were all toddlers. Oh, loads of them."*

Mollie Ingham lives at Oakwood, which is sited at the south end of the the village centre, just before the railway, now. This is what she said about it.

**Mollie Ingham**:

*"... a school took it over, a school from Sunderland, and I think they would have been neglected children, they had so many women looking after them, they had to have one girl to four children or something like that. [...] They were self supporting, the kids used to plough the front of the house. Next door where Diane lives, that's my oldest, they built that for the gardener and cook, the cook lived there and it was it was all self-supporting.Then it couldn't take any more children there was no more room. It was just little children. Well like primary age."*

I think it's time to tell the Oakwood story because I've have found out some things. This is what I know, starting with the story of Oakwood House itself.

Chapter 2 – A Croft Childhood

# Oakwood and the Dixon-Johnsons

Oakwood, up until the school closed and the house and land was sold to the Valente brothers in 1968, belonged to the Croft Estate. I have been able to establish that there was an earlier house on the site called Plum Tree House up to at least 1861 and that Oakwood House and Lodge was advertised for sale or let in 1866, so it must have been built in that five year period.

The house was taken in 1867 by Colonel William Williamson who had recently retired from 25 years in the army and married for the first time. He and his wife Sarah had two children before he died in 1873, aged 49. In 1882 the third baronet of Croft and Witton Castle, Sir William Chaytor (1837-1896), and others, agreed a ninety-nine year lease to Cuthbert Greenwood Johnson, who seems to have been living there with his family for a few years beforehand also.

Mr Johnson came from Durham, and he was descended from the Dixon family of Aykley Heads, a large house on Framwellgate dating from 1700 which, in modern times, became the basis of the headquarters of Durham County Council. The Dixon family had extensive estates in Durham. Mr Johnson was born in 1844 at Aykley Heads to Francis Dixon and Agnes Harrison Johnson. In 1866, he married Maria Grey Smith (b 1843), the daughter of the Reverend John W Smith of Dinsdale. She was born at Dinsdale Rectory, one of a family of four. As a young woman she and her family were photographed several times by the son of the Rector of Croft who was friendly with the Smith family. These photos still exist. The son's name was Charles Lutwidge Dodgson, now better known under his pen name, Lewis Carroll. In his diary entry for 3 August 1857 the latter notes that the Smith children were "much what one might expect from their free country life, strong, active, handsome and with a strong aversion to books".[36]

Cuthbert and Maria Johnson lived first in Stockton and then in Sedgefield where they had 3 children: Anna Grey (b 1867), Cuthbert Francis (b 1871) and Charles William (b 1875). What brought them to Croft is unclear. Certainly Maria might have known Croft as a girl when her family were friendly with the Dodgsons. But there's another connection which is this: an executor of Cuthbert's father's will was a man called George Duberley, and George Duberley was also Sir William Chaytor's (the third baronet) agent and manager for his Durham estates. Either way, the Johnsons moved to Oakwood around 1879 and in 1882 took out the 99 year lease from the Croft Estate as I mention above. The house would have suited them because Cuthbert Greenwood was a keen agriculturist, an innovator in the field of 'ensilage', a keen huntsman and the owner of many horses.

On 18 December 1893, Cuthbert Greenwood Johnson changed his name by deed poll to Dixon-Johnson, signifying his inheritance of the Aykley Heads estate which had been associated with the Dixon family since the early eighteenth century. This inheritance took place after his father died on 19 November that year. However, in 1899 he, Cuthbert, unexpectedly died, aged 54, whilst on a visit to Paignton, Devon. He was a yachtsman, and had moored his vessel there. But he became ill with peritonitis while on shore. This left his widow Maria as the tenant of Oakwood and she lived there until her death in 1932. She was a significant but not very visible figure in Croft, contributing to local causes, attending church and so forth.

Although Maria lived until she was 89, her life was not without tragedy. Her two sisters Fanny and Anne both died young and they are commemorated by two impressive stained glass windows in Dinsdale Church. Her father and mother died in the 1890s. Her husband died relatively young as I've noted but she also endured the death of her daughter in 1899 and youngest son Charles who was killed in Flanders during the World War 1.

Charles William Dixon-Johnson was a Rifleman – a Private – in the Prince of Wales Own (West Yorkshire) Regiment, 1st/7th Battalion. He died on 9th October 1917, is buried in Flanders and commemorated at the Tyne Cot Memorial. He was 40 in May 1916 when conscription for married men began, scraping into the qualifying age by just a few months. He turned 41 in October that year.

Charles had married Christian Elfreda Grey (known as Elfreda) of Kirknewton, Northumberland in 1907.[37] They lived first at Oakwood and then at some time around 1910 they moved to Croft House, the large house facing the Tees in Hurworth Place, owned by Sir Ernst Cassel and demolished in 2008. At that time they had a son, Cuthbert John, and while at Croft House, Elfreda gave birth to twin daughters called Elfreda and Christian. The Dixon-Johnsons must have had the prescience to discuss what might happen to his family if Charles was killed, because Elfreda became the beneficiary of a family trust whereby the estates of Charles, his mother and elder brother all provided money for her. Elfreda did not re-marry and died in Edinburgh in 1955. I imagine she moved to the Berwickshire estate of her Grey family, called Middle Ord.

Anna Grey Dixon-Johnson, Maria's only daughter, married William Hopper Williamson – the son of the Colonel Williamson mentioned above – in 1891 and they lived at Over Dinsdale Hall, having three children. But, as noted, she died in 1899. So Maria's widowhood and old age at Oakwood was shared by her elder son, Captain Cuthbert Francis Dixon-Johnson. He was a career soldier, a graduate of Sandhurst, a Captain in His Majesty's 6th Inniskilling Dragoon Guards and a veteran of the Boer War. His obituary in the *Darlington and Stockton Times* noted that was a keen horseman, yachtsman, shot, beekeeper and angler who supported many local causes but was rarely seen at public events.

In 1934, two years after his mother's death, Cuthbert moved to Tunisia where he owned orange groves, leaving Oakwood empty but for his staff. He did not marry or have any children. He died on 30 November 1939 at Nabeul, Tunisia. His will bequeathed annuities to all of his former servants – at Oakwood, in the army and in Tunisia – with his nephew Cuthbert John Dixon-Johnson, Charles's son, his main beneficiary. However, his obituary noted that "At the outbreak of the present war, he placed his Croft house and staff at the disposal of Croft Rural District Council for the reception of evacuees".[38] And it was his express wish, added as a codicil to his will, that the house should continue to be used in this way.

Chapter 2 – A Croft Childhood

# Sunderland children come to Croft

At this point then we can pick up the story of Oakwood School.

The arrival of evacuees in Croft on 4 September 1939 undoubtedly stretched the village's ability to offer accommodation. I reflect on the impact of the evacuees in the next chapter. However, it is enough to know here that the 1939 Register, which was taken at the end of September, after evacuees arrived, indicates that there were indeed a range of evacuees at Oakwood. I think we can also conclude that it was Cuthbert Francis Dixon-Johnson's servants who were hosting them, because two of the servant names match those in his will: Annie Raine and Edith Grainger. In addition there is another maid and two 'voluntary helpers'. That leaves 10 evacuees, the eldest being 14 and the youngest 5. There are 5 names, and five redacted entries which can't be seen. The children, and quite possibly the voluntary helpers, will have come from Sunderland, probably, because Sunderland had requested specific accommodation for children that needed some support beyond that available in a third party household. This was the first use of Oakwood as a place for children in the war.

However, many of these evacuees would have gone home again by the beginning of 1940 (see next chapter). In early 1941, another role as Sunderland Nursery School was served by Oakwood.

The story from the Sunderland side is that, with prospect of aerial bombardment a real one in a place like Sunderland, their Education Committee saw an urgent need to relocate the Sunderland Nursery School which had been set up up in 1939 at Hawthorn Towers, Seaham. This was a large gothic-style house built in 1821. In notes from a meeting of 16th January 1941, the view of the committee was that the place of relocation would be Minsteracres, then a large house owned by the Roman Catholic Silvertop family, situated near Riding Mill. At a meeting of Sunderland Education Committee on 25 February 1941 it was noted that:

> *Due to the breakdown of heating it is not possible to transfer children from the Nursery School at Hawthorn Tower. As it is essential to secure alternative accommodation arrangements have been made with the Senior Regional Officer of the Ministry of Health, Newcastle to house the school in premises known as 'Oakwood', near Croft, North Riding of Yorkshire.*[39]

The first time Oakwood is mentioned in Croft RDC minutes after the start of the war on 27 May 1940. The committee had been talking about hostels for evacuees from Sunderland and Captain Parlour notes that he has been 'offered' Oakwood. It was agreed that Oakwood should be made a hostel. Then later at the Council's meeting in March 1941 it was reported 'the Clerk noted that he had requisitioned Oakwood on behalf of Sunderland Education Committee as a Nursery School' and that there were now 30 children there. So Captain Dixon-Johnson's wishes were being honoured. I have yet to find out exactly what the Nursery School was, but clearly the children were small and not with their parents. It maybe that there were older evacuees also.

Then the war ended and another new phase in the history of Oakwood school began.

On 1st March 1945, the Director of Education for Sunderland City Borough Council (Mr W. Thompson) wrote to the Ministry of Education to make the case for a permanent school at Oakwood. He wrote:

> *My Committee have been considering very closely the future of [the Nursery School at Oakwood], and while the numbers at present are small, we have deliberately refrained from sending more children pending the approval of a permanent scheme. It is desired to keep the premises, for a time at any rate, in order that we may send out in the main debilitated children under the age of 5. So much benefit has accrued to this type of child at Croft that [...We] are strongly of the opinion that such a type of school is necessary, and the School Medical Officer has suggested that there are sufficient children to keep it full. [...]*
>
> *The school from which these children were drawn initially was a voluntary Nursery School for which we accepted responsibility for the period of hostilities. This has now ceased existing at the premises, which were of a very temporary nature, taken over by the War Department and opened as a War Nursery [...] we are of the opinion that there would be sufficient children from a town of this size to warrant the continuance of 'Oakwood' as a Residential Open Air School for children up to the age of 5.*[40]

A great deal of correspondence followed, and the further facts emerge from that: (a) Sunderland only ever had access to Oakwood House. Oakwood Lodge and gardens were separate and at the time of Mr Thompson's letter the latter was let to Mr R.Geldard (b) Captain Dixon-Johnson's interest in both properties were being handled by his trustees, a friend – Mr W.F. Parrington – and his nephew Cuthbert John Dixon-Johnson (c) The school was run by Miss Alice Lee and a group of 4 additional staff (including 2 qualified nurses) plus a domestic staff of 5.

At this stage you may be wondering what an 'Open Air Residential School' was. The Open Air School movement was a response to the large numbers of children who suffered from debilitating diseases in cities and places of poor quality housing and overcrowding. The idea was that an Open Air School would give 'delicate', sick children frequent access to clean fresh air, good food and natural surroundings that would heal them. The movement started in 1904 in Germany, gained popularity in Europe and the US in the period before World War 2, and declined in the late 1950s and 60s.

The children could be at the school for a few months or years, depending on their condition and the living conditions they might be sent back to. Some of the children might be recovering from pulmonary tuberculosis, pneumonia or other respiratory diseases. Others may have had one of the childhood infectious diseases – diphtheria, polio, scarlet fever or measles. We forget that childhood infectious diseases were still a major threat to children up until the 1960s. And that was true in Croft too. The Medical Officer for Croft RDC issued a report each year and these show that, while Croft Rural District was a pretty healthy place for children, there were still cases, and deaths from these specific diseases, but they were generally counted in numbers of less than 5 per year from 1930 onwards, with exception of a few more serious outbreaks of measles and scarlet fever. The equivalent reports for Sunderland County Borough, an area some 5000 acres smaller than Croft Rural District but with 100 times the population, count instances of TB in dozens, infectious diseases in hundreds, and additional hundreds of cases of other diseases such as rheumatism, arthritis and skin infections.[41] Disease followed poverty and overcrowding, a principle still in evidence today, but all the more so before modern medical services could provide mitigation.

A paragraph in the medical report for Sunderland schools in 1950 explains what Oakwood was about in more detail:

> *The Oakwood School, Croft Spa, has continued to do good work [...] children are admitted from poor homes or are of a delicate type. After a stay of three or four months, in fresh surroundings, with adequate meals and under controlled rest they are returned to take their place in ordinary schools. During the year much has been done to the buildings and in the grounds for the benefit of both staff and children. Regular visits by Members of the Committee* [I.e. Sunderland County Borough Council Education Committee] *have maintained interest throughout the year, many visitors have been received from the Darlington Training College and also a party of administrators of Local Government from Germany.*

Just after World War 2 there were almost 100 Open Air Schools in England and Wales. One was at Beaumont Hill in Darlington.[42] Another was at Joicey Road School in Gateshead: those school buildings are still there and are Grade 2 Listed.[43] There are also a number of first hand accounts of being at one of the schools online.[44] Children had lessons either in buildings with large windows, or actually outside. They would wear specially designed warm overclothes with hoods for winter, as did the teachers. They were also encouraged to work outside in kitchen gardens. Three home-cooked meals a day were part of the benefit for pupils, who may not have been well-nourished at home, so growing their own produce was part of the approach. Hence Mollie Ingham's point about the school being 'self-sufficient'. The Oakwood site was in four acres of ground and access to good quality, local food would have been another advantage of the site. Coupled with the walks through Spa Woods, the path past the house to Standalone Farm and Vince Moor and Croft's continuing association with the Spa, mineral waters and peaceful recovery, it is no great wonder that Sunderland were keen to continue.

The Ministry had some reservations about Oakwood which were mostly that it was very small (21 pupils advised at present, extending to 40 if alterations could be made, and so economically only just viable), and that Oakwood House was in need of upgrading to provide a modern and suitable education to these children. The HMI Inspector allocated to Oakwood, Mr Plumbley, noted in comments appended to Mr Thompson's letter that "I have visited Oakwood … the site and surroundings are most attractive, but it is evident that considerable work would have to be done before the premises could comply with Building Regulations". There was also a concern that the 99 year lease had 35 years left to run, and what would happen after that?

The Ministry decided to grant temporary extension of the school while a longer term plan was

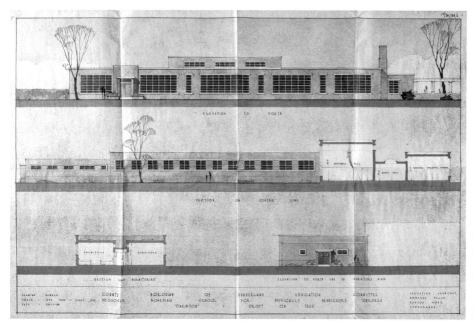

This plan was submitted by Sunderland Council in 1949 as a significant expansion of Oakwood School, then housed in the converted houses of the Oakwood site.

drawn up. After discussion, it was decided that Sunderland should apply for a compulsory purchase of Oakwood using powers for the acquisition of land granted through the 1944 Education Act. On 20 December 1946 a notice appeared in The *Northern Echo* announcing this and giving the address for any objections. The objective was to sweep all the interests – the Croft Estate's tenure of the land, the Dixon-Johnson trust's tenure of the lease and the awkward let of the Lodge recently in the hands of Mr Geldard – under the Compulsory Purchase Order, providing certainty for the future before public investment in the school was made. There were objections, particularly notably from the landowner, Kit Chaytor. Captain Dixon-Johnson's trustees had already offered the house to Sunderland for the modest sum of £1,500. An extended legal wrangle ensued.

This longer term plan, it turned out, would mean quite a change. In January 1948, the County Architect for Sunderland wrote to the Ministry with a design for a completely new school building, meeting the needs of 100 children and staff. This was to stand on the 4 acre site of Oakwood House, to the west of the existing building. The cost was £62,000.

However, nothing came of this. I couldn't find any documents about a compulsory purchase but it may have happened. For the next 18 years Oakwood school continued in Oakwood House, with another person – a Mr Barningham now – in the Lodge. In those 18 years the school did various improvements. In June 1954, the schools drainage was connected to the new main drainage in Croft and in June 1953 a major application was made for permission to build a caretaker's house. About this time there was an invitation to tender for the demolition of the old Lodge.[45] A letter asking for funding from the Ministry of Education notes "The present accommodation provided for the Caretaker, his wife and three children consists of two rooms having a total area of 288 sq.ft. and sanitation is not provided". The cost of building the house was £1999 6s 2d.

The only other story of note in the post-war life of Oakwood School was the story of the rat. On 10 November 1948 the Sunderland Echo reported that a four year old child had been bitten on the face and hand by a rat while in bed in a dormitory at Oakwood. The parents were horrified and Councillors made statements to the press. An inquiry was launched. The cause of the problem was that the tenant at The Lodge had been storing animal feed in outhouses and these had become infested with rats. When vermin control were called they laid out poison, and the amount consumed led them to believe they had killed around 75 rats, but just one within the school. The parents were satisfied that the school was not to blame. All returned to normal.

I'm not clear when Oakwood School closed but it was in the mid 1960's, probably 1966. If you think about the reasons for an 'Open Air Residential School', many were now not so pressing. By the mid 60s slums had been cleared, sanitation improved, medical treatment had become preventative as well as curative plus vaccination programmes for polio, smallpox, whooping cough and diphtheria had been successful in virtually eradicating these diseases. The scourge of childhood illness had been shrunk from a monster to a domestic animal.

On 5 April 1967 the Croft Estate – Bill Chaytor – sold Oakwood House and land to brothers Natalie and Marcello Valente with their business associate Leslie Wardle. The Valentes had a cafe and restaurant business in Durham. It's not clear why they bought the property and they did not keep it long. On 15 July 1968 they sold the main house to Ralph Ingham (Molly Ingham's husband) and the buildings to the north of that, including the caretakers house, to Barry and Diana Chapman (Molly's daughter and son-in-law).

And that, for the period we are interested in in this book, is the story of Oakwood. And we have come to the end of this section, with an account of what it was like to be a child in Croft, to go to school from Croft and what Croft gave back to children just by being what it was.

In the same year that Enid Blyton was accurately lampooned by the Comic Strip (1982), a film of *The Island of Adventure* was released, with a reworked script updating the story and erasing the social attitudes that now made people feel uncomfortable. It was fairly successful. So those core themes of freedom, independence and adventure in a less than perfect world that attracted me and millions of other children 30 years before proved enduring, however things progress.

Enid Blyton once said that she didn't accept criticism from anyone over 12. The evidence from our Croft voices is that, even when the world changes around us, what makes a good childhood is remarkably consistent.

---

**Endnotes**

1   Doris's mother was Lillian Bramley before she married, and I believe the Bramleys lived in Hurworth Place.
2   Charlie said he was born in the front bedroom too.
3   http://www.rockliffecourtsurgery.co.uk/Info/Practice-history/151, accessed 23 May 2022.
4   Mr George Stairmand's market garden was on the land north of Waterside, on the Northallerton Road (aka Dalton Road). In the 1939 Register it appears as 'Park View' and Stairmand (who was born in 1865 in Gilling and died in 1947) lives there with his unmarried daughter Mabel and one or two other gardeners. He also had a son Victor. George married Annie Cottam from Durham in 1893 and they came to Croft, to Park View, after that. Mabel was born in Croft in 1896. I believe the house and market garden was between Waterside and 'Strawberry Cottage' which was occupied by the Thorntons. In 1963 both, which were rented from the Croft Estate, were there, with Mabel Stairmand at Park View and J Thornton at Strawberry Cottage. [*Croft RDC RB 1963*].
5   North Walmire.
6   This was North Walmire - I talk about the disappearance of North Walmire Farm in Chapter 5.

7   Clervaux Castle was demolished in 1951 and I discuss this in detail in Chapter 4. I think Doris's memory will relate to the time before the Castle was used by the army in World War 2, maybe 1939.
8   The 'New Spa' bath-house, off Northallerton Road on the left as you head to Darlington. I discuss the demolition of the New Spa and conversion of Spa Cottages in Chapter 4.
9   Monk End Farm, so Clow Beck, by the pack horse bridge.
10  *North Eastern Gazette*, 6 April 1939, p10. The club was still going after World War 2 but I'm unsure when it ceased to exist.
11  Prince Charles married Lady Diana Spencer on 27 July 1981.
12  This was a flood prevention measure, but was also to preserve Croft bridge which was taking the full force of flood water at the Hurworth end. This is discussed in Chapter 5. This work was done in 1977.
13  This was at Newtown. Ron was, employed as a woodsman by the Croft Estate and worked for Kit Chaytor before Bill took over.
14  The Anchorage was built in 1927/28 for a Miss J F Mathewson [Croft RDC RoP]. Miss Mathewson appears to be Janetta Fraser Mathewson b 1864 who was a career nurse and Matron at the Stockton Fever Hospital [ancestry.co.uk, 1901 and 1911 Censuses]. She died in 1936. Mr Reginald Reynolds was a Chartered Surveyor, according to the 1939 Register. He and his wife were both born in 1911. Margaret also noted that another advantage of having Heather as a friend was that Mr Reynolds was one of the few people in the village with a car.
15  Then a private girls' school in Darlington.
16  Margaret thinks that the Young Wives group was started by Reverend Charlesworth's wife Dorothy, so this would be in the 1950s.
17  "Parents' 'right to choose' schools for their children has been enshrined in government policy since the 1988 Education Reform Act in England and Wales – and the 1981 Education (Scotland) Act." From "British Social Attitudes 28" https://www.bsa.natcen.ac.uk/media/38964/bsa28_4school_choice.pdf accessed 06/02/2022
18  There is a lot of material in NYRO about the school's history.
19  A good resource for understanding the history of National Schools is Lois Louden *Distinctive and Inclusive: The National Society and Church of England Schools 1811-2011*. See Bibliography.
20  The Terrace.
21  From evidence I saw in the National Farm Survey of 1941 (see chapter 5), all the land sweeping up the hill behind the hotel (which came down to South Parade where Carroll Place and the new Primary School are now) past the Terrace and South Terrace was considered a farm and Turnbull is the name of the farmer. So that's what Peter is referring to I think.
22  Eryholme school closed in 1936 and its eight remaining pupils transferred to Croft. See AJ Pollard, *A Perfect Paradise* p107.
23  Margaret still remembers all the words to *If* by Rudyard Kipling and *Home Thoughts from Abroad* by Robert Browning.
24  This was Mr Fell's predecessor, who evidently did not last long.
25  TNA, ED21/43236, document dated 28th July 1921.
26  TNA, ED21/46236, letter dated 5th April 1930.
27  PC minutes, 14 July 1982 (NYRO PC/CRO)
28  Croft RDC, RoP number 285A. Permission applied for in December 1944.
29  NYRO, PR/CRO Letter dated 9 February 1955.
30  NYRO, PR/CRO 12/5/68.
31  Miss Allen had had a range of teaching jobs but her job at the time of applying for the Croft role was as a peripatetic teacher in Darlington.
32  NYRO, PR/CRO 5.
33  Cockleberry was the community that formed on the Aerodrome after the RCAF left. I explain about Cockleberry in Chapter 4.
34  Catherine Beatrice Chaytor (1907-1983) known as Betty. David's mother was Margaret Clare Chaytor (b 1918). 'Granny' was Dorothy Elizabeth Chaytor (widow of Alfred Henry Chaytor).
35  There is more about this, and the previous village halls in Chapter 6.
36  Roger Taylor and Edward Wakeling, *Lewis Carroll, Photographer* Princeton University Press, 2002, p137.
37  Elfreda's Grey family have an interesting history of their own which can be viewed at http://milfieldgreys.co.uk/index.html (accessed 01 March 2022). Her father was George Grey.
38  D&S, 9.12.1939.
39  Tyne and Wear Archives, Sunderland Borough Council, Education Minutes 1940-42 (CB.SU. 17/18).
40  TNA, ED32/2450 - this is a large file on Oakwood, the continuation of the school and requests for approval/funds to develop it.
41  Annual medical reports for both Croft and Sunderland can be found at www.wellcome.org. Many thanks to Peter Sykes for finding this rich resource.
42  See an 'Echo Memories' article on the school dated 3 April 2002 at https://www.thenorthernecho.co.uk/news/7079060.open-air-schools-cold-comfort-pupils/ (accessed 08/03/2022).
43  See https://historicengland.org.uk/listing/the-list/list-entry/1392603 (accessed 08/03/2022).
44  Verbal accounts of being at an Open Air School are here: http://www.formerchildrenshomes.org.uk/open_air_schools_memories.html (accessed 08/03/2022. A search of the Wellcome Collection or British Library Catalogue will also reveal a good number of works about Open Air Schools in general and specific schools.
45  The whole discussion or a new house for the Caretaker is contained in the bundle of records at TNA numbered ED32/2451(517/7005).

# CHAPTER 3

## THE IMPACT OF WORLD WAR II

War between Britain and Germany was declared on 1 September 1939, the opening move in what was to become known as the Second World War. The impact on Croft was immediate. On Sunday 3 September the British government put Operation Pied Piper into action and around 40 evacuees arrived in Croft, along with helpers and teachers, from Gateshead and Sunderland. Croft, along with most of rural North Yorkshire, was a 'reception area' – a place that was deemed to be safe for evacuees to be sent to.

Before I start, let me say that there are probably more books published on subjects relating to the two World Wars than any other subject. The British Library catalogue lists 15,694 items with 'World War 2' in the title, slightly less than the number of items listed against 'World War 1'. It's very unlikely I will say anything generally about World War 2 that will be new, but I hope there will be things about Croft readers do not know, or hadn't fully appreciated and that appropriate background is given to bring out the full picture. Books I have consulted are in the footnotes and the bibliography.

In September 1939 the chances of any bombs or aircraft attacks on Croft seemed very small. It might be war time but life went on pretty much as it did before, with adjustments for rationing and the black-out. By September 1945 the story was different and in this chapter I will explain how the war effort crept into everyday life in the village.

But change started with evacuees. Evacuees and Civil Defence.

## Evacuees

The arrival of evacuees in early September 1939 had been planned for many months. At their meeting in December 1938, councillors of Croft Rural District considered the first communications from the Ministry of Health (MOH) about the evacuation of large towns in the event of war, requesting information about the potential amount of accommodation that could be made for evacuated children and their helpers. The RDC responded to the MOH by reporting that organisation of billets for evacuees was more than their limited staffing and funding could support. At the January 1939 meeting the discussion was on the 'organisation of a national register', which we now know as the 1939 Register. Then in February a sum of £15 was to be awarded to Mr W Dobson – a council employee – as remuneration for organising evacuations, and he was to attend a conference in Newcastle at the end of

March on the project. In April, Captain Parlour, Reverend SC Joad (Stapleton), Mr W Miller were to create a plan for reception of evacuees in Croft Rural District, and, to this effect, Captain Parlour held a meeting on 19 April 1939 attended by 'many women and the WVS'.[1] They had been told to expect '500 evacuees from Tyneside, detrained at Darlington'.

Children were evacuated by school, and teaching staff to continue their education were evacuated too. Along with helpers to deal with all the practical things that children would need to be organised. It makes sense that evacuee teachers were billeted in Croft where the school was, because the school would be providing for evacuees billeted in Dalton, Girsby, Over Dinsdale, and Eryholme as well as Croft. I have looked at the 1939 Register for Dalton and Eryholme and found only a couple of un-redacted evacuees.

Charlie Headon, who first alerted me to the fact that there were evacuees in Croft, said that while evacuees were in the village the local children got school in the morning and evacuees had school in the afternoon. This is corroborated by George Fell's entry in the school logbook for 20 September 1939, the day the school reopened after closure on 30 August pending the declaration of war. He wrote 'Owing to admission of evacuated children from Garden Street, Sunderland and Harlow Green, Gateshead the following arrangement has been made: Seniors, full-time; Juniors and Infants half-time'.

The 1939 Register was taken on 29th September as a means of creating a central register whereby identity cards, ration books and the tracking of evacuations and other population movements could be administered in time of war. The date meant that initial wave of evacuees were recorded at their host addresses. Below is a list of evacuees and their teachers and helpers that are clearly visible in the register. This will be a subset of the actual number, because there are names redacted due to data privacy (if the person's birth date is within 100 years of today and they are not known to be dead then the name is redacted). I have put a # against each address where I think a redacted name might be an evacuee, and where there is more than one I put multiple #s. There are 38 names here of which 15 are teachers or helpers. So it seems likely there were about 30 evacuee children in Croft village centre. I cannot find any evacuees at the farms. I asked Doris if there were any evacuees at Vince Moor. She said 'my mother wouldn't have them. She said we had enough on without evacuees.' I'm guessing that was a common sentiment amongst farmer's wives. As I explain in Chapter 5, farming was in the frontline of the war effort, although in September 1939 they were only just beginning to understand the challenges that they would be facing. However, feelings in the farming community about the demands made on them by the evacuation came through from other areas of the North Riding. There was one letter in the D&S on 7 October which certainly did not hold back:

> *Sir,*
> *It is appropriate at this stage in the evacuation scheme that consideration should be given to the position of residents in the reception areas. In the view of many people this forcing of total strangers into an Englishman's home is opposed to the teaching of generations and there is bound to exist in* ▶

Chapter 3 – The Impact of World War II

A group of chidren standing outside Monkend bungalow ca early 1940. The girls on the right at the back and on the end of the second row are 'Connie and Betty' who were evacuees. Margaret Headon (Chapman) is front right and her brother Charlie is on the left of the second row.

*the minds of householders the feeling that liberty is gone.*

*Evacuees have openly stated that evacuation would enable them to have a few months holiday before winter came and then they could go home if to proved to be lonely. Many of the children proved to be verminous and were not even house trained and the mothers were idle, too idle to clean their children ... They appeared to expect they should be waited on by already overworked farmers' wives and in some instances the farmer's wife cleansed the children of their vermin while the evacuated mother took trips to the town.*

*For years the country districts have been grossly neglected as regards electric light and a clean water supply, yet as soon as war breaks out these areas are expected to house numbers of townspeople who look upon these services as absolute necessities. [...]*

*Camps ought to have been constructed in safe districts and the evacuees mothers brought in in relates to act as cleaners, cooks etc. This would have put the work of looking after the children upon those who should bear it namely the children's mothers. It would then have been interesting to note the number of parents who came forward to look after other people's children, which the country housewife was expected to do with enthusiasm.*

*Yours etc. 'Once Bitten'.*

If you are feeling that this is an uncharitable letter, it should be noted that hosting families did have considerable challenges with the evacuees. Children from the harsher parts of Sunderland and Gateshead did not behave like the children of Croft. At worst, they came with inadequate clothes and shoes; they were unaccustomed to washing much; they had unusual toilet habits and were sometimes malnourished, so always hungry. Worst of all, many of them had infestations of lice and sometimes infectious diseases. Coupled with the fact that hosts received only 8/6 per week per child, the problems started to build up. The papers were full of complaints, and this was a national phenomenon, not just in the North Riding. In the edition of the D&S in which 'Once Bitten' had held forth there was a report from Croft RDC about a home where the adults had caught the measles from evacuees. 'They welcome strangers into their home, and *this* is their reward complained Councillor HG Coates. In fact, an outbreak of measles at this time was a specific problem for the school. Mr Fell writes in the log book for 30 October 'Reported several cases of measles' and then on 11 November 'School closed on account of measles, by order of Dr Wilshaw, local MoH'. The school reopened on 27 November. A hospital for infectious cases needed to be found and the favoured place was Ellerton Abbey, near Grinton in Swaledale. The Reverend Joad complained that children were dirty and verminous and their habits were dirty as well.[2]

There is not much sense of a united people all doing their bit for Britain here. But we should remember that what happened after the swift evacuation of September 1939 was the Phoney War. The expected air raids did not occur, people started to feel it was all an over-reaction, parents missed their children and many children were not happy away from home, quite apart from the consternation of the receiving hosts. The evacuees started to go back. Figures that emerged at NRCC level were that, of 16,160 children evacuated to the North Riding in this first wave, only 13,896 remained by 23 September and by 20 October this had fallen again to 9,233. Within Croft Rural District 200 children had been billeted on 3 September but by 20 October only 127 remained.[3] The Croft School Admission Register is helpful in this regard because they record the names, admission dates and dates of birth for every admitted evacuee. They also record the last attendance dates for most of them. So I can reveal that on 20 September 1939, Croft School admitted 50 evacuee children aged 5 to 14 (29 from Gateshead and 31 from Sunderland). Also that by mid-October 28 of them had gone home. 8 are registered as having stayed until April 1940.

It should also be noted that not everybody was negative. Sir Bedford Dorman, Chairman of the North Riding County Council, recognised that the evacuee scheme was hard work, and that although immediate danger seemed far away people should not relax. All of this work was needed and he appealed to women's institutes, voluntary services and other institutions to organise entertainment and welfare for children so that they might stay put rather than hanker for home.[4] 'Knowing the North Riding and its folk as I do, I have no doubt whatever of the success that will be achieved' he said, hopefully. The Croft Young Farmers Club held a dance to raise funds. A man from Kirbymoorside wrote to the D&S pointing out that there would be labour shortages after the war and that maybe, if treated well, some evacuees would develop an interest in working in agriculture. The WI organised parties and activities for the children

There is no evidence that people in Croft had resentments against evacuees similar to some of the examples I've given here, but there must have been tensions from the clashing together of town and country in this way. I tried to find some evacuees to get their story but have not succeeded. However, there are lots of materials that give you first hand accounts of what is was like to be evacuated and to host evacuees.[5]

This is the list of evacuees and evacuee teachers/helpers in Croft parish at the end of September 1939:

| Address | Host | Evacuee Name (Role) | DoB |
|---|---|---|---|
| The Anchorage, SP | Reginald Reynolds | Mary C Davies (Helper) | 11.01.1880 |
| | | Beatrice M Davies (Teacher) | 01.10.1912 |
| Monkend Farm | Walter Eeles | George Steel | 08.09.1928 |
| High Thorn | Frederick A Inness | Maurice McCulley (Teacher) | 12.06.1914 |
| Monkend Gardens # | Henry A Inness | Harold Verne-Jones (Teacher) | 26.07.1904 |
| | | Claire W Verne-Jones (Household Duties) | 12.08.1903 |
| Schoolhouse | George Fell | William Hall (Headteacher) | 13.07.1892 |
| | | Georgina Hall (Household duties) | 12.01.1894 |
| St Kitts, Monkend # | Ernest Payne | Agnes Coatsworth (Household duties) | 04.09.1907 |
| ? South Parade | Thomas Notton | Sidney Oates | 14.01.1932 |
| 9 South Parade # | Ralph Geldard | Isabel Cowell | 12.05.1934 |
| | | Nancy Cowell | 22.02.1930 |
| 12 South Parade # | Redacted | Isabella Turnbull | 16.04.1926 |
| | | Joe Turnbull | 19.11.1929 |

| Address | Host | Evacuee Name (Role) | DoB |
|---|---|---|---|
| 13 South Parade | Edward Marrett | Edward Holt | 22.10.1928 |
| | | Christopher Blair | 23.01.1926 |
| | | Mathew Robson | 27.12.1928 |
| 7 South Parade # | George Mosley | John Kirkhouse | 21.05.1930 |
| 2 Monkend Terrace | Tom Barningham | Thomas Devine | 23.05.1929 |
| 4 Monkend Terrace | William Haynes | William Adamson (Head Schoolmaster) | 12.11.1880 |
| | | Alice Adamson (Household Duties) | 22.02.1888 |
| 6 Monkend Terrace | Charles Lazenby | Ethel Bewick | 03.10.1926 |
| | | Ernest Bewick | 14.08.1928 |
| Pear Tree Cottage | Tom Falshaw | Marjorie Lumsden | 08.12.1925 |
| The Poplars (aka Bridge House) | Frederick Steggall | Joseph Botcherby (Teacher) | 21.08.1900 |
| Croft Hall ## | Dorothy Chaytor | Harold Stanks (Teacher) | 25.05.1904 |
| | | Freda Stanks (Helper) | 01.08.1908 |
| Oakwood #### | Annie Raine | Florence Bews (Helper) | 13.11.1893 |
| | | Irene Bews (Helper) | 18.09.1920 |
| | | Jean Blackstock | 09.05.1926 |
| | | Wilhelmina Blackstock | 09.05.1926 |
| | | Ethel Williams | 25.01.1927 |
| | | Ellen Robertson | 09.11.1929 |
| | | Elizabeth Dixon | 20.09.1929 |
| The Spa | Mary Riseborough | Thomas Green | 27.03.1926 |
| | | William Green | 31.10.1928 |

After the initial not-entirely-successful evacuation of 1939 things went quiet for a bit, and then in 1940, further billets were requested, and in early 1941 another nine evacuees arrived at Croft School – 1 from Gateshead and 8 from Sunderland. Evacuees were a feature, even if not a hugely prominent one, of Croft's war experience.

**Margaret Chapman** remembers two girls particularly who she and her brother Charlie were friends with:

*"During the war because* [Louisa Fyfe, Margaret's Aunt] *had a bedroom free,*[6] *you had to have an evacuee. And she had two. Two girls. Connie and Betty Barron, I called them. And I've got a snap of them here. Connie's the one there, at the front in the skirt. And* [Betty]*'s*[7] *the dark one, you'll recognise, standing at the back, 'cos they look quite alike. And Charlie's at the front somewhere, and I'm at the front. And I would be about six to seven on that one. Betty wouldn't stay long 'cos she was about school-leaving age, you see, it was only schoolchildren that* [were evacuees]*."*

The North Riding Education Committee had overall responsibility for the evacuees, while Billeting Officers, reporting via their councils to the Ministry of Health, were responsible for local organisation. In December 1939 a report was delivered to councillors for discussion at the NRCC meeting on the 6th of that month. It showed that, initially, the plan was that 12,000 children would be billeted in the

North Riding from Gateshead and Hull. However, on the planned evacuation day, 1 September, 7,500 children arrived from Gateshead and 5,000 from Hull. On 8 September, a further 7,000 children were evacuated from Middlesbrough, Sunderland and Hartlepool, plus 550 from independent schools. All of these children travelled with teaching staff and helpers. The report concluded that 'As far as can be judged the evacuated children are happy enough in school and there has certainly been a great improvement in their health and physical condition'. But by the date of the report, only 57% of evacuated children were still at their billets and this dropped further after Christmas. The Croft School Log Book entry for 9 February notes that 'W. Hall, Assistant Head Teacher of Harlow Green School, Gateshead returned to his own school duties' and that 'H Verne-Jones of Garden St School Sunderland has been transferred to Barton School'.

However this first wave of evacuees got on, September 1939 was not the only push for evacuation. As air raids became more extensive in 1940 and beyond there were still calls for children to evacuate to the countryside. But numbers were not high. When talking to interviewees I found few people that were aware of evacuees in Croft, perhaps because they were very young themselves during the war, but you can see from the evidence above that evacuation made a distinct impact at the time.

# Doing your bit

The Billeting Officer was an important role in the administration of the evacuation, and as time went on it was needed again. Mr Dobson was the Billeting Officer for Croft Rural District and his job was to canvas the local population for those willing to take an evacuee – and later, Land Army girls, and others – to organise the settlement at billets and deal with all issues arising. Mr Dobson was, I believe, a council employee. A vote at Croft RDC on 6 February 1939 gave him remuneration of 15/-, and I assume this was extra pay per week. But there were many other war roles that Croft people signed up for. The ARP and the Home Guard are well known. There was also the Auxiliary Fire Service, the WRVS, Red Cross, Special Constables and the Observer Corps, for example. Again the 1939 Register gives us some clues, this is the list, although it would certainly grow bigger as the war went on. It should be noted that the Home Guard was not set up until May 1940, so no names in the 1939 Register will not have that role.

| Name | Address | Auxiliary role |
| --- | --- | --- |
| Reginald Reynolds | The Anchorage, SP | Auxiliary Fire Service |
| Walter Eeles | Monkend Farm | Special Constable (North Riding) |
| Frederick Inness | High Thorn | Special Constable (North Riding) |
| George Fell | Schoolhouse | Observer Corps |
| Sarah Fell | Schoolhouse | First Aid |
| Marcus Matthews | SP | ARP |
| Richard C Whitworth | Corrie, Monkend | Observer Corps |

*Crofts Crossing*

| Name | Address | Auxiliary role |
|---|---|---|
| William Horne | Sunnybrae, SP | ARP |
| Daisy Horne | Sunnybrae, SP | ARP, First Aid |
| Elizabeth Dougill | 5, South Parade | Nursing Reserve |
| Richard Mosley | Tarlogie, SP | Observer Corps |
| William Parlour | Monkend Hall | District Controller, ARP |
| Gladys Parlour | Monkend Hall | ARP |
| Rodney Laing | Monkend Hall | Officers Emergency Reserve |
| Tom Hesp | 2 Rectory Cottages | Special Constable (North Riding) and Observer Corps |
| Walter Smith | 1, South Parade | Observer Corps |
| Mary C Smith | 1, South Parade | Red Cross Nurse |
| Laurence Headon | 2, South Parade | ARP, Auxiliary Fire Service |
| Charles Lazenby | 6, Monkend Terrace | ARP |
| William Adamson | The Mill | Special Constable (North Riding) |
| George Saunders | The Mill | Special Constable (North Riding) |
| Lawrence Arnett | Monkend Stables | Head warden ARP |
| Edward Steggall | The Poplars | Observer Corps |
| Henry Garrington | 3, The Terrace | ARP |
| Dorothy Chaytor | Croft Hall | ARP, Ambulance Driver |
| Catherine B. Chaytor | Croft Hall | ARP |
| Maurice Pease | Waterside | Special Constable (North Riding) |
| James R Taylor | Spa Road | Observer Corps |
| Percy Minns | The Limes | Special Constable (North Riding) and Observer Corps |
| George Chilton | Weigh House | ARP |
| Thomas Holiday | Plumtree Cottage | Special Constable (North Riding) |
| Joseph Binks | ? Halnaby | ARP |
| Johan Lindboe | North Lodge Halnaby | Scandinavian Interpreter to NR Police |
| Henry Abon | Newtown | Observer Corps |

This list would have grown as the war progressed, and, of course, some organisations – like the Home Guard – did not start until 1940 or later. However, there was an expectation that the populace would step up to aid the war effort. At a meeting in 1941 the RDC discussed participation in Civil Defence and:

> *several members referred to the fact that there was still a small proportion of the male population who had not as yet enrolled in any of the Civil Defence services, and expressed the opinion that the duties and obligations of Civil Defence should be shared by all male members of the community. It was resolved that, notwithstanding the provisions of the Civil Defence Duties Compulsory Enrolment Order 1941, His Majesty's government be urged to take steps to compel all able bodied male persons within prescribed age limit to undertake some form of Civil Defence duty and that a copy of this resolution be forwarded to the Minister of Home Security.*

## Chapter 3 – The Impact of World War II

Of course, many men in Croft would have joined up. Kit Chaytor had joined the Army Service Corps for example. Jack Headon was also one of these and he joined the RAF. However, his brother Jim was a motor mechanic, which was an occupation that was needed at home, so he joined the Home Guard. The Home Guard had many men who were needed on the Home Front, especially farmers, plus those who were too young or too old to join up. In this latter group were many who were veterans of World War 1. And the Home Guard were just one body of many who constituted what is generally known as the Home Front: the organisations, processes and daily personal resolve of the British people required to get through the dangers and deprivations of war.

**The children of Lawrence and Ada Headon, who lived at 2 South Parade, pictured at the back of the house in May 1941. Jack, the eldest, is in RAF uniform. Jim, exempted from call-up because he was a motor mechanic, is in Home Guard uniform. The two youngest, Margaret and Charlie, are in front.**

**Colonel Sir William Worsley addresses the men of C Company 12th North Riding (Gilling) Home Guard and attendees at the At Home event, in the field to the side of Monkend Hall in summer 1943.**

Captain William Parlour and his brother-in-law Lawrence Arnett were heads of the ARP and Home Guard respectively.

Air Raid Precautions (ARP), and the accompanying force of ARP Wardens, had started activity in the early planning stage of the war, as early as 1935 in central government, but in 1938 in Croft. It was at the beginning of 1939 that Captain Parlour became District Controller of the ARP. A role he took very seriously. The ARP was a Civil Defence organisation and all civilians – including women – were eligible to apply for it. They had arm bands and helmets but not a military uniform.

However, in early 1940 Winston Churchill recognised the need for a reserve force who could be called on if Germany tried to invade and the Home Guard was formed. The Home Guard was a civilian militia designed to hold up the Germans while the regular army organised for battle, and to assist in helping the civilian population following invasion. They had a uniform like an army uniform, did exercises and drills like an army platoon and had ranks like the army. Lawrence Arnett achieved the rank of Major.

Let's just say that there was a bit of rivalry between Captain Parlour and Major Arnett. And this rivalry was all the more interesting because the two men were related to each other, shared a profession (auctioneer), and also a good part of their lives.

*Chapter 3 – The Impact of World War II*

# The Parlours and the Arnetts

Captain William Parlour was born in 1890 in Hurworth Place, to William Parlour (b 1861 in Dalton-on-Tees) and his wife Mary Elizabeth (nee Nesom) of East Cowton. He was one of 3 children, including his sister Dorothy, 10 years his junior, and the only son. Their sister Mary died of TB when she was young. In the 1911 census his father William is listed as an auctioneer residing in Croft, with William junior aged 18 and described as an 'agricultural student'. By 1921 William Senior is an 'Auctioneer and Estate Agent' and an Employer. In a 1902 Kelly's Directory William Senior appears as 'auctioneer and brick maker' and his address is Tees View (Hurworth Place). It was William Senior who negotiated a long lease with Sir Walter Chaytor (5th Baronet) about 1912 for some land next to River Tees, near the railway bridge. On this land he built the house Waterside, submitting plans for approval from Croft RDC on 9 September 1912. And that is where he was in the 1921 census, and where he died.. On 4 December 1914 he bought the land from Sir Edmund Chaytor freehold to obtain full ownership.[8] When he died, on 26 August 1925, he left an estate worth £126,526 (over £8 million in 2022 money).

William Parlour Junior joined the army some time in 1915. He was posted to the Army Service Corps (it became the Royal Service Corps in 1918) became a Lieutenant and then just before his discharge, Captain. The job of the Army Service Corps was to ensure the tenure of land, supplies and transport to all army units. William Parlour's job was to buy hay for horses. In an army still with cavalry units and which depended on horse-drawn transport in the main, this was an important job.

On leaving the army, maybe as late as 1921, Captain Parlour seems to have taken up his father's profession as a land agent and auctioneer but he can't be found in the 1921 census. On his marriage certificate he is described as 'Estate Agent'. He is sometimes mocked for always calling himself 'Captain', but it was an easy to way to make his identity clear. There could be confusion with his father and probably several other relatives as well. There are a good number of Parlours in Croft and Dalton history and they recycled the same names in every generation. Confusion is always possible! This William Parlour was known either as 'Captain' or, if you knew him well, 'Will'.

We know that Captain Will Parlour married Gladys Gotto in London on 11 June 1919. How they met is not clear.

**Sally Still**, his niece, does not know either:

*"I don't know how they met. Was he in Cornwall for some reason? Maybe again, looking for hay, I don't know. She was a very grand lady. And she really was a lady. Anyway, they obviously fell in love. He was at least a head shorter than her. She was in her youth sort of 5 foot 9 or 5 10 easily? Anyway he proposed to her on a railway station and produced a potato out of his pocket. Because they were like gold dust you see. And she said yes. And anyway, she was an a Cornish lady – they married in London in 1919. And, you know, the church, St Saviour's, I think it was behind Harrods."*

Gladys was the only daughter of Christopher Lamb Gotto and his wife Helen Mary. She was born in June 1886. The marriage certificate records Mr Gotto's occupation as 'Gentleman' and Gladys's place

**The marriage of Lawrence Arnett to Dorothy Parlour in 1937. Captain Will Parlour is at the left of the picture and Gladys Parlour is second from the right. The party are posing in front of the then new swimming pool at the Croft Spa Hotel.**

of residence as Launceston, Cornwall. Evidence suggests that that residence in Launceston was not permanent throughout her life. Gladys was born in London, St Pancras to be specific, where the family lived in Gordon Square. She had one one brother, Christopher Hugh, who became a Brigadier in the Devonshire Regiment and who was awarded the Military Cross during World War 1. On Gladys's and Hugh's baptism records their father is listed as a Merchant, but on a later census he appears as 'Stationer'. That is because Gladys's grandfather – Hugh Jenkin Gotto – founded the company of Parkins & Gotto. They started as Stationers and Printers on Oxford Street, London, with a printing and manufacturing unit on Rathbone Place. They began by specialising in printed stationery: things like annual almanacks, calendars, greeting cards, personalised stationery and business books like ledgers. They soon diversified into writing slopes, stationery cabinets, furniture, card tables, toys and games, tennis sets, croquet sets and billiard tables. They were very well known in the second half of the nineteenth century, occupying several premises on Oxford Street and a cursory google will yield many pictures of items made by them which still fetch good money. Gladys's father ran this business from 1894 but it declined in the early twentieth century and is not mentioned in trade directories after 1912. As for Gladys herself, she seems to have been at boarding school in 1901 in Farnham Royal, Buckinghamshire and in 1921 was living as a boarder at 118 Queen Anne Gate in London (She was already married then, of course). The link with Launceston is that her parents were living at Yeolmbridge House, near Launceston at the time of her marriage and that

## Chapter 3 – The Impact of World War II

is where both of her parents died (her mother died in 1922). There is evidence that the Gotto family had this house as a country residence for some time, maybe from the late nineteenth century. Christopher Lamb Gotto died in 1941 leaving an estate of £26,000 and a will that named his executors as Brigadier Christopher Hugh Gotto (Gladys's brother) and Captain William Parlour.

On the subject of how Will and Gladys met, here's a theory: Gladys had a cousin, also born in 1886, called Guy Wolfe Gotto, and he was in the Army Service Corps like Will, also joined in 1915, as Lieutenant and then Captain. It's not inconceivable that Captain Parlour and Captain Gotto knew each other, and that the latter invited the former to some social event where he met Gladys. I can't think of better explanation.

It was six years into their marriage when Will and Gladys bought Monkend Hall, the place where they could live the life they aspired to live and which they made available to Croft for many purposes and events. The deed of conveyance is dated 11 March 1926 and the buyer on this is Gladys Parlour. The sellers were the children of Richard Bowes, who presumably held the Hall in trust as the result of Richard Bowes's death on 18 November 1925. Why Gladys is the buyer I don't know. Certainly her husband, following his father's death, would not have been short of money but perhaps it was earmarked for other purposes. Gladys would undoubtedly have had money of her own. When she died, on 14 August 1974, her estate was valued at £124,723 and her will specified that the Hall be made available to her husband for his lifetime. She still seemed to be the owner.

Lawrence Wilfred Arnett was born in Middlesbrough in 1893, the eldest of seven boys born to William Heslop and Sarah Hannah Arnett. In the 1911 census he is 17, living at home in Middlesbrough and working as a clerk in a wire works. His father is a butcher aged 50. He joined the army in 1915, as part of the Yorkshire Hussars (9th Battalion, West Yorkshire Regiment). He served at the Western Front.

Following discharge from the army Lawrence was apprenticed to William Parlour Senior as a land agent and auctioneer. In the 1921 census he is living in Croft as a boarder at 17, South Parade and is listed as 'Pupil Land Agent and Auctioneer' with his employer given as William Parlour. Certainly we know he was successful in this career as he headed a succession of auctioneer businesses up until the 1950s – Wallis & Arnett and Arnett, Calder and Twizell etc had regular advertisements in the D&S for many years. On 7 October 1937 he married Captain Parlour's sister Dorothy at Croft Church. They lived at The Stables, then known as Lawn Cottage I think, next to Monkend Hall. In 1947 they moved to Pond House in Hurworth.

And so a remarkable team came about during those war years – Will and Gladys Parlour, Lawrie and Dorothy Arnett, all related by marriage and by blood, and by profession. Will and Gladys did not have children; Lawrence and Dorothy had Daphne (married Anthony Scott-Harden in 1965) and Sally (married Simon Still in 1974). Sally remembers: *"My aunt was 'Deedle-Dee', my uncle was 'Onk', my mother was 'Snooks'. They all had nicknames."* And during World War 2 the Parlours and the Arnetts set to with war work. They featured heavily in all activities in the village.

A great deal of attention was vested in the ARP during the run up to war. Captain Parlour was a District Councillor at this time and there were many discussions at council meetings that detailed their activities. In December 1938 he was appointed as 'Honorary ARP Officer'. Honorary, I imagine, because paid ARP Officers were part of the Civil Defence hierachy and worked for the County Council. Civil Defence generally was the responsibility of the Home Office. Captain Parlour accepted his title with the request that Mr Arnett be called the *Assistant Honorary* ARP Officer.

Captain Parlour liked to take things on, but then he liked to have control of those things. He had developed his own ARP scheme for the District and it was clear that if the County Council hierarchy didn't deliver what he wanted in terms of support he'd follow that plan anyway, insofar as he could. An example: if Captain Parlour hadn't been granted the number of stretchers he wanted for the ARP, he moved that the RDC should pay for them and order them directly. If the County Council ordered that Fire Guards should be bought uniforms, Captain Parlour disagreed, he moved that no action could should be taken (they had helmets and arm-bands I believe). When NRCC laid down standards for how civilian deaths might be dealt with, Captain Parlour responded that it was all in his plan, and he'd made arrangements with Darlington Memorial Hospital to take any casualties.

During the war the National Fire Service, including the volunteers of the Auxiliary Fire Service, was placed under the jurisdiction of the ARP organisation and the local authorities, for planning purposes. So Captain Parlour led both. He recruited the volunteer fire guards and took responsibility for their training and equipment.

Petrol rationing was introduced from 3rd September 1939, the first day of the war, before food rationing actually. As priority for use of petrol was to be given to the armed forces and civil defence, Captain Parlour also became Fuel Controller for the Rural District. Not least because he didn't like what the County Council were proposing with regard to petrol for the ARP and he needed to make sure the Croft RD had everything it needed.

In May 1943, the Divisional Officer of the National Fire Service had written to the district council to say that the Home Guard were storing bombs and live grenades in a hut to the rear of the Croft Spa Hotel, and this was in close proximity to the NFS and residential homes. He asked the council to take steps to minimise the danger. Captain Parlour said that the Home Guard would have stored everything 'with due regard to regulations' and resolved that no action be taken. This was carried by his fellow councillors.

Captain Parlour was very much his own man with regard to deciding what was effective, or not. In May 1941, he was elected as a County Councillor to represent the Croft Electoral Division. A post he held until 1953 when he was elevated to the status of Alderman (until retirement in 1974).

Sally Still noted in her interview that her father Lawrence Arnett was a more easy-going and light-hearted man that Captain Parlour. He was better at getting on with people. He enjoyed winding up his brother in law on occasion, and Captain Parlour did not always see the funny side. Although Sally did say that her uncle was also very gregarious.

Mr Arnett was the Croft Parish Clerk from September 1925, all through the war and into the 1950s. He knew a great many people in the village and was happy to serve. An example of him in action was a big meeting in January 1939 to plan Croft village's civil defence. Mr Arnett was in the chair. The Women's

Institute was represented by their chair, Gladys Parlour, the British Legion was there, the District Nursing Association in the person of 'Miss Parlour' (not sure who this was). Together they planned in great detail what would happen if Croft was in danger, how it would defend itself from aerial attack, how casualties would be dealt with, who would handle communications, who would organise transport, who would find shelter for anyone displaced, who would offer support to the bereaved. They emerged with so much achieved that the plans hardly needed to be re-visited again – only to factor in a new ruling, a new role or some piece of detail they'd missed. A tribute to community co-operation and effective chairmanship.

It's no surprise then, that when the Home Guard was formed the following year (1940), it was Lawrence Arnett who was put in charge, not just for Croft Home Guard but for 'C' Company, 12th North Riding (Gilling) Battalion. He had attained the role of Lieutenant before leaving the army in World War 1, but within the Home Guard he attained the rank of Major. As the Home Guard had been formed specifically to deal with the possibility of a German invasion, to hold up the Germans until the proper army arrived, the sense of urgency in Croft cannot have been all that great at this time. It was not Warmington-on-Sea or some other coastal town on the English Channel. And it was the case that people, particularly children, in Croft may not have been suitably respectful as the Home Guard paraded up and down the street. *"We used to laugh at them"* said Margaret Chapman, noting that they would march up and down South Parade, *"and Mr Coates, his initials were HG, so we called him Home Guard Coates"*.

The spell of *Dad's Army* persists in the British national consciousness when it comes to the Home Guard. It is not fair to laugh at the Home Guard because they were a significant part of our defences. And had Germany invaded they would have been in the hot seat. In 1942 the British government believed that invasion was imminent and the Home Guard was a key part of the plan to fight back. I've seen some of those plans. 'C' Company consisted of Croft, Barton, Great Langton, North Cowton and Stapleton, but most members of the main company seemed to be in Croft.[9] 'Battle headquarters' for the Croft company were at the Half Moon Inn in Barton. The Germans were expected to land on the east coast and the job of 'C' Company was to obstruct them, without actually getting involved in direct fighting. Croft Bridge was a key obstruction point. I heard an interview with Ernie Hodgson from Hurworth Place where he described the setting of explosives on the bridge that could be detonated to prevent the Germans crossing the river.[10] However, it was the Durham Home Guard who were responsible for that, and indeed all crossing points on the Tees. 'C' Company was to man designated 'strong points' and defend them; to observe and report information to Battalion Headquarters; to assist the military when they arrived, for example, by manning road blocks. C Company consisted of 269 men who had 104 rifles, and 5 Lewis Guns between them. Each man was to carry 4 grenades. The main 'strong points' were Barton and Atley Hill and the latter was also the designated Observation Post for the company.

The documentation shows that serious and viable plans were made and that there was important work to do. But still there is a little bit of Mainwaring-esque self-importance in it all contrasted with some homely detail. Before setting out to defend our nation, men were to be reminded to take sandwiches, as food might not be readily available. The part-time soldiers must have felt quite excited by it all especially perhaps by Phase 3 of the Defence Scheme in case of invasion. It states that *'Should the enemy break through and fighting become general, the Home Guard would be used as Guerrillas employing ambushes etc.'.* It's possible they might have felt slightly disappointed that Hitler's invasion did not happen, and the chance to show what they could do never came.

Although there *were* domestic applications for Home Guard skills it seems. David Coates tells a story about his father Bert, who was a Home Guard enthusiast.

**David Coates**:

*"I don't know why I remember this but mum wanted the chimney cleaning. And evidently Dad came home with what I think you call a thunder flash from the Home Guard, and stuck that up the chimney. It made a bit of a loud bang. It certainly cleaned the chimney because I can remember seeing the kitchen. It was just like raining soot. It was a disaster."*

I don't have a list of who was in the Home Guard in Croft. I know Jim Headon was, Bert Coates, Peter Parlour from Townend Farm in Dalton and probably many others, but there's no list available. However, on 25 July 1943 there was a major event at Monkend Hall involving the Home Guard, which was attended by the Northern Division top brass. The programme records some names.

In addition, Charlie Headon recalled that his brother Jim was heavily involved in the Home Guard and was a Sargeant.

**Charlie Headon**:

*" ... my next brother to me, eight year older than me, he was a sergeant in the Home Guard. That was Jim. I think they used to have a bus go and pick the men up 'cos they were mostly farmers and didn't have cars, and I used to go out on the bus on a Sunday morning 'cos me brother never got up in time, so I was the bus conductor, which I enjoyed. And on Sundays he'd bring them up here* [South Parade] *when they were out some nights in the summer and he'd drill them outside our house* [No.2], *so me sister and I could see out the bedroom window."*

**Front page of the programme for the Home Guard At Home event held at Monkend Hall.**

Dave Headon, Jim's son, said that his father continued to talk at length about the Home Guard into

## Chapter 3 – The Impact of World War II

his old age, not always to a fascinated audience. *'If my father started a sentence with the phrase "During the war...", the room would empty'*.

After the war, Lawrence Arnett was awarded an MBE for services to the Home Guard. There's a copy of his recommendation in the National Archives. The recommendation was made by the commanding officer for the 12th North Riding Battalion HG. It says this:

> *Major Arnett has commanded 'C' company of this battalion since it was formed in 1940 and has given up a vast amount of time to Home Guard duties in spite of being a very busy man.*
>
> *The company covers a very large area, chiefly agricultural, and considerable tact, patience and perseverance is required to get the necessary response from this type of man. Major Arnett has been particularly successful in producing an extremely high standard of efficiency in his company and is indefatigable in his efforts to maintain this.*

The recommendation was accepted and Lawrence Wilfred Arnett went to London to get his MBE.

While all of the above are the 'official' side of war work, the role of women's organisations on the Home Front should not be forgotten. In Croft this was principally the Women's Institute (WI), as I can't find anything about the local Women's Voluntary Service (WVS). There definitely was a Croft & Darlington WVS, but I can't find anything about them. In early civil defence planning in Croft Rural District a 'Miss Mowbray' was the WVS representative. However, there is evidence that the WI was active in many ways and was well attended. The D&S carried occasional reports of their activities, and RDC minutes often note the contribution of 'the Ladies' Committee' to key activities. The WI was not only a key organisation for encouraging and administrating voluntary work but also a vital support for the women who were busy trying to maintain a stable home life at a time of food, household and clothing shortages. It was the WI who were almost solely responsible for organising the practicalities of dealing with the evacuees. And whenever there was practical organising work that was not specifically about dealing with attacks or armaments, the WI stepped in to assist. Gladys Parlour was the Chair of the WI at this time and Monkend Hall the usual meeting place for members.

There were two other war-related organisations active in Croft village during the war: the Royal Observer Corps and the Auxiliary Fire Service.

There was an Observer Corps post at Croft-on-Tees. It was a post and not a control centre. The Observer Corps was a civil defence organisation, mostly manned by civilian volunteers but annexed to the RAF. Their job was to provide intelligence to the RAF on air activity within British airspace. They were part plane-spotters and part spies. An Observer Corps post maintained a constant team of observers. The observers had radio equipment and were trained to identify planes and anything else visible in the skies. When something was spotted they had a specific protocol for reporting it to the Observer Corps control centre. At the control centres they calibrated all of the reports, mapping them and detecting patterns of activity, maybe attack. This intelligence was used in decisions about military strategy both immediate and long term. It was a vital contribution to the war effort.

# Crofts Crossing

The Observation Corps post at Croft fed into a control room like this: observations were plotted on a map, interpreted, and intelligence fed to the armed forces.

You can see from the list on pages 9 and 10 that several men in Croft village were part of the Observer Corps in 1939, and once the aerodrome started I imagine this number would have increased. The entry pictured below comes from an official history of the Observer Corps. The figure Z.309070 is a National Grid reference and it indicates a spot on the west side of the A167, just south of the Eryholme Lane turning that occurs just before/after Dalton. A similar reference is given on Wikipedia.[11] I had heard that the Observer Corps post was at Clervaux Castle, but this doesn't seem right according to the official information. Ann Carnelly (Reed), whose father was in the Observer Corps at one point said that the observation post was in the field to the south of the Tees Railway bridge, before you get to Pepperfield Farm.

*Croft*
Opened Dec 1936 Z.309070, 9/Z.3; 9/V.1 Feb 1945; 20/J.4 Nov 1953; U/G July 1961; 23/S.4 March 1967;

**Ann Reed (Carnelly):**
*"it looked like a balloon. It was a dome in the field. Between, just past the railway bridge, first field before you come to Pepperfield. [...] It was the observation capsule thing."*

The grid reference recorded below probably refers to a cold-war bunker that was built after World War 2, to provide additional intelligence about Soviet or similar activity. I think this is what is meant by 'U/G July 1961'. It was still in use in 1976 when the book was compiled. Another online source – *Subterranea Britannica* – provides some pictures of the bunker taken in the 1990's and says it that fell into disuse in 1991.[12] Who would have manned the cold war bunker? And why at Croft? Questions I can't answer I'm afraid. None of the people listed in 1939 as being members of the Observer Corps in World War 2 are still alive, but maybe some of their relatives would know.

**Margaret Chapman** has distinct memories of the Auxiliary Fire Service, which was situated at the back of the Croft Spa Hotel:

*"They were at the back of the hotel. It was high walled all the way around. And you know, where the village hall is now, and they had railings somewhere round there I think. Then at the back of the hotel, just had gates going in [...]. And through those gates it was the Auxiliary Fire Service. Yes. And they went through and there were all huts. Built on bricks this high. Down the side – the right hand side. And I suppose I never saw fire engines because you weren't allowed in there. But yes, the NFS service. And then suppose they didn't need them anymore."*

According to the 1939 Register, there were also a group of 16 women whose address was 'Croft Spa Hotel', but they are listed separately – two pages away – from the main Hotel listing of staff and guests. The entries all say '11th E.R. Coy A.T. S.'. It's not possible to see the right hand side of the entries that gives roles. However, I believe this group to be members of the Auxiliary Territorial Service. The ATS were the forerunners of the WRAC (Women's Royal Army Corps), but they were, I believe voluntary.

# Food, Food Control and Food Production

The Food Control Committee for the Croft Rural District dealt with all matters of food rationing. This included ensuring people got their ration books, that they had access to the food they needed, and to prevent the sale and production of food outside of the designated food controls. The Ministry of Food were responsible for food control policy and local authorities enacted it. Captain Parlour and Mrs Dorothy Chaytor (the widow of Alfred Henry Chaytor and mother of Kit) were the Croft members of the Rural District Food Control Committee throughout the war.

Food rationing started immediately war was declared and tightened in the ensuing years, so by 1941 it was a major challenge for the ordinary housewife (or servant) to put a palatable meal on the table. The district Food Control Committee felt that rationing procedures were too focussed on people in towns and did not suit the Croft Rural District where there was a 'dearth of shops'[13] that people could use to get provisions. The distribution of ration books seemed to take place in Darlington, and there were concerns about people being able to get there within distribution times.

However, Ian Dougill told me that Croft was not so badly off in the war when it came to food. 'You could always get extra food if you needed to'. This was because Croft had several market gardens and small farms. You could do a bit of barter for some eggs, or bacon, maybe vegetables. Gerry Andrew, Mr Stairmand, Mr Henry Inness and his son Frederick and Mr Adamson at the mill all kept chickens and pigs and had fields of potatoes and cabbages. It was not permitted for them to supply local people outside of the Food Control rules, but it may have happened. Owners of pigs were allowed to keep half when it was slaughtered. And who was to know how many eggs a chicken had laid?

**Margaret Chapman's** brother Jim had become engaged to Mary Kirk and she was invited to spend a week at Mary's farm:

*"I went to Mary's farm. Mary married Jim you see, the second son. Mary lived at Bullmire Farm. When I was seven [1941], I think I can remember going on my little bike and my mum taking me on her bike. I had a week, a week at Bullmire. And oh, she said I came back with full cheeks. I mean, I had milk every day. Butter, eggs, every day, which you never got when you're in rationing time."*

Children on farms had better access to food, no doubt. However, the farms were not allowed to slaughter animals just for their own use. They could slaughter chickens and offal was not rationed. Bargains within the parish were probably struck. However, if you were stopped by the police and found to have illegal levels of food about your person, it was a crime. The Food Control Committees also set up undercover inspectors who would attempt to obtain food illegally, and report any offenders.

One other contribution to Croft's food supply is to be noted. Captain Parlour had acquired a great acreage of grouse moors in Durham, Northumberland, Yorkshire (more on this in Chapter 5). And he, with friends, went shooting regularly. During the war, and beyond, he applied for a licence to sell game from Monkend Hall. The important point here being that *game* was not rationed at all.[14]

The Government was also keen for everyone to have allotments and for all grass to be turned over to food production. In response to a Ministry of Food circular on the matter, the RDC sent back a message that 'in a district like Croft' there was no need for allotments. They did not engage in encouraging them or trying to find land for them. So in March 1941, they politely declined an invitation to attend a conference on food production through allotments, to be held in Newcastle, and continued to hold out against lobbying over the next 3 years. I know that the Rectory garden had some allotments on it and I believe these were operational in 1950, but when they started I don't know. The Croft Millennium Book contains a lovely photo of Robbie Carter on his allotment in the Rectory Garden. However I assume this would have gone when the garden was sold off for building plots in 1969. It is minuted in the Croft Parish Council records that on 13 September 1978 Bill Chaytor offered the parish 9 allotments with fencing and water for the rental of £50 per annum. And those are the allotments in use today.

Of course, farmers were on the frontline too, an issue I deal with in the Chapter 5. They needed to feed a nation that had, before the outbreak of war, been dependent on imports for its food supply. Pre World War 2, 70% of Britain's food was imported. 90% of wheat came from the USA, Canada and Australia. Sugar was produced using imported sugar cane and, incredibly, 90% of butter was produced abroad.[15] Now we had to feed ourselves and demand for farm labour was higher than before, at a time when many men were absent on forces duty or tied up in other war work.

The Women's Land Army was revived in June 1939, having been originally formed during World War 1. I have verbal evidence from Mary Andrew, Bert Walker, Jane Parlour and Margaret Chapman that Land Army girls were active in Croft parish but the details of who, when and where are not complete.

**Mary Andrew**:

*"There was just a Land Army girl down at Home Farm and it was you know, the Home Farm for the* [Halnaby] *Hall. And she married the son, Michael Banner's uncle. Land Army girl did. Raymond Banner. And then they emigrated to Canada."*

It's also not clear where the Land Army were billetted. In February 1943 the Croft RDC were asked to provide billets for the Land Army by the Ministry of Food, who were responsible for organising them. The council replied to this request by saying that there were no more billets available in the villages, and that the best place for Land Army girls was a hostel. But they would see if any farmhouses had capacity. I believe there was a Land Army hostel at Sadberge near Darlington, but whether this was the one used by the Croft assignees I don't know.

However, the Land Army was still not enough to fill the gap. Prisoners of War had started to arrive in Britain in 1941 but numbers greatly increased as the war progressed. The first prisoners were Italians, then Germans. It should be noted that 'German' POWs included many nationalities since Germany had conscripted citizens from occupied territories. All treatment of POWs was governed by the Geneva Convention which had been agreed before World War 1. Britain was largely a scrupulous adherer to the Convention, not least because it did not want reprisals against British prisoners captured by the Germans. As early as 1941, Britain took the view that POWs might help reduce the chronic labour shortage. In that year, Britain agreed to take 50,000 Italian POWs for exactly that purpose.[16] The network of POW camps started to grow: the major camp nearest to Croft was the Gilling Camp at Hartforth Grange. However, our Croft voices talked about Kirkbank at Middleton Tyas as a place POWs lived. There is certainly evidence of POWs living around the area and I believe Chris Lloyd has written about these. By 1944, the government authorised the use of Prisoners of War as labour, not just on the land, but in numerous jobs where they could contribute skills. The POWs were paid fair wages – the same as any other casual labourer. They paid for their keep and were allowed to put the rest into account they could use when they were released. A small amount of pocket money was allowed for their leisure use. Later on, it was permissible for POWs to live outside their camps or shelters as long as they followed rules and civilians were happy to have them. Not every POW had the right to work. Prisoners were assessed and graded as to what risks they posed to the community. Only the lower risk prisoners, for example ones that would not try to escape or pass information back to enemy sources, were allowed to work.

**Mary Andrew:**

*"And then the prisoners of war were at Kirkbank, the Germans. And they used to bring them around in a wagon, you know, an open back wagon to work on the farm. I remember, I can see that one coming yet. And they dropped them off at the farms and we had two at Waterloo.*

*Yes, Albert and Bruno. They were lovely. And again, I don't know how long for, a few weeks or maybe months? I don't know. But then mum said to them if they would be allowed to stay at the farm, you know, to live with us, would they like to do that? And of course, oh yes, of course they wanted to do that. […] And there was two up at Creaking Tree Farm. Yeah. And there was two at Brook House living in. […] I think when mum started with our two, they stayed as well. And then on a Saturday night, one of the farms, you know, would have them all. They all came to Waterloo one to two Saturday nights. And mum would put some food on for them. Yeah, they were lovely were those two. I can't remember how long they stayed or when it was but I know we got two Italians after when the Germans went back. And they weren't half as friendly as the Germans were. No the two we had were really nice. And well, I don't know how we managed with the language really, but we must have done. Me father was very deaf. But anyway, they made him understand, or he made them understand what he wanted from them.*

*We didn't have tractors much then just horses. […] I think both of them maybe had some, you know, agricultural background but yes, they could work the land with the with the horses and do the field work and they fed the cattle. And I don't know whether they did any milking because Mum always did the milking, but they were they were good all right. One horse we had, I can always remember her, this particular one, we called her Jean. And dad said to one – he must have made him understand, or maybe they could speak a bit of English, I don't know – but he said you know 'be careful with Jean, 'cos she bites' and this Bruno says 'no … Jean good horse'."*

The Walker family and helpers take a break during haymaking at Birch Springs, ca 1949. L to R: Edward (POW), John Walker Snr, Bert Walker, Laurie Walker, Horner Walker, Sally Walker, John Walker Jnr.

# Chapter 3 – The Impact of World War II

**Bert Walker**:

*"Aye, we had an ex-German prisoner, he was a good man. Aye, he was very good, 'cos he'd been a farmer in Germany. And he used to make baskets and do all sorts in his spare time. He used to go brambling and mushrooming and sell them you know, door to door on his bike. He lived with us, at Birch Springs, in the farmhouse. Edward Schumpeter.*

*It was something like that. I just remember him as Edward, it was always Edward.*

*Yeah, he was from Germany. Well, it was Lithuania where he came from. But he was a farmer out there, and things weren't very good, I don't think, when he was farming. He said potatoes are what they grew, they used to hawk them about round the towns and sell them. And he said sometimes if they stopped at a house and made them walk up to the horse and cart, they wouldn't bother with him anymore [laughs]. So, it was pretty tough for him over there. But then, he was called up in the army and was taken a prisoner of war, and that's how he ended up here.*

*I don't know where he was kept quite, but I know when they took him, they wouldn't let him have any knives or forks to eat a meal with. You know, in case of, you know, what he might do with them. Yeah, yes, that's right, 'cos it would be – I don't know what time, what it would be [when he came to work for us]? It would be possibly just after the war finished when he came to work for us, 'cos he'd worked at another farm before he came to us. That was at Browns [Jolby Farm].*

*He went back, well, he met a girl from Germany in this country, and he wanted to marry her. So, whether he ever married her or not, 'cos he couldn't write in English and we lost touch with him, although when he went back he said he would certainly keep in touch, but he didn't."*

Margaret Chapman and Ian Dougill both remember Italian POWs being brought on a wagon into Croft village to work on Gerry Andrew's market garden, and that the children in the village used to shout things at them and shake their fists.

**Ann Reed (Carnelly)** also remembers having a birthday cake made for her by an Italian POW:

*"There was a prisoner of war camp. It was on [the Leggott's] land. And behind there is where the paintball is now. And me fifth birthday was spent there because my mother and father used to go out there and they did a party for me on me 5th birthday [1945]. And it was an Italian chef. And the officers ... they would be the guards. And [the Italian chef] brought me birthday cake in and it was three tiered like wedding cake. I said 'Is that ice cream' and he said 'have you stuck your finger in it'? 'No', and it was ice cream. And they did me a bracelet. It was plastic wire with a clasp. And it had little brass hearts on it."*

Quite a few Italian POWs were taken on in catering roles. The place where Ann had her birthday party might not have been a POW camp. In the position she describes, in 1945, it was likely to be the NAAFI facility for the Aerodrome, that would be why her parents went out there, and the Italian POW was probably employed there because he could cook. The NAAFI site was called Communal Site No 2 and is described in detail, with a photograph, in Alan Todd's book, page 204.

**Ian Calvert**, who was a child living in Banks' Terrace during the war, also remembers prisoners of war:

*"If you were out at a certain time on the street on a morning, there would be trucks going down from Hurworth, with the prisoners of war on the back end. There was a prison camp down at the scar there. Well, they were all Italians and they used to to bring them out on a morning. And they had these badges on the arms to identify them as prisoners. Was it a triangle or something? And we used to shout at them as they went past. [...] They used to take them to Fell's farm on Darlington Road [Oxneyfield]. And then the farms around here.*

*And there were Germans but they were a different kettle of fish. There must have been Germans because at the end of the war there were two, or several, men who fought on the German's side who stayed in the villages. Married local girls. At least two. And it was probably a lot more. They were Ukrainians, captured by the Germans and put in the German army to fight against the Russians and the Brits. They hadn't joined out of their own choosing I don't think, they were conscripted into the German army. I only know by the name of Henry. Henry Vischok is it? And he ended up living at Pilmore Cottages."*

Jane Parlour's family have been at Village Farm, Dalton (previously known as Townend Farm) since the mid 1800s. She recalls her father, Peter Parlour, who was born in 1918, talking about prisoners of war working on the farm in, maybe after, World War 2.

**Jane Parlour**:

*"He always used to tell me that about prisoners of war that they had, or foreign nationals, shall we say, that I guess were prisoners of war, but would be working on the farm. And he would kind of rate them in terms of how hard working they were. And that to him was how you earned your respect. You had quite high esteem for people that worked hard, you know, he didn't treat them like slaves. But if they were capable of doing a day's work, like everybody that had to do a manual job then they would be of higher esteem. And he mentioned a lot about Ukrainians and Germans. And they were always the hardest working and strongest. He said all these Ukrainians were big lads. And they were strong, you know, and this is at times when they used to carry what they called sugar sacks up and down the granary steps. They weighed 16 stone, which is unbelievable. It was hard graft. It wasn't just sitting on a tractor. So the idea was that these Ukrainian lads were up to the job and they could do it. And then the Germans, he said the German prisoners of war were hard grafters as well. [...]*

*And he was very, very upset post war, when a lot of the Ukrainians were returned to the Soviet Union. I don't know where they went to. Because he said they, they didn't actually want to go back, a lot of them. They were kind of worried for their safety. And I think there was something about, I wouldn't say that the Ukrainians were collaborators with the Germans, but there was some of that territory. There was one in particular that was here, that actually ended up marrying a local girl, I don't know a name, and was able to settle and stay here. And I think they went on to have a family and my dad became the godfather of their eldest son. And you know, till the day he died, which was 1986, I remember my dad having never a good word about the politicians of the time who actually sent these Ukrainians back to Stalin, basically, because they knew that something bad was gonna happen. And I have heard from somebody else who's studied the period, that they were actually massacred at the docks, a lot of them. They were they were seen as collaborators, and they were shot."*

There is a lot to know about the situations that Bert's Lithuanian and Peter's Ukrainians were going back to, and it graphically illustrates how the war impacted people on the continent of Europe, as opposed to us, the British, in our island fortress. There are a number of studies to refer to and I offer a summary here, with the references in the footnotes.

POWs started to be repatriated from the second half of 1945 and by the end of 1946 they had mostly gone. This would have been a timetable dictated by the Geneva Convention. But some prisoners did not want to go home. Bert's Edward did not want to go back to Lithuania, he said. This might have been because Lithuania was now part of the Soviet Union.

The situation with the Ukrainians was a bit more complicated. Ukraine had suffered many deprivations as part of the Soviet Union in the interwar years. When Hitler invaded western Ukraine many felt that the Nazis would tolerate an independent Ukrainian state and saw them as the better of two evils. So a Ukrainian Division – sometimes called the Galician Division – of the German Army was formed in May 1943, first with volunteers, and then with forced subscription. The idea was that this Division would be specifically focussed on fighting the Russians. As the Nazis were driven back, the allies took many of these soldiers prisoner. Britain agreed to take around 30,000 of them towards the end of the war, in an attempt to fill up chronic labour shortages during the later stages of the war, although it's not that clear that that number ever reached these shores. Prior to that only a few thousand Ukrainians were amongst the PoWs in the Britain. As prisoners started to be repatriated after Victory in Europe – from 1945 – the assumption was that labour shortages would disappear as our own soldiers returned. But they didn't. In May 1946, the Foreign Secretary gave figures to parliament that showed net emigration to e.g. the US, Australia and Canada outstripping any immigration to Britain. The estimated Labour shortage was 140,000.[17]

The government started to work on providing schemes that would allow European displaced persons (including POWs) to work in the UK, with rights and pay like any British worker. Between 1 July 1947 and 31 December 1950 some 81,000 such workers settled in the UK, with another 4,000 'sponsored' as individuals by British citizens.[18] Only a subsection of this number would have been Ukrainian, possibly as few as 10%. However, there were organisations in Britain, such as the 'Brotherhood of Ukrainian Veterans' who were formed specifically to look after the interests of Ukrainian migrant workers. As the organisations associated with the war – such as the War Office – were closing down these organisations took on a co-ordination and monitoring role, with resources to intervene in cases of injustice.

It may be that Peter Parlour's Ukrainians fell into the gap between May 1945 and July 1947 and were repatriated. Certainly it was the case that when the Russians captured members of the Ukrainian Division during the war, the latter were shot as traitors. We can't know what happened without a further account. Let's just hope Peter's perception of their end was wrong.

It's not possible to know more about the *individuals* who were POWs because the agreement post-war was that the information about who was held where would be repatriated along with the prisoners. We are reliant on the memories of those in this country who are willing to share their experiences.

But, whatever the PoWs were up to, there was another sort of war work going on in Croft in the early years of the war. There was an airfield to build.

# Bombs, billets and buildings

The Crown and Anchor was the pub in Dalton-on-Tees during the war. It is now the Chequers Inn. In the 1939 Register it is shown that there were four men lodging at the Crown and Anchor on the day of the census. Robert Robson (Engineer Aerodrome), Thomas Davison (Excavator Driver), George Thew (Motor Driver) and William Lough (Timber Feller). These men were probably all part of the early work to build Croft Aerodrome.

Following World War 1, the RAF had taken on the mantel as the premier armed service. The view was that future wars would be won from the air and that bombing was the main defence issue for Britain. Harold Macmillan wrote in his memoirs that 'We thought of air warfare in 1938 rather as people think of nuclear warfare today'.[19] Hence the early planning and focus on Air Raid Precautions. The plan was also to increase Britain's airfield capacity and this dates from the early 1930s.

The first mention of the 'RAF Station' in the RDC minutes is at the November 1940 meeting, when they consented to Richmond Rural District Council supplying the aerodrome with water, and generally they did not say much about it until the war finished. They had some ongoing complaints about pollution of Dalton Beck from the aerodrome to deal with but, actually, very little was said in council about the aerodrome until after the war.

I do not intend to detail the operational life of Croft Aerodrome from an RAF/RCAF perspective in this book. There is already a detailed exposition of airfield operations in Alan Todd's book *Pilgrimages of Grace*, which is well worth reading. We now also have Bob and Dan Middleton's book *Luck is 33 Eggs* which gives you a detailed and vivid account of what it was like to be an RCAF Navigator flying from Croft.[20] I intend rather to discuss how the aerodrome altered life in Croft, the dangers of living cheek-by-jowl with bomb stores, bombers and nightly sorties, how the Canadians interacted with people in the village and the continuing life of the aerodrome immediately *after* the war.

Not only did the aerodrome get built very quickly, it created a huge amount of disturbance in the building. Almost overnight there was the the thunder of lorries and trucks bringing excavating equipment, hardcore, cement and labourers.

## Chapter 3 – The Impact of World War II

**Peter Metcalfe** remembered it well. He was a child of around 9 when it all started and his farm at Pepperfield was right next to the action:

*"In 1939 when the aerodrome started [my father] was the only one who got a job on the aerodrome. Bearing in mind we hadn't any money. He got a job carrying bits of cement about the aerodrome. Because you would not believe how they got all that stuff [...] to build that aerodrome. And one of the main runways is more than a mile long and the stuff that's in there – the stone – you wouldn't believe. [It came from] Durham way somewhere but they came in through Halnaby, through Doris Hobson's. Well, they were still building it when the war was finished. They built 36 dispersal bays for the bombers to stand. And this never got as much advertisement is as what they called Goosepool – Middleton St. George. Because that was the main bit. This [Croft] was supposed to be just an offshoot. There were hundreds of labourers. They came down from Sunderland and Newcastle in buses every day. There were some queer lads, rough lads. They had no toilets, just went in the wood, you know."*

The land had been requisitioned under the Defence (General) Regulations 1939 that gave the government the powers to take land and buildings for any use 'in the national interest' in the state of war. Certainly there would have had to be contracts and compensation with the landowners but there wasn't an option to refuse the requisition. In Croft parish at this time the chief landowners would have been Christopher William Drewett Chaytor for the Croft Estate and Lady Catherine James Crawford Wilson-Todd for Halnaby with Thomas Harold Hobson for Vince Moor West (the Hobsons owned their farm from 1920). There were a few other requisitions from farms in Dalton parish, but as you can see from the map on p226, the bulk of the land for the aerodrome lay in Croft parish. And you can also see from the map how close to existing farmhouses the airfield came. Once the war finished, the emergency requisition was no longer valid, and other arrangements for retaining the land had to be made if the land could not be handed back immediately. However, it was years before Croft Aerodrome completely closed and farmers got back what had been taken. This resulted in the Air Ministry having to temporarily purchase some of the land, and then sell it back when it was finished with. I explain in greater detail in the next chapter.

**Alan Todd** explains some of the background:

*"At the time in the beginning of the war, there was a desperate need to develop airfields and they appraised a lot of flat areas around at one point well, they they decided on that area, which by my reckoning, probably ought to have been called Walmire rather than Croft. [...] It was decided eventually to earmark Middleton St George, or the the the farmland around Goosepool Farm, and the all the farms around Walmire, at the same time, but they decided to create a permanent base at Middleton St. George, and Croft, initially, was supposed to be in a satellite for Middleton St George. Just to stem an urban myth that seems to have grown up more and more over the last generation, Middleton St George was never called RAF Goosepool, it was referred to as Goosepool by the locals because that was where it was. By the*

*same token, Croft aerodrome was referred to by the locals as Dalton. But during the build up of all these airfields around this area, there was another airfield being built at Dalton on Swale near Topcliffe. And in order to avoid confusion, they kept the name Dalton for Dalton on Swale and Dalton here became Croft."*

The first airfields to be built in Yorkshire came well before the declaration of war. For example, Dishforth was opened in September 1936 and Linton-on-Ouse in May 1937. This was all part of the Air Ministry's Expansion Scheme. The view before the war actually came was that it would be primarily waged from the air, and that it would involve massive destruction, and that bombing rather than fighter planes would be the agent of that destruction. The Expansion Scheme plan was to build airfields from which a bomber could reach Berlin in a longitudinally straight line, so the eastern counties, notably Yorkshire and Lincolnshire, were selected for concentration of supply.[21]

Building the airfields was put out to tender, and the names of the senior suppliers are still familiar: John Laing & Son, Taylor Woodrow Ltd, Richard Costain Ltd and George Wimpey &Co. There was then a huge number of sub-contractors, and hordes of labourers. Heavier bombers required tons of concrete.

**Jonathan Falconer** estimates:

*"the following figures are typical of the quantity of work involved in the building of one RAF bomber airfield in 1942: 603,000 sq yd total area of surfacing; 242, 000 cu yd of concrete; 1,030,000 cu yd of excavation; 34 miles of drainage work; 10 miles of cable ducts and 7 miles of water mains."*[22]

**RCAF ground crew working at the aerodrome bomb stores take a break. Vince Moor East farm house is behind them.**

## Chapter 3 – The Impact of World War II

A group of off-duty RCAF air crew photographed by one of the Pearson family, summer of 1945. Air crew were men who flew in the planes. Ground crew serviced the planes and kept the base operational.

Croft was meant to be a smaller airfield, but it still needed 3 runways, hangars, maintenance bays and bomb stores for 36 bombers plus accommodation for 1,892 service personnel.[23] Peter's account is a testimony to the local disruption that building the aerodrome would have caused. However that was not so great in comparison to what was to happen when the airfield became operational.

Middleton St George airfield opened on 15 January 1941 and Croft was ready for operations on 7 October 1941. At this point it housed Number 4 Group of the RAF who remained there, with modest numbers of bombers and personnel until 1943. It had taken twenty months to build, but was still incomplete. And it provided far from luxurious accommodation for crews.

**Bob Middleton**, a Royal Canadian Air Force (RCAF) Navigator from Toronto, remembers seeing Croft for the first time in September 1944.[24] He thought it was an old World War 1 aerodrome:

*"I expected to see, what was his name, Errol Flynn, walk out and get into his Sopwith Camel. And I thought 'what a dump'! But I'll tell you this, After two weeks it was home. I found every airport was the same. After you get used to it, it's home. [...] I can't believe they put officers in a Nissen hut. I thought, 'good God, what are we'? Anyway, it was fine. We had a dandy time."*

However, the food in Britain was a big shock, particularly the way it was prepared at Croft. Bob became afraid of mutton:

*"And our eggs were a powder. Made from a powder. And the bread, I think it was made with shavings from the woodmill. You had to enjoy it, there was nothing else to eat. And then about twice a week they had this bloody mutton, you know, streaks of fat and then streaks of meat. And when we came home, I said to Pat I said: 'there'll be no mutton in this house'."*

Reg Harrison, another Canadian airman I interviewed, developed similar feelings about Brussel sprouts.

Perhaps this is a good time to explain the title of Bob's book – *Luck is 33 Eggs*. Under food rationing, the British public had to make do with powdered eggs, unless they had their own chickens. Bob Middleton hadn't reckoned with the powdered eggs and food restrictions when he set off for Britain, nor had most of his colleagues. It was, however, common for air crews to get a meal with a real egg and bacon on completion of a bombing raid. Sometimes farmers left out the eggs and bacon for the crew to take when they got back. Sometimes it wasn't taken, and that's when the farming families knew a plane had gone missing. Bob got his egg and bacon in the mess when he completed a mission. He flew 33 consecutive successful missions in six months with no loss to crew, a remarkable record which he said was mostly good fortune. So Luck is 33 Eggs.

Vince Moor, as you'll see from the map in Appendix B, was right on top of the airfield. The Pearsons were farming there at that time, and much of their farm had been taken as part of the War Office requisition. However, the Pearsons made friends with 'their' air crew. Mrs Pearson was one of the farmers' wives who put out eggs and bacon for the airmen to take when they came back from a raid. The pictures here show the camaraderie and proximity of operation.

But on top of it all the food issues, it was cold. At one point, on return from a mission, Bob's crew could not return to Croft because it was snow and fog bound, so they put in at RAF Winthorpe near Newark:

**Air crew from RCAF 434 Squadron outside their Nissen hut at Croft Aerodrome.**

**Bob Middleton**:

*"It was such a warm pleasant place after freezing at cold and damp Croft in our non-insulated corrugated steel Nissen huts. During the 1944/45 winter at Croft the only time we were ever really warm was when we were up flying. [...] During the month of January 1945 there were a few big snowstorms, and the temperature was mighty cold below freezing. This was the worst winter in years. At Croft that winter for a few days most of the plumbing froze and there were only three toilets working. We were at Winthorpe for three days and we did not have to do a thing except relax. [...] We burnt all of their wood, ate all of their food and drank all of their beer while there. [...] In our experiences the Americans had the worst food. The RAF by far had the very best food and the best Officers' mess. The food at our Croft Officers' mess was somewhere in the middle."*[25]

## Chapter 3 – The Impact of World War II

Later in his book Bob notes that there was one tiny coal stove for heat in the Nissen huts and that the weather that winter was 'cold and rotten'. And this was a Canadian who said that.

Canada had entered World War 2 on 3 September along with Britain and other Commonwealth nations. Shortly afterwards, the British government made an agreement – called the British Commonwealth Air Training Plan – with Commonwealth nations such as Canada, Australia and New Zealand that they would support the training of air personnel from those countries, and that in return the respective national air forces would fight as part of the RAF. Canada trained more air personnel than any other Commonwealth – 131,500 of them. The RAF had not had a successful run with bombing raids early in the war. The plan was to utilise Canadian air crew and new aircraft. So the RAF withdrew and the first Canadians arrived at Croft on 30 September 1942. Number Six Bomber Group was all Canadians. They were to stay until June 1945 when the last Canadians went home. From December 1943 there were two squadrons – 431 Iroquois Squadron and 434 Bluenose squadron.

So the Canadians were in Croft for less than two years, effectively, but they made a big impact. All of the Croft voices who were alive in the war have a story. Bob Middleton (who was only in Croft for 6 months) and his crew tended to stay on the base, but others liked to come to the Croft Spa Hotel, the Comet or the cafe in the Methodist Chapel. Some Canadians were actually billeted in Hurworth Place, maybe in Croft too, and there are clear memories.

Charlie Headon remembered that his mother, Ada, worked in the Methodist Chapel in Hurworth Place where there was a cafe for service people. Also that RCAF Officers drank at the front bar of the Croft Spa Hotel, rank and file at the back bar, and that there were dances put on for the servicemen.

**Ian Dougill** thought the Croft Spa Hotel might have been a hot spot:

*"Of course this place [the Croft Spa Hotel] was a watering hole. It was alive with Canadians during the war. Because that's where you met the local girls. It used to be an absolute riot. Well, you know, you would let go a bit wouldn't you? If you knew you probably wouldn't be alive in the next few hours. You could understand what a fevered atmosphere it must have been. In those days it was run by somebody called Mrs Bradley.[26] She was a Tartar. She had everything: none of your snowflake, modern management. I think it belonged to a firm called Deuchars. And they were based in Sunderland as well. Mrs Bradley was sort of Carry On Managing... the equivalent of Hattie Jaques. She ruled with a rod of iron. Well, you had to. It must have been pretty riotous in there at times."*

Reg Harrison was stationed at Croft from 12 March 1944, but he did not come into the village or go to Darlington. He stayed on the base unless he was on leave. He spent leave with his uncle near Hull. His view was that many of the younger non-officer crew went drinking and maybe looking for girls because it was their way of dealing with the stress and danger. He noted that there were no prostitutes working the Croft and Darlington area that he had heard of. If you wanted to meet them you had to go to Middlesbrough or Leeds or Manchester and those places were out of bounds for Canadian servicemen. So this backs up Ian's view.

However, **Chapman Pincher**, whose parents ran The Comet in the 1920s and 30s, remembers that it wasn't just airmen who frequented the Croft Spa Hotel. He was in the army in World War 2, based at Catterick:

*"One of my joys at Catterick was the proximity of Croft. My father had relinquished The Comet on being recalled to the army as a major, but most of my friends remained in the village, being involved with agriculture, so I switched my allegiance to the more splendid Croft Spa Hotel, just across the bridge. Many dances and other rather wild festivities were held there to offset the austerity and one of my squad who had a car enabled us to enjoy them as often as we wished. I introduced other Army friends to its pleasures and the Richmond Flyer, the little train to Darlington which stopped at Croft, became known in my unit as the Flying Fornicator."*[27]

Some of the Canadians did not live on their base, they were billeted. It seems as though this was mostly in Hurworth Place. Ian Calvert was a young boy of 3 when the Canadians arrived in 1943, but he remembers being told about this.

**Ian Calvert**:

*"And then during the war of course because* [our house in Banks Terrace] *was a house with quite a lot of rooms, and we had Canadian airmen billeted. We were confined as a family to the downstairs basement, which was always a kitchen area and there was a sitting room area and when a large pantry. And then the airmen lived on the first floor in two large rooms on that floor. And then they also had rooms in the attic area. Well, it was one large room, one small room. And these were British descent Canadians, because there were also French Canadians and they didn't mix. So I remember my father saying we had to either have the English speaking Canadians, or the French Canadians, you didn't have the two in the same house because there were goings on. Especially on the High Row in Darlington when they were on leave. [...] They got the meals at the aerodrome and a good part of that was they used to get food parcels sent by their parents. And if we were lucky they would hand the food parcels over to my mum. So every now and again – tinned peaches or corned beef, or things like that, which you're supposed to declare. But we didn't. So every now and again, we would get a treat when they got supplied with the food parcels from Canada."*

**Margaret Horseman** also remembers being told about Canadians coming for tea:

*"And* [mum and dad] *used to have the airmen come and visit here – they were supposed to do their bit, you know – to come and have a cup of coffee or tea or whatever. And mother gave me quite a few names of people that they got quite friendly with [...] But yes, they used to come over and visit and I think my aunts were quite popular or they found themselves quite popular with them. Because they would be young, in their early 20s, late teens, sort of thing. So that did happen."*

It seems that local people were welcoming to the Canadians., and there was quite a bit of interaction. There was definitely interaction through the fence between the people who lived in the farmhouses adjacent to the aerodrome.

## Chapter 3 – The Impact of World War II

**Doris Cameron** had a range of memories. She was about 13 when the Canadians arrived, and Vince Moor West was right by the boundary fence to the aerodrome:

*"... in the Sunday afternoon, you'd see the airmen were getting ready, the pilots and things, so they used to come and load up. And they stored the bombs over there [points], which used to go down the bomb dumps, and some lovely badger setts down there, they've all gone. And so I used to go in the aeroplanes. With the dog."*

**Me**: "So presumably not with anybody's permission ..."

**Doris**: *"No. Well you wouldn't get permission would you?*

*"And I can remember going in and, you know, going. And then I used to collect for the Red Cross, and take it to Mrs Tompkins, the parson's wife at Croft. And I'd go round with me pony for them. I used to go round the airmen, you know, when they were working on the aeroplanes. [...] And then my sister was six years older than me, and she had a friend. And I used to send them round the planes 'cos they were much older and much more glamorous. And I once got a letter to say I'd got the most, collected the most money.*

*And, so my mother knew the ground crew very well, 'cos she used to be here alone. And you used to have a way through the barbed wire, 'cos there was masses of barbed wire. So the man who was working there he used to just be lonely, he was from Canada, they were all Canadians. And he used to come for afternoon tea with mother because, you know, he was missing his family life. [...]*

*We had a Whitley that had crashed nearly into the farm buildings there. It would be about the start of the war when they were just starting to build. And they guarded this Whitley because it had to be guarded, and nothing had to be stolen from it. So my father used to sit every night guarding the Whitley, and he used to sit with them and chatting away, and by the time they'd got the Whitley away I don't think there was much left because, I think we did pretty well. I think I got the first aid boxes out and all sorts. And then there was a raid. Cos the people on the next farm used to serve tea to the airmen every morning. They had morning break, and they used to cycle over and go for a lovely home cooked breakfast – at the Pearson's [Vince Moor East]. Then there was a railway line going up to Richmond and there was a station at Eryholme. And when they were bringing this food up to be taken to this farm, you know, they were checking, and they discovered that some people were having the parachutes. Cos the aeroplanes came back and they'd crash 'cos the bomb was underneath, and some people got parachutes. So they started to try and find where the parachutes were being kept because the material made lovely undies. So, my sister and I, and our mother, decided we'd better do something. So there was the toilet down there [outside in the yard] with the two seater, so we wrapped the parachute, which of course we had, we were making undies from, up very carefully, and put it under the seat where you sat. So when they came and inspected they never found the parachute. So then we continued making undies."*

Bert Walker was 15 when the Canadians came and his farmhouse at Birch Springs was also right next to the aerodrome. When Bert Walker retired, in his nineties, he lived in a new bungalow close to the old farmhouse which is built in the position where a bomber used to stand. Bert and his wife Jean said that 'their' bomber was a 434 Bluenose Squadron Lancaster, WL-Y. It went missing on 11 Mar 1945 and all the crew were killed bar one, who was taken prisoner. Bert and his wife Jean had a painting of the plane on their living room wall, done by Mr A.M. Alderson of Girsby. Jean told me she'd told their son and daughter that the picture, with its commemorative plaque for the airmen, is never to leave the house, whatever happens to them, because that's where it belongs.

Bert explained that the crews working up by Birch Springs had a way to go to get anything to eat or drink. The mess was down near West Lane. So his mother helped them out.

**Bert Walker**:

*"They used to come down, there was an odd pilot or two, one off the stand here and one further up there used to come down. They used to get a glass of milk, my mother used to make teacakes and cut a piece of teacake. 'Cos that saved them going down to the canteen right a way down that main road."*

So Croft people got to know about the Canadians. But what were the Canadians told about us? The fact was, all Canadian servicemen were given careful briefings about the British, especially the women. These were briefings were very clear about the dangers of associating with British women and made them sound as unattractive as possible. The reasons advanced were:

(A) The women may be prostitutes, in which case you would be highly likely to get VD. In Canada prostitutes had to report when they had VD by law, and they received free treatment if infected. This was not the case in Britain.

(B) The women might be single and away from home (for example in the services or working in munitions) in which case they would be likely be trying to get you and/or your money

(C) They might be nice girls, but if you marry them they might not fit into Canadian life well and therefore be a burden on you and the Canadian taxpayer.

(D) (For French Canadians) They may not be Catholics.

Whatever they'd been told, plenty of Canadians were happy to associate and there were a great many war brides who married Canadians. Nationally there were 7,197 RCAF wives (5,814 marriages in May-Nov 1945 alone) and 2,466 children taken back to Canada after the war. There was a Canadian Wives Bureau which arranged passage and visas etc. There were 32 Wives Clubs. In fact, there were more Canadian war brides than American ones.

One young woman among many who married a Canadian airman was Muriel Adamson. Florence Muriel Adamson was born in 1920, and lived with her father and mother, William and Selina Adamson, at Croft Mill. She worked at the NAAFI in Middleton St George, presumably where she met her husband George Densel Le Roy, known as Ben. They married in Thirsk in April 1945. Muriel settled in Quebec and died in Shawville, north west of Ottawa, in April 2004. She came back to England with her four year old son Michael in 1950, for how long I don't know.

**Ian Dougill** has this memory, demonstrating that Croft ties are not easily broken. Ian went to

Canada after graduating and was living in Montreal. In 1967 he got a message from his parents, asking him to meet Mr Adamson at Montreal airport:

*"Mr Adamson was another irascible bloke, we used to steal from his orchard, he used to chase us away. But he was an amazing man, I have a picture of him upstairs somewhere. He arrived in Montreal in 1967 on the plane. His wife had died* [in 1964]. *Once the marriage had gone, his livelihood had gone. But he was getting near to retirement age by then* [he was born in 1889]. *He came to Montreal in 1967 for the World Exhibition. And his daughter came down to Montreal from upper Quebec. And we had supper in his hotel room."*

Lastly, **Margaret Horseman** had this story:

*"I can remember when we were little, and we had a Christmas tree in* [the front room]. *We had boxes of silver aluminium tape, and it's what they used to throw from the planes and that radars would check that they used to throw. Is it flak? It was aluminium strips, and it used to confuse the radars and we have boxes of it in the cellar. Obviously they'd given them to mum and dad and we* [Margaret and her brother] *used to cut them into strips and then tear them into tiny little strips put on the Christmas tree. That's what we use to decorate the tree with. Quite a few years ago when I was clearing the cellar up for one reason or another I found some ..."*

**Bob Middleton** can explain everything. He has a whole chapter on the aluminium strips.[28] They were called Window:

Bob Middleton, sitting in his house in Toronto just a few years ago, holds up a strip of 'window'. See the text for an explanation!

*"Early on in World War 2 the German scientists and engineers had developed extremely accurate and deadly radar. On the German radar screens our bombers would show up as individual bombers or groups of bombers as came into the range of the radar as we crossed the French coast. [...] The radar operators directed the Luftwaffe fighter pilots where to find us and the direction we were heading. With that information the Luftwaffe fighters would set up an intercept course and shoot us out of the sky.*

*In the early 1940s British scientists developed a method named Window to create a confusing image on the German radar screens. [...] The foil reflected the German radar signals that were beamed into the sky looking for the bomber stream. [...] Window was not used until 24 July 1943 as it was feared the German bombers over England would start to use it as well to fool British radar operators.*

*When we were dropping Window into the sky the reflections from the thousands of strips of window would show up as a cluster of targets that would swamp their radar screens. This made it difficult to guide the fighter pilots to exact locations of our bombers [...]. We convinced ourselves that the Window helped protect us. After any operation there were tens of thousands*

*of strips of Window all over the target and the path to and from the target. It looked like Christmas decorations hanging from houses, hedges, trees and wires."*
And later on a tree in a house on Tees View.

Another thing about the airmen, they were fun. A glimpse into a world not quite so stuffy as dear old Blighty. Margaret Chapman recalled seeing the Canadians on the back of wagons as they were transported to Darlington or wherever and the local Croft children shouting 'got any gum chum?' At them. Sometimes they would be thrown gum or sweets. Ann Carnelly recalled that the Canadians used to provide a Christmas Party for local children, with presents. One such party, at Oakwood, is described, with photographs, in Alan Todd's book on p127.

The other aspect of having the aerodrome nearby was just the danger and the disruption of having all those bombers taking off night after night, and landing again 6 hours later.

**Bert Walker** remembers:
*"... when they were going out on a raid, they used to fuel the planes up by the ground crew, and bomb them up and take them to the runway. And park them up there, and then the crew has come round in what we call a pilots van, it was like a big minibus. And that was what they took over to the plane from there. We used to go up to just our field end, and watch them go up most times, you know. And if they were going off in daylight."*

**Peter Metcalfe** and his brothers had their own vantage point at Pepperfield:
*"There was a stable and the granary on the end of th'house. And there were steps up to it which are now demolished. And we sat on the step to watch them all go. So when they set off to go, up to 30 bombers, be it Halifaxes, Lancasters, whatever. And there was a lot of them that was sent up, more than the Middleton St George, I'm sure this was bigger. And yeah, 30 Lancaster's at the finish going off, one after the other. The sky was full of bombers, circling to get height, and then they'd follow the railway down there, tailing off to go down. And the noise was brilliant."*

And of course there were many accidents. There is a full list of aerodrome explosions in Alan Todd's book, but Bert remembers one in particular.

**Bert Walker**:
*"There was one [bomber] came down over North Walmire with bombs on. And one of the bombs went off, and it blew all the building roofs off North Walmire Farm. And [the family] came down here, about two o'clock in the morning, they had to get out of the house because, you know, there was a lot more bombs and they were frightened of them going off. They stayed here 'til next morning, but that was Mr Biglin who farmed there. And he couldn't get back quick enough because it had blown all the roofs off of the farm and he wanted to get it tidied up a bit, somehow. I don't know why it crashed there. But it crashed. [...] it had bombs on, so it was bombed up to go out on a raid."*

## Chapter 3 – The Impact of World War II

It was not the case, however, that enemy aircraft came over Croft or that the village was in danger from enemy fire. Except for one incident. Ann Carnelly Reed lived in number 1 Richmond Terrace after moving from Spa Cottages in the early forties.

**Ann Reed (Carnelly)** remembers one particular incident when she was about 5 (1945):
*"Because my Dad was invalided out of the army he joined the Observer Corps. And our shelter was the cellar under Richmond Terrace. And we were down there one night. And Dad was looking up through the grating. And he spotted a plane. 'It's alright. It's one of ours.' Then he says 'bloody hell … there's jerry on his tail'. And the jerry crashed near Rockcliffe, in a field there."*

This incident is well documented from several angles. There are some local stories about it, for example, that the German fighter came down and everyone was killed and that some schoolboys found a boot with a leg still in it. This is what actually happened.

Very late in the war the Luftwaffe decided to use a strategy that had that had been discussed earlier on but not deployed. They had discovered that their fighter planes could avoid British radar by flying above the bombers as they returned to base. The deployment of this late strategy was called Operation Gisela, and it came right at the end of the war. On the night of 3/4 March 1945 it was executed to devastating effect. Alan Todd explains in his book: '… the night of 3/4th March proved highly successful for the [Luftwaffe's] last ditch marauding night fighter force. [They] mounted an operation comprising 200 night fighters to follow the returning Allied bombers'.

These night fighters had a very successful night. One of the units badly affected was 346 (Free French) Bomber Squadron who were based at Elvington airfield south east of York. As two Halifax bombers lay ablaze on Elvington's runways, two other Halifaxes were told to divert to Long Marston, and then to Croft. Both planes were dangerously low on fuel by this time.

*At 02.10 hours one of the French pilots, S/Lt P Gridelet, successfully landed his NR232 at Croft, but as his colleague Captain P. Noelle's aircraft NR229 'H7-D' with an all-French crew was in circuit at about 2,500 feet turning into the westerly wind towards the well-lit runway. Unbeknown to the Frenchmen, they were being stalked stalked below by Feldwebel [Gunter] Schmidt's crew, who pounced on the unsuspecting Halifax at about 100 yards range and fired [...] the Halifax crash-landed at nearly 100 mph through some bushes on the County Durham side of the Tees at Rockcliffe Farm [...] Luckily the crew scrambled out of the fragmented wreck, carrying the unconscious pilot Captain Noelle, just before the fire started in earnest.*[29]

So that is why the plane *'had a jerry on his tail'*. The pilot, Captain Noelle, was able to write about the incident in his own logbook. Even more remarkable, the logbook of Feldwebel Gunther Schmidt 12/NJG3 still exists.

## Crofts Crossing

**Feldwebel Schmidt** wrote in his logbook:

*On 3rd March 1945, I took off with a Ju 88G-6 at 23.42 hours despatched to perform long distance night fighting over the British mainland. Landfall over the British coast was made 01.50 hours.*

*At 2.00 hours the Bordfunker, when spotting some Verey pistol shooting, saw an aircraft overhead, which shortly after was identified by the entire crew as a four-engined one with a twin tail fin. My altitude was 200 metres, that of the enemy aircraft about 800-1000 metres. I managed to approach from below and let the first burst go from about 150-50 metres at 02.05 hours, the enemy aircraft proceeding against the landing direction within the traffic pattern (Drem circuit) altitude 500 metres. Hits were observed in the port wing and the and some debris was also lost. The aircraft turned to the the left. The second attack was started some distance from astern. Hits in the rear turret and fuselage. Small fire in the fuselage with dark red flames. Third attack from the rear also from a distance of 150 – 50 metres. Again hits in the port wing and fuselage. Almost immediately it crashed and exploded north of the airfield, within the traffic circuit. I was in a position to watch the enemy aircraft until it crashed. There was no defence. The airfield where the combat occurred was located roughly 10km south of the city of Darlington and had, along the west side of its Drem system, the identification letters 'CR" formed by white lamps."* [30]

Bob Middleton noted in his book: "The Luftwaffe fighters attacked aircraft as far north as Croft. The fighters came down and strafed Croft but luckily no-one was injured. I was away on leave that night and missed the action." [31] And Alan Todd summarised: "The Luftwaffe had wreaked havoc with many of Croft's charges on their way to or from their targets but this was the only time the Third Reich presence was actually to be felt at Croft and two shells from Schmidt's cannons were later confirmed to have burst on the airfield."

So Croft had a lucky escape. And a childhood memory takes its place in a chain of experiences that makes a small part of the tapestry of a world event.

But we should not forget the ultimate impact of what those airmen, the ones that brought food parcels and talked to farm families through the wire, and held Christmas parties for children, were there to do. Bomber Command helped win the war and stop the bloodshed, finally. But while they were flying and bombing the crews were under incredible stress and the nature of their night's work should be considered.

Bob Middleton recalled a specific Bomber Command mission, on 23 February 1945, a 9 hour round trip to

**The statue commemorating the contribution of the RCAF to victory in World War 2 at Dalton-on-Tees.**

*Chapter 3 – The Impact of World War II*

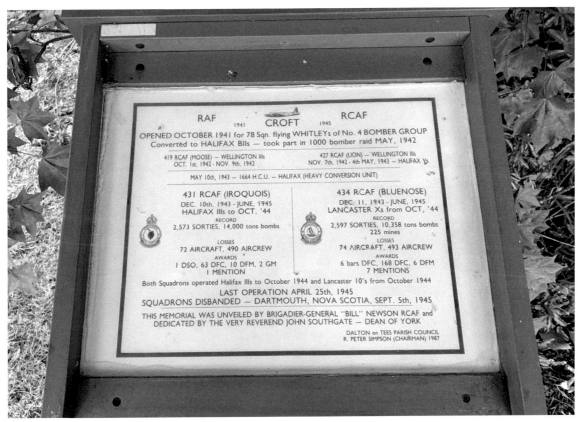

A summary record of deaths and sorties associated with Croft Aerodrome. This plaque stands next to the RCAF memorial in the previous picture.

Pforzheim under the illumination of a full moon. A total of 356 bombers left Britain that night and Bob's plane was one of 12 that left Croft. Bob entered in his log book: "That was our best attack yet out of 32 operations. Of all the Bomber Command operations this was the third in terms of loss of German life on the ground, after Dresden and Hamburg. About 18,000 people were killed. In my logbook I wrote, 'Best attack yet'." [32]

Bob's book gives a first hand account of what flying those missions really entailed. As a 21-year-old there was great excitement, great skill to be learned and used, great camaraderie amongst the crews. But there was an aspect that wasn't talked about, that was kept in check. When an airman did not arrive back there was no announcement, no ceremony. There was just a gap where he used to sleep or where he sat. Bob explained that for every mission, the target was not revealed until a few hours before take-off, and that's when it all started to feel very real.

**Bob Middleton** recalls:

*"I found that after the briefing you went to the bathroom at least twice. And I used to say to myself long after the war, I said, were we scared? Well, you're a little worried. And then it dawned on me one day, you wouldn't go to the bathroom if you weren't scared. And that's the way it was. Anybody that says they weren't scared? Well, they got no feeling."*

A group of off-duty RCAF air crew photographed by one of the Pearson family, summer of 1945. Air crew were men who flew in the planes. Ground crew serviced the planes and kept the base operational.

I spoke to Flight Lieutenant Reg Harrison in July 2022. He was just 6 weeks off his 100th birthday and at that point was, I believe, the only surviving member of the RCAF squadrons based at Croft. Reg had near perfect recall. I asked him how he felt about his 'job'. He said he didn't think about it much but he was also sure that as crew, they didn't really know whether bombs hit target with any accuracy. They didn't know what the effect was on the ground, they just dropped them and tried to get back safely. They were told they were bombing a depot or railway line, and were given co-ordinates, but they didn't know whether there were civilian targets mixed in, or how widely the bombs fell. That sort of information never came back to them, there was a great deal that wasn't discussed. He also noted that for years after the RCAF squadrons were disbanded, no-one in Canada wanted to talk about the war. He said his own daughters did not get taught about World War 2 at school. Then in the eighties some people started to interview the veterans, and the stories started to come.

Bob's home in Toronto in 2021, when I interviewed him via Zoom, had many pictures and mementoes of his time as an RCAF Navigator and it's clear that that was the formative experience of his life. But I asked Bob whether he ever doubted what was doing, when he saw the bombs hit their targets. I told him that my own father, who was in the Navy, had said he wasn't proud of what he did in the war, but that you just got swept along in things, you just did it because you had to.

**Bob Middleton**:

*"Well, that's right. You have to do that to maintain your sanity. But this happened in a shopping centre* [in Toronto]. *And I was first in line, there was a woman behind me. And she said, 'Oh, this shopping is getting too much for an old person.' I said, 'Do you think you're old? I was a navigator on Lancasters during the war'. And the woman behind her said* [loudly] *'Did you bomb innocent*

*women and children in Germany'? And you have to be prepared for those questions. And I came back with 'Yes, we did. They started it, we finished it'. And it's surprising how an answer like that shuts them up. So it wasn't something that you did with relish. It was something you did. I remember one night we set out. We were flying over the north side of the Alps, on our way to Munich. And it was a beautiful moonlit night.*[33] *As the moon reflected off the snow, it was like the Night Before Christmas. The most magnificent, beautiful sight that you'd ever want to see. And we're flying over this and I'm almost mesmerised looking at it. And then you think, Oh, my God, look at the beauty of the scenery. And what am I doing? I'm taking six tons of bombs to drop on a city in Germany. That makes you realise war is hell, you know?"*

Bob Middleton left Croft on 12 April 1945, travelling to Eryholme station by lorry and finally by train to Liverpool to get a ship home. His tour of duty – 33 missions – was complete and there would not be another one. On the 8th of May the Germans surrendered and the war in Europe was over. By the end of June the last Canadians left Croft. There is a memorial to them at Dalton, unveiled on 26 September 1987 when some survivors came back to meet old friends and remember once more.

David Walker was very involved in that day of remembrance when the memorial was unveiled. He met the veterans and families of veterans and was impressed by them. He continued to correspond with some of the veterans. But he particularly recalls a letter he received from a man called Hamish Mahaddie, a decorated RAF veteran of some repute, who had been there at the ceremony.

**David Walker (right) with Croft RCAF airman Fred Lewis and his son, early 1990s, by the memorial for Pilot Officer Andrew Mynarski VC at Middleton St George.**

Mr Mahaddie wrote to David as an organiser of the day and this is what he said:

> *I thought the Croft weekend was very special, and the Canadians were very impressed, not only with the memorial but all the other facilities and arrangements that had been laid on. I feel that possibly the one thing that shattered them was the sincerity and deep feeling of gratitude that the locals were so keen to make known to those that attended the unveiling ceremony.*
>
> *The Yorkshire folk normally do not wear their hearts on their sleeves, indeed they go a long way towards concealing their innermost feelings but I know they felt in meeting the locals at Croft, at York Minster and at the Evening Service in the Croft Church and possibly, most of all, at the Cemetery in Harrogate, that there is a deep and indelible link between the broad acres of Yorkshire and those distant Canadian relatives that left their seed-corn in Europe.*

Croft aerodrome continued to exist after the war finished and the Canadians went home. It had another life. Eventually of course, in the sixties, it became a motor racing circuit and other buildings were repurposed as industrial units. Unwanted parts of runways were either demolished or gradually absorbed into the landscape. Between 1946 and 1962 it was home to many people: the 'squatters'. Their story comes in the next chapter. But there was more RAF activity after 1945 and here is a story about it

As the buildings that had housed maintenance depots and stores became disused by the RAF, businesses or organisations took them over. One was the Darlington Aero Club and there are RDC minutes discussing the arrival of Abbot's buses and garage services. However, the aerodrome runways were still intact and for a number of years planes that had taken off from Middleton St George landed there. Middleton St George had been redesignated '205 AFS RAF Middleton St George', where AFS stands for Advanced Flying School. In the late 1940s and early 1950s they had a particular job to do. They needed to retrain hundreds of RAF pilots to fly jets.

**Ian Dougill**:

*"And actually what I do remember from Croft very very distinctly, that's the jet planes replacing the propeller. Yes, because I worked in Titchmarsh's market gardens* [at High Thorn] *as a schoolboy, to earn extra money. And I remember distinctly that the aircraft started making a totally different noise. And I think they were called the Meteor. I'd say they would be based at Middleton St. George. Goosepool. But I think probably Croft would be an additional facility. I don't think the airport at Croft was ever run after the war. No, I think their responsibility was transferred to what was then Goosepool for these Meteors. It would be the very first British jet plane.*

*So they could still land at Croft. And the Goosepool planes flew over the market garden. And you know, you looked up, because it was a completely different sound. And you kept wondering, how on earth do they fly?"*

The Gloster Meteor was indeed the first jet plane commissioned by the RAF. Some were used in the last year of World War 2 and after the war ended the RAF set about modernising their whole fleet to jet

## Chapter 3 – The Impact of World War II

planes. Middleton St George was one of a number of Advanced Flying Schools providing the relevant skills update to match.

On 25 January 1951 a Gloster Meteor F4 crashed in Croft village, making impact on the bank just in front of The Terrace. It was about midday. The pilot was killed and two children were slightly injured. It's an incident often talked about.

**Ian Calvert** was on the scene:

*"I was a schoolboy. I used to sometimes cycle home from Hurworth [Secondary Modern] school to Banks Terrace and have a sandwich for lunch. On this particular day, I was just about at the Grange, before the Grange, and this jet came screaming over so low and so loud it was unbelievable. I just saw it went over the top of the trees almost. And then there was a God Almighty explosion. And I pedalled like hell to see what it was and it was by that tree. There's a tree planted in exactly the place over there.* [This is the tree in the centre of the field in front of The Terrace.] *In the ground there was a big hole. A big hole and the Earth was all heaped up over the road. There's nothing at all you could see, just the hole in the earth, and pieces of metal – there was nothing to show. You couldn't see it was a plane. It must have exploded when it hit the ground."*

**This murky photograph is all we have as pictorial record of the crash of a Gloster Meteor in 1951. You can just about see that the plane came down in front of The Terrace.**

Janet Mackenzie was a toddler, and they lived in Carroll Place. She remembers a big noise and her mum looking frightened.

The *Evening Despatch* was also on the scene and they reported 'A 13 year old girl and her ten year old brotherhood had a narrow escape from being killed by a Meteor Jet plane from Middleton St George RAF Station which crashed in a field near the Croft Spa Hotel near Darlington today, killing the pilot.' The girl and her brother were named as Joyce and Kenneth Barker, who lived in Richmond Terrace. The report continues 'The children saw the plane coming down with smoke billowing from it and turned to run [...] Joyce's coat was splattered with oil and one leg slightly injured.' The paper also reported that the Coates family, who lived at 3, The Terrace, saw it all and it was Carol Coates who rang the police and the fire brigade. It was reported that the police tried to recover the pilot's body from beneath the wreckage but also that 'the pilot was buried deep in the earth under the flaming wreckage'. It's not clear that they ever recovered a body, maybe just some bits.

A day later the name of the pilot was released. He was 24-year-old Pilot Officer Arthur A McKernan from Belfast. The youngest son of Isabella McKernan and her late husband James, of 28 Adelaide Avenue. He joined the RAF in 1948 and received a commission three months before he was killed.[34] Another newspaper report in *The Irish Times* noted that he had been in the air for less than two minutes.

I found the Operations Book for 205 AFS Middleton St George in the National Archives. The incident was recorded at 12.05:

> *Student, Pilot Officer A.A. McKernan (3504720) was killed when his aircraft Meteor Mk.IV VW255 dived into the ground shortly after take off. The aircraft exploded on impact with the ground, the cause of the the accident is unknown.*
>
> *A Court of Inquiry assembled, President Wg. Cdr. WSG Maydwell, DSO, DFC, to inquire into the accident which resulted in Pilot Officer McKernan's death.*[35]

**The death certificate of Arthur McKernan.**

The weather for that day, 25 January, was recorded at the head of the month's entries as 'Cloudy, with light mist and occasional drizzle'.

The findings of Wing-Commander Maydwell's inquiry are lost. There are many inquiries into Meteor accidents that survive but not this one. The National Archives say that not all Air Ministry files have made it to them, and this looks like one of the missing ones. There was also a Coroner's inquiry. This will become available for the public to view in 2026, as it is marked as closed for 75 years.

The fact is, there were a lot of accidents involving the Gloster Meteor. In 1951 as a whole there were 490 RAF accidents – that's any accident outside of conflict – with 280 fatalities.[36] I counted 25 accidents in 1951 involving the Meteor F4 – the same plane that crashed in Croft – with 17 fatalities, mostly pilots. 5 of these involved planes flying from Middleton St George, with 4 fatalities. There were many other accidents involving other types of Meteor and this went on for years. The statistics could not be ignored, so in 1956 the Air Ministry commissioned a full report entitled *Meteor aircraft accidents involving structural failure in the air*. This report was not declassified until 2004. It includes the Croft accident. For most Meteor accidents covered, a cause is found and there are conclusions about structural re-design that is required. VW255 (the Croft plane) appears in an Appendix III, which is a list of accidents where causality is not clear. It records against VW255: 'Crashed after take off for an exercise to climb to 30,000 feet'. In the body of the report it says:

## Chapter 3 – The Impact of World War II

*Appendix III lists 50 uncontrolled high speed impacts with the ground of Meteor aircraft. The explanations offered for these accidents generally suggest pilot error, and while this will be true in some cases, there appears to be no reason why Meteor aircraft should have a much higher than Vampire aircraft for this type of accident.*[37]

The report then notes that there were a number of malfunctions registered where jets flying above 6,000 feet experienced sudden loss of control and in many cases the aircraft dropped 3-6,000 feet before recovery. These were all to do with problems with the undercarriage. If a plane was flying at less than 6,000 feet at the time of the malfunction, it would have hit the ground, and as these planes tended to explode on impact, it was not possible to get evidence about what happened. The final conclusion in the report being:

*It appears logical therefore, to suppose that some at least of the uncontrolled dives into the ground had their sources of trouble in the primary failure of an undercarriage leg or an undercarriage door.*

There is a local opinion that Pilot Officer McKernan was a hero, that he steered his plane into the bank in order to miss the primary school which was just a hundred yards to the north of where he crashed. That could be true but we don't have the evidence that would prove it definitely was. Whatever happened, a young man was killed tragically, and his remains may be there still under Croft earth.

---

**Endnotes**
1. Women's Voluntary Service – stalwarts of all kinds of welfare work in war time and beyond. It didn't become 'Royal' (WRVS) until 1944
2. D&S, 7 October 1939
3. Croft RDC meeting 6 December 1939
4. D&S, 13 October 1939
5. Specifically relevant to Croft is *Wish You Were Here: An Account of Sunderland's war time evacuation* by W.W.Lowther (Walton Publications, 1989). Croft is not mentioned but there is much about the North Riding. Try also https://spartacus-educational.com/2WWbilleting.htm for first hand accounts (accessed 25 March 2022) and there are many other accounts online. The Museum of Rural Life at Reading holds many materials on evacuation but nothing about Croft.
6. This was at Monkend Bungalow, aka Appleton Cottage. Margaret also said that Connie and Betty were from Gateshead.
7. Margaret remembered Connie as the elder girl, but the school register shows that Connie is the younger one.
8. NRRD, Vol.260, p827, #290
9. TNA WO 199/1522: details of 12th Battalion briefings for Defence Schemes and a few other papers.
10. *Memories of Croft*, audio CD available from Croft Productions. Thanks to Viv Craggs for giving permission to quote and to Ian Calvert. for lending me his copy. See http://www.croftproductions.co.uk.
11. The image is taken from D.Wood *Attack Warning Red: Royal Observer Corps and the Defence of Britain 1925-75*, Macdonald & Jane, 1976. The wikipedia entry is at https://en.wikipedia.org/wiki/List_of_Royal_Observer_Corps_/_United_Kingdom_Warning_and_Monitoring_Organisation_Posts_(A–E).
12. https://www.subbrit.org.uk/sites/croft-roc-post/ – accessed 29 April 2022.
13. Croft RDC, 1 May 1939.
14. For a complete list of what was rationed and not rationed see https://www.bbc.co.uk/history/ww2peopleswar/stories/84/a4537884.shtml, accessed 6 June 2022. The reference to game is under 'Further Notes'.
15. *BBC History Magazine*, March 2022, p42.
16. My major information source on POWs and their work in the community is: Sophie Jackson, *Churchill's Unexpected Guests: Prisoners of War in Britain in World War II*, The History Press, 2010.

17. J.A. Tannahill, *European Volunteer Workers in Britain*, Manchester, 1958, p4.
18. Tannahill, p132.
19. Quoted in Jonathan Falconer, *RAF Bomber Airfields of World War Two*, Ian Allan, 1992, p8.
20. AAB Todd, *Pilgrimages of Grace: A History of Croft Aerodrome*, Alan Todd Associates, 1993 and Robert J Middleton and Daniel R Middleton, *Luck is 33 Eggs: Memories and Photographs of an RCAF Navigator*, Self-published, 2021 (available via Amazon).
21. I've taken most of the description here from Jonathan Falconer, *RAF Bomber Airfields of World War 2*, Ian Allan, 1992.
22. *RAF Bomber Airfields of Work War 2*, p11.
23. See David Brown, *Aerodromes in North Yorkshire and Wartime Memories*, David Brown, 1996, p19.
24. See Bob's book: Robert J and Daniel R Middleton, *Luck is 33 Eggs: Memories and Photographs of an RCAF Navigator*, self published, 2022. This is available print-on-demand via Amazon.
25. *Luck is 33 eggs*, p322-333.
26. Mrs Alice Bradley. She was a widow born on 28 August 1895 (1939 Register). She seems to have been the manager at the Croft Spa Hotel for a number of years.
27. Chapman Pincher, *Pastoral Symphony: A Bumpkin's Tribute to Country Joys*, Swan Hill, 1993
28. *Luck is 33 Eggs*, Chapter 18.
29. Pilgrimages of Grace, p135.
30. Simon W. Parry, *Intruders Over Britain: the story of the Luftwaffe's night intruder force – the Fernachtjager*, Kristall Publications, 1987, p149.
31. *Luck is 33 Eggs* p220.
32. *Luck is 33 Eggs*, p347.
33. This is probably the mission to bomb Pforzheim which Bob talks about earlier as 'best attack ever'.
34. *The Belfast Telegraph*, 26 January 1951.
35. TNA, AIR 29/1773
36. James J Halley, *Broken Wings: Post War Royal Airforce accidents*, Tunbridge Wells, Air-Britain, 1999.
37. TNA, BT 218/11

# Chapter 4

# Bust and Boom

In the immediate aftermath of World War 2, the British people did not have many comforts in ordinary life. We had celebrated Victory in Europe in 1945 and Victory in Japan in 1946, but for the average Brit life didn't feel very victorious. The country was almost bankrupt, rationing was to last until 1953 and the promised improvements to infrastructure and housing conditions seemed to be on hold until further notice. There were shortages of food, shortages of clothes, shortages of money, shortages of building materials and, generally, shortages of fun. When the boom years of the late fifties and sixties arrived it was no wonder people wanted to sweep away the grey, overcoated Britain of this time for something more colourful, modern and free.

One of the topics that most weighed on people's minds – and on those of the government – was post-war housing. The lack of it, that is.

*This was about a lot more than bricks and mortar. The war separated husbands and wives, deprived children of their parents and had in general shaken the family fabric of the country. Some 38 million civilians had changed address, a total of 60 million times. Many marriages had broken up under the strain of the war. Yet people wanted a return to the warmth and security that family life can offer. There were more than 400,000 weddings in 1947 and 881,000 babies born; the beginning of the 'boom' that would reshape British life in the years ahead.*[1]

Inadequate housing was not a new thing. Following the end of World War 1 there was a similar shortage and the government introduced subsidy schemes to build 'affordable' housing that 'the working class' could utilise. It was between the wars that the first council houses were built also, and town centres cleared of primitive, insanitary dwellings. Public opinion supported 'homes for heroes' and public policy followed suit. However, the post World War 1 housing problems had not been fully dealt with before World War 2 started. There was still much poor housing stock and living conditions, not least in rural areas. The poor quality of agricultural workers' housing was a national concern and the National Union of Agricultural Workers was lobbying hard for improvements. Mindful of the situation following World War 1, the war time coalition government started to think about post-war housing early, estimating that hundreds of thousands of houses would need to be built. On 19 April 1943 Croft Rural District Council considered a letter from the Ministry of Health (which was then responsible for housing) asking them to start planning for post-war housing. At that precise point, the only council houses in the Rural District that I know of were in Barton. In April 1943, the RDC assumed that the only post-war need would also be in Barton.

It is therefore surprising to read in the May 1943 minutes that the plan for council houses, communicated to the Ministry of Health, was as follows: 16 to be built at Barton, 8 at Croft, 6 at Stapleton, 2 at both Cleasby and Eryholme, 4 at Manfield. Only Barton had an existing site in council ownership that could take the planned increase. Everywhere else had to find a new site. The problem was resolved quickly because in August 1943 it was reported that sites had been found for all houses. In Croft, the land was to be gifted to the council by Kit Chaytor. A conveyance dated 21 June 1945 details the transaction: CWD Chaytor transfers to Croft Rural District Council one acre, between the School and the bus garage, 'as a housing site for the erection of houses under the Housing Act 1936 or any subsequent enactment thereof'. Two restrictions were applied. First, that the land could only be used for the stated purpose and secondly, that the bus garage be given appropriate light and air.

Actually building the houses took over three years, a rate of progress that was quite good in comparison to the national picture, where shortages of building materials – particularly timber – and labour were creating major delays to the Labour government's ambitions for 300,000 council houses. In July 1946 the RDC had been lobbied by the National Union of Agricultural Workers (NUAW) who wrote to point out that there was a lack of agricultural provision in Croft district and asking them to press ahead with their council building scheme. In response to this approach the RDC resolved to tell NUAW that 'the Council's housing programme progresses and to assure them sufficient number of houses will be reserved for occupation by agricultural workers". By November 1947 a shortlist of 12 applicants for the 8 new houses in Carroll Place had been drawn up. In January 1948 the committee sub-group of Kit Chaytor, Captain Parlour and Mr R Alderson met to decide who should have the last four houses, four having been already allocated. The initial list of occupants was:

| House # | Occupant | House # | Occupant | House # | Occupant |
| --- | --- | --- | --- | --- | --- |
| 1 | JR Taylor | 4 | J F Booth | 7 | W Pearson |
| 2 | A Pearson | 6 | J R Headon | 8 | A Abon |
| 3 | W E Cooper | | | | |

Two of the houses went to members of the Pearson family from Vince Moor East. Janet McKenzie was born to the Pearson family who moved into number 2. She recalls this about living in Carroll Place in the early years:

**Janet McKenzie**:

*"My dad lived on Vince Moor East. And my mum was from London. […] I was actually born in London, Islington in 1946. And then when I was a few months old they came to live at Vince Moor. And then when dad came out of the army … 1947 … those houses in Carroll Place were ready. And they were for land workers. So Mr. Taylor had number one. He was railway worker. Dad was on the farm. He worked for Simpsons at Old Spa Farm. Jack Cooper was a bus driver.*

## Chapter 4 – Bust and Boom

*Jack Booth – I can't remember what he was. Jack Headon – can't remember what he did. Bill Pearson my uncle lived at number seven. He was working on the farm, Spa Farm. And Alex Abon was at number eight. And he was a Market Gardener.*

*We knew everyone. You didn't need to shut your doors. You see, doors were open all night, until five o'clock in the morning. People just going in and out of each other's doors. It was fantastic. You know, you knew everybody, knew where they lived."*

In 1980 the newly elected UK government, under Margaret Thatcher's leadership, introduced the 'Right to Buy'. This was a policy that allowed council house tenants to buy their council houses at a reduced sum, become owner-occupiers and sell them them on if they so wished. The District Council calculated a market value for them, and then the tenants were given a discount based on the years they had paid rent. I don't know the exact fate of all eight houses. I can say that on 26 September 1983 a person named Willment bought 4, Carroll Place.[2] They paid £10, 150 for the house, discounted from an estimated value of £17,500. The national average for a house in 1983 was £27,500.

There was no further social housing in Croft until the building of the eight old people's bungalows in Lewis Close in 1982. The land for this was sold to Richmondshire District Council by the Croft Estate (then headed by Bill Chaytor). The issue of accommodation for elderly people in Croft Rural District first came out of the centralised planning of the war years. As early as 1943 the council were asked to look at providing more. By the time the RDC were abolished, and housing matters passed to Richmondshire (in 1974), there was no provision for the elderly in Croft. I believe there was in Barton. During the 1980s the Parish Council, notably Charlie Headon, became very involved in the push for Lewis Close. Again, the issue of housing for agricultural workers took a prominent role.

**Bill Chaytor** remembers:

*"On my farms I had a problem when I had elderly people who were retiring – yes, elderly tenants and employees. And some of them wanted to live in the village and I hadn't got housing for them, and so I said to the district council would they buy from me the land on which Lewis Close houses are built, on the condition that they built it and I would sell it to them cheap. And I remember I sold it to them for what was lower than the market price at £16,000, and they built those houses on the understanding that I could approach them initially and five or six tenants or employees lived in them and the district council were always very good about it and helped me with my difficulty of housing. 'Cos I adopted what farmers have adopted nationally I think, or used to, which is that if somebody has worked on the land for a life, you house them free. And I have done that hitherto, and the last one now who is living is in fact not living in one of those houses but lives up in Hurworth. I've given him a house for life."*

So Lewis Close was built, and remains as social housing in Croft, allocated to tenants by the council on the basis of need. No further social housing, other than these two schemes in Carroll Place and Lewis Close, was built. However, after the war, there were a great many people in the parish of Croft who were desperate for a place to live.

## The Squatter's Tale

This is the story of Cockleberry, a place that is rarely mentioned by Croft people, but which forms a part of the history of the parish in post-war years.

**Ian Dougill** remembers:

*"Well, Cockleberry was the squatters' camp. In those days, we did use the word 'squat' [laughs]. It's very, very frowned on today, but we were told they were squatters. They moved into ex-air force accommodation, and there wasn't a village there, it's a sort of junction, isn't it, Cockleberry, it's the far end of the airfield. It'd go to Cowton, very near the railway line. And oh yes, they were the Red Indians of the day. You know, we didn't mix with Cockleberry, no. I think some of them, some of those buildings became big pigsties, which didn't help the image. [Laughs] But I believe some of those houses are still left, temporary as they were meant to be."*

The thing about the 'squatters' was that they weren't squatting. They paid rent and rates like any other council tenant, they were just in temporary housing on a disused airfield, because there wasn't anywhere else for them to go. But the name stuck: how did it come about?

*The first stories began to appear in newspapers in July 1946. Out of the blue, fed up with having nowhere decent to live, around forty-eight families had marched into disused army camps at Scunthorpe. Then it happened again, in Middlesbrough, when thirty families moved into a camp. Homeless people in Salisbury took over thirty huts there. At Seaham Harbour, just up the coast from Newcastle, eight miners and their families chalked their names on empty huts and began unrolling bedding. And so it went on, from Chalfont St Giles to Fraserburgh. People wanted accommodation, and accommodation was sitting there empty, so they moved in. By early autumn it was estimated that 45,000 people had illegally taken over empty huts, flats or other shelters."* [3]

In London, the whole 'squatter' movement took on bigger proportions and became politicised when the Communist Party took up the squatters' cause. Many people were appalled at the lawlessness, rattled by the politicisation, with many letters appearing in the press. However, there was also considerable sympathy for the families that were taking matters into their own hands. I came across a Pathe newsreel from 1946 that interviewed some of the families living in Nissen huts at the former Chalfont St Giles army camp.[4] The newsreel said it was a 'controversial' subject but gave a sympathetic hearing to the families – people who had had two rooms for a family of five, families who were living in accommodation with toilets and baths shared by many others, and where every head of family was an ex-serviceman.

However, from the point of view of government administrators, things were more complicated than the public thought. I tracked down some documents in the National Archives at Kew that might tell me what sort of conversation the would-be hut dwellers and Croft Rural District Council were wrapped up in. It was clear that from 1945 onwards the latter were in frequent contact with the Ministry of Health

## Chapter 4 – Bust and Boom

about what to do, what they were expected to do and the practical issues of people wanting accommodation on Croft Aerodrome. When I turned up at Kew I was expecting to see quite a few papers – but I was amazed by the two stacks of documents that greeted me. There were hundreds of papers: inter-departmental meeting notes, ministerial briefings, press releases and letters from all sorts of people. The issue of 'squatters' after the war was a huge one, with high political and financial stakes, and it was not one that could be solved easily. I could not process all of these papers – the subject almost requires a book of its own – but I read enough to understand the background to Croft's particular challenge in the matter.

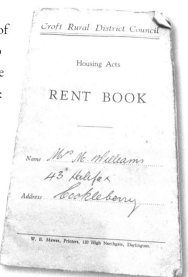

**An example rent book for tenants at Cockleberry.**

Following the Labour Party's landslide victory in the general election of July 1945, the Minister for Health was Aneurin Bevan (in 1947, as plans for the NHS took off, housing became part of a new Department of Housing and Local Government and Bevan's responsibility passed to Ellen Wilkinson). Mr Bevan was subject to many personal appeals from Labour voters. For example, a letter dated May 1945 from a Mr Crane of Ware, Hertfordshire:

> *I am an ex-soldier with a wife and two children and I am living in one room and sleep in the same. I am a lorry driver and I travel all over the country. I cannot find any other accommodation but I notice quite a lot of disused army huts. There are some quite near here. I wondered if it could be possible for me to rent one of these places. I have had notice to quit this place because we are overcrowded. Will you please do your best for me as I don't know what will become of my children if we are put out.*

Another letter was from an ex-quartermaster in the army to the Permanent Secretary for MoH dated November 1946 noting that he had suggested, over a year previously, to the Ministry of Health (MoH) and Army colleagues that vacated camps could provide temporary accommodation with some adaptation for struggling families. He offered his services again in achieving this.

Lastly, a Mr Reynolds made a particular appeal to Bevan and his party:

> *Probably you will have seen a possible Nissen lay-out in today's Daily Express. This, and the fact that only two days ago I and my fiancee were talking over the possibilities, has prompted me to write to you.*
>
> *So, please Mr Bevan, see what your department can do to provide us would-be householders a home of our own quickly, however temporary. We can't wait for permanent houses, we can't afford to buy one privately, we look to you for speedy action, please don't let us down. I voted for and welcomed the Labour Party back to office, looking to it as the only party likely to act drastically enough.*[5]

These are just examples of the letters being received. It is also clear that the local councils were writing frequently on the topic. They had long waiting lists for public housing and wanted to know if the empty camps could be used to reduce them, if only temporarily.

Pressure began to mount on the government to act but MoH were at pains to point out that, although camps looked vacant, it did not mean they were unallocated to other purposes. An MoH press briefing explains:

*Many camps which are vacant or only partially occupied are still required for government purposes and have not yet been declared as redundant. The demands for this type of accommodation are considerable and are tending to increase as it becomes necessary to find accommodation for British workers, Poles and European voluntary workers who are being placed in agriculture, coal-mining, wagon manufacture and essential export industries.*

In addition, the briefing goes on, the camps are not always fit for habitation by civilians and their families, and local authorities needed to become more involved to manage the standard of accommodation, safety of sites and applications for placement. It would become difficult if the government were seen to sanction unfit accommodation, or if there were accidents on sites that were never designed for civilian use, or if people being allocated huts were seen as 'queue-jumpers' by those already on housing waiting lists. It was clear that local authorities had to take on management of these hutted sites as they would any other public housing site, that money would need to spent on making huts habitable and sites safe. But this created another dilemma: there was a national labour shortage, and labour used to adapt the disused camps was labour not then available to the national house-building programme which was significantly behind schedule.

The issues were passed to and fro between the War Department, the MoH and the Ministry of Works for some time, with public and local authority pressure building all the while. Eventually, via a Liberal MP called David Renton, the case for sanctioning use of the abandoned camps and allocating a budget to make the huts decent and the sites safe was put to Parliament, on 9 December 1947. There was a debate, but not one that resulted in any legislation. It was up to the new Department for Housing and Local Government (created to allow the MoH to concentrate on setting up the NHS) to create the policy and manage it through the local councils. And so it was that Croft RDC received authority to adapt Croft Aerodrome for occupation as temporary housing. In January 1948 the first site – Site 5 – was approved for adaptation.

By October 1948 Croft RDC received official word from MoH that they were to take control of all viable sites at the Aerodrome. They were to commission works for the 'hutments' to be made suitable for habitation. They also needed to set rent and rates, arrange for their collection and put in place all the services that social landlords need to administer their properties. Allocation was through a waiting list following application to the council. 'Squatting' was no no longer the means available for accessing this type of housing. If people tried to occupy buildings that were not adopted by the council, and

## Chapter 4 – Bust and Boom

which could be dangerous, they were to be prosecuted. By adopting this approach, the government was regularising arrangements and managing the risks of random occupation of unsuitable accommodation. Investment on making the 'hutments' weather-proof and habitable was significant.

There is evidence that the local community was supportive of the temporary housing site and took practical action to help. A bus service from Cockleberry into Darlington was run by Abbot's bus company from Hurworth, and Abbot's had a depot at Cockleberry, situated in, I believe, the old RAF transport service garage. In the early days, however, people living on the aerodrome were miles from any shops. Given the practicalities of the time – rationing and no refrigeration – frequent visits to shops were needed to feed a household. I found an article showing a 'Food Flying Squad' set up by the Darlington Borough Council and WRVS, which is reproduced here.

'Food Flying Squad' set up at Cockleberry in 1954 would have helped people on the site get a decent meal.

One of our Croft voices, Peter Percival, was born at number 23, Halifax Site, Cockleberry in 1951. His family were among the last to be re-housed – at Barton – in 1960. Peter said his mother Nellie Percival had come from Newton Miers and her first accommodation was on the Technical Site to begin with, and that his uncle Edgar Percival was also at Cockleberry and lived on the Communal Site. These different sites were parts of the aerodrome complex of huts and other buildings. If you look at the Aerodrome map in Appendix B, you'll see that the various groups of buildings were given site numbers. Once they had taken over the accommodation, the Rural District Council gave the sites names. In the 1950 rate book there are the following named sites: Woodside, Whitley, Wellington, Lancaster, Lincoln and Halifax. Woodside and Whitley were in Croft civil parish and had 47 occupied hutments. The rest were in Dalton civil parish and had 82 occupied hutments – so 129 homes altogether. Nearly as many as there were in the village centre at Croft and certainly more than there were in Dalton. Halifax was the biggest single site. In 1950 only one Percival was listed, at number 28. It seems from the rate book that some people stayed less than a year, and Peter's evidence suggests a number of changes between 1950 and when he was a small child. It may be that 129 was not the highest number of hutment homes on the Aerodrome.

**Peter Percivial** can remember the hutment with some clarity:

Peter Percival (front) and his brother in front of their 'hutment' at Cockleberry, ca 1954.

*"It was obviously some sort of fabrication, you know, and I know that they were cold in winter. We had the water, the water was freezing up. You went in, there was the living room which had a cast iron stove over to the right on the wall there, with a chimney going up the middle of the room on that wall. And then we had a pantry as you went through the door, and it had a door on. And then if you went back there was the two bedrooms. But that was the full living area. There was a sink, a sort of big porcelain, white porcelain sink you know, as in years gone by*

*As far as I'm aware there was only the one tap [a cold water tap]. What I do remember was just the one window in the kitchen. And it was the old galvanised steel. And then again, obviously for the bedrooms at the back there was the galvanised windows, little eight inch square windows. We had curtains up. The walls were distemper. The toilets were across the road, you know, which was a wash house and the toilets. Tin bath in the house. I do remember when me my sister Linda was with me and I was only little, you know, like five year old, so she was sat on one side and I was sat on the other side with my father giving us a wash. [...] There was one of the houses, is it was empty next door so [for washing] it was just a posser and a wringer. No washing machines as far as I knew. [...] The stove had a oven at the side. You'd open the front to let the heat out, but on top you used to lift the ring off with a little poker thing, lift it off and put the kettle on. And then you had a oven at the side. Right. And my mam used to bake while the fire was on – she would bake cakes and bread."*

Peter had happy memories of kind neighbours and playmates at Cockleberry. The older children in his family also made friends with local farm children. His sister was friendly with someone who lived in the station house at Moulton. When the site was at its fullest, the Council made provision by rejuvenating the facilities of the old RAF base. There was a store and also a cinema. Rev Charlesworth, the Rector of Croft, had established and consecrated a church – St Thomas's – a project that required significant powers of persuasion from him. Some of the older children worked beyond the Cockleberry site on local farms or other businesses. Later, a sawmill – Cockleberry Sawmill – started up near where Westwood Timber is now I believe.

## Chapter 4 – Bust and Boom

**Peter** remembers going over on a weekend to help out:

Children play out at Cockleberry, ca 1953.

*"When I was a kid, I'd only be about nine, give or take. And I used to walk across the field from the back of the house over to what was the rolling stock then. And then on a Saturday I used to shovel the sawdust out of the sawmill for them, and they used to pay me right? I thought it was great because when it come to bait time I was in the bait cabin with the men and right comfy. I had me a bottle of water and nice sandwiches that mam made us. And I thought it was great because I was sat with the men. And there was a fella there and I don't know who he was, I would love to have found out. He was a big hefty fella and, and he used to, when I went over, he'd tap the fellow beside him and he would hold his hand out and say 'give us some money' and he would give him a shilling or sixpence. And he'd say 'here you are Peter'. And that was me, you know, and sometimes I came home with a couple of bob."*

But Peter's family were not offered alternative housing in Barton until late 1960. They were one of the last families to leave Cockleberry. The RDC were being pressurised by the government to clear the site so that it could be decommissioned entirely but there were no facilities that the council controlled in which to rehouse people, so progress was slow.

Peter was clear that most people at Cockleberry had jobs. They had to pay both rent and rates on their hutments. Nellie Percival paid 6/6 a week which I believe was 1/- a week less than tenants in Carroll Place (who had three bedrooms and indoor bathrooms). An item in the RDC minutes for October 1952 shows that Cockleberry people were seen primarily as people who worked in Darlington:[6] '...it had always been made clear to the Ministry that the Council could not accept responsibility for re-housing the occupiers of the hutments practically all of whom came from Darlington and continued to work in the town.'

What Peter saw as a child was that neighbours and playmates were moving away, and the centre of the Cockleberry community was being knocked down.

*"I had a friend Eddie, I still keep in touch with him now. They moved to Darlington because I think they were building houses at Firth Moor, and a few people went. And there's others went to, if I'm not mistaken, Wycliffe or maybe Eaglescliffe. [...] I can remember it being a built-up area in the centre, you know, over at Cockleberry. But before we come away they started knocking them down.. And then once we moved, we were the first family to move to Barton."*

Even when he got to Barton Peter was picked on as somebody who came from Cockleberry. He always felt the people on the council estate generally were looked down on, but Cockleberry people particularly. He left school at 16 and got a job on the farm across the road.

*"Rose Villa. And the old fellow there said 'You were squatting' and I says 'No we weren't. We paid rent'. 'You were squatting.' And I said 'No, we weren't.' 'No, Peter, you were all squatters up there.' And he got very insulting, you know? And I said, no, I said, we paid rent. 'No, you were squatters'. He just carried on like that. To me, that wasn't insulting me – it was insulting me mam. You know, and I was annoyed about it."*

The Cockleberry site was completely cleared by 1963 and much was demolished. Some of the buildings in the centre were repurposed as industrial units. The runways continued into the seventies and by then Croft Circuit was established and using some of them for motor racing. Others were dug up and the land turned again to agriculture. Some parts of the runways are still roads linking Vince Moor with Birch Springs. David Walker told me that one of the bomb dumps was re-purposed as a common sheep dip for several nearby farms that kept flocks of sheep. But eventually, the old structure and presence of the aerodrome melted back into the landscape.

There are quite a few people from Cockleberry living in the vicinity of Croft but few speak out to identify themselves. Most people in Croft know little or nothing of the lives that were led there after the war. So The Squatters Tale needed to be told.

# From post-war to 1990: development and destruction

Against the national trend, which saw over 4 million council houses built nationally up to 1980, Croft Rural District Council did not build many more council houses after the initial post-war flurry. However, also against the national trend, there were fewer new houses built in Croft in the two decades after the second world war than there were in the two decades before it. Furthermore, in the period following World War 2 there were also many *destructions* of old buildings, some of them notable features of Croft's history.

A difficulty for the local historian of Croft is that the Ordnance Survey did not re-survey the Croft area between 1912 and the Pathfinder Series of maps in 1975. This means that the development of dwellings in that period can't be tracked reliably via OS maps. To cover this gap I have created a map myself, using data from the Croft Rural District Council Register of Plans, that shows the village in 1930, with tables of houses and construction dates. And this is in Appendix B. I hope it will do as illustration. In addition, I have an aerial picture of Croft dated 1951, which I have annotated to augment my hand-composed map. These are all in Appendix B and are the best way of understanding how the village centre changed from 1930 to 1990.

## Chapter 4 – Bust and Boom

In addition to all the new houses that appear via the maps, there were lots of small changes to dwellings and larger changes to village infrastructure. Mains sewerage was re-engineered and made available to all houses in 1954. Electricity was extended to the more remote houses and farms in the period 1959-1961. During the sixties and seventies most houses in Croft applied to build a garage, and, if they didn't already have one, an inside toilet and bathroom.

Why did the village centre develop in the way that it did? I have a theory: see what you think of it. First, Croft Rural District Council did not do large-scale development or development strategy. It may be that the North Riding Council didn't do it either but I have not assessed that. Croft RDC preferred to develop small and piecemeal, house by house. In the inter-war years there were two schemes for larger residential developments in the village proposed by private individuals. These were:

1. A scheme to build 22-25 houses in the field next to Monkend Hall and behind South Parade. The plan pictured below shows what this would have been. The idea was to build houses that would attract a government subsidy and the landowner was Richard Bowes, owner of Monkend Hall from 1888. This plan was submitted on 03 March 1923 with a letter stating 'It is proposed to erect 22-25 houses at a cost of between £800 and £1000 either detached or semi-detached'. This plan was submitted shortly before the 1923 Housing Act was made law. That Act set out subsidies for people building houses for private ownership by 'the working classes'.

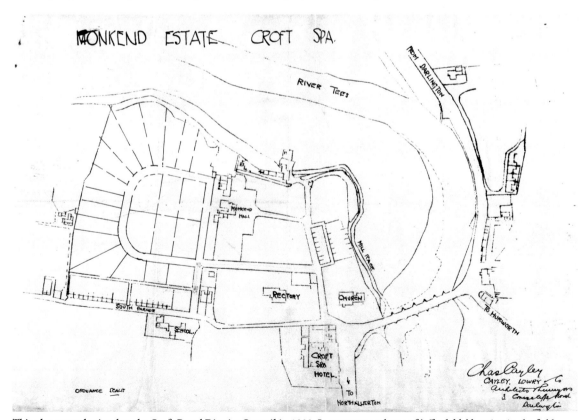

**This plan was submitted to the Croft Rural District Council in 1923. It proposes a scheme of 'affordable' housing in the field behind Monkend Hall.**

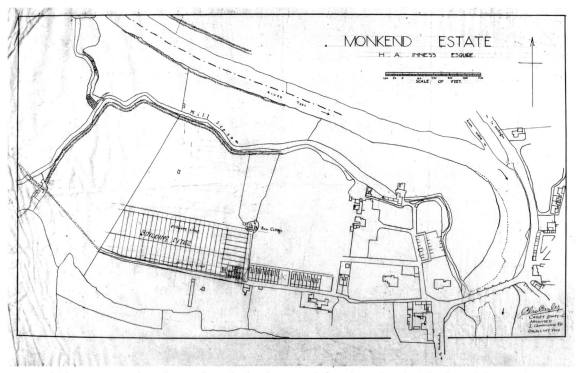

Henry and Ada Inness put in this ambitious plan to develop the west end of South Parade on land that formerly been market gardens.

2. Another proposed development at Monkend, this time to the west of South Parade, pictured above. It was submitted on 29 November 1926 in the name of Henry Atkinson Inness, with the same architects as Richard Bowes's scheme – Cayley, Lowry & Co of Coniscliffe Rd, Darlington. The landowner was Henry's wife Ada Mary Inness. In the case of this development all houses would be semi-detached, keeping prices low enough to get the subsidy.

A reason for these proposals was that the government of the day were keen to build houses and had asked local authorities to take the responsibility and the initiative in planning public housing. But they also provided incentives for private landowners, architects and builders to build houses in the form of financial subsidies for new building. There were multiple Housing Acts between the war as governments of

Henry Inness, of Monkend Gardens, does some digging. Date 1929. I'm unsure where he is but that looks like the two terraces of South Parade behind him, so he may have been in the large garden attached to 1 South Parade.

varying colour considered who should be building the 'homes fit for heroes'. In 1919 responsibility and subsidies went to local authorities. In 1923 – an act anticipated by the first of the schemes listed above I would surmise – local authority subsidies were withdrawn from local authorities in order to incentivise private development that would be affordable for the 'working classes'. In 1924 an act balanced the approach of the two previous ones – this act was credited as having seen through the clearance of many slums and the erection of 700,000 houses. In 1930 the money swung back to local authorities. By the beginning of World War 2 the country's housing problems still hadn't been solved and a housing act in 1947 again mandated the building of temporary and council housing.

Whatever wave of housing policy the developers of our two Croft schemes were hoping to catch, they didn't succeed. I'm not sure what happened with the first scheme, it doesn't seem to have been discussed at council, but the second scheme got a flat 'no'. 'Over intensity' was a phrase used and generally, they just didn't like that scale of change. Their refusal led to the next reason for the bit-by-bit development in the twenties and thirties.

Secondly, landowners sometimes need to 'liquidise their assets' for personal reasons. In the case of scheme 2 above Ada Inness sold much of the land that would have used for the larger development anyway, and individual builders put up new houses for people to buy, often designed to those individual buyers' specifications. This resulted in an assortment of buildings in the same vicinity. We got Thorneycroft and Corrie, Durley and St Kitts, Brentwood, Shirley Cottage, Normanhurst and Sunnybrae, The Anchorage and Rosedale. It's a stark contrast to the approach taken by Richard Bowes of Monkend Hall and his builder, Albert Edward Oates of South Shields, in 1901. This is when the plans for the second terrace on South Parade (numbers 9 to 16) were submitted and approved. The plans proudly say the houses are 'to be the same in every respect'.[7] Individual plots of land were offered to buyers before building, but the style of house was not to be customised: it was a complete terrace, unique in Croft because numbers 1 to 8 developed piecemeal, and so did Monkend Terrace.[8] But, anyway, Ada Inness's land sales led to all those individual houses at the west end of South Parade I've mentioned above. Here's why she sold…

Ada Mary Inness bought what is now Monkend House (then Monkend Gardens) plus two very large tracts of land in the area known in general as Monkend Gardens, both sides of the 'Proposed Road' that was the Stapleton bridle way, in 1906. The story of this land and how she got it is complicated and not for these pages. It is enough to know that Ada Mary Inness, the wife of Henry Atkinson Inness, and mother of Fred, Henry and Cosmo, also did a lot of mortgaging in the period 1912 to 1937. She took out something like 8 different mortgages, and she wasn't always paid up on them. So by the 1920s she needed to sell some land. The big scheme (shown on p118) that would release the value of her investment was the housing development. When it was rejected by the District Council she was left to sell individual plots, some to builders, some to individuals like Miss Mathewson, for The Anchorage, or Miss Boagey for Brentwood. When Ada's son Fred bought some land to create 'High Thorn' in 1937, he bought directly from the Darlington Equitable Building Society who were, according to the conveyance, 'exercising their statutory right to demand a sale'. I.e. the Building Society wanted payment of some of the arrears. Fred bought the land for £225. He sold 'High Thorn' to John and Lilian Titchmarsh in 1947 for £4500.⁹

Ada died on 26 February 1955 in Newcastle but not before selling Monkend Gardens to Wilfred and Elsie Hauxwell on 12 January 1954. The Hauxwells lived at Monkend Gardens (the house, now called Monkend House in aid of disambiguation) until 2017. They also sold much of their land: in July 1954 for the pair of semis Dellwood and Pinedell, and then, after the millennium, the 3 house development called Monkend Gardens.

Bill Chaytor also proposed a small residential development along Northallerton Road, between The Limes and Waterside, in 1966. The story behind this was that that stretch of land had several dilapidated properties on them, with elderly residents who could no longer maintain the agricultural businesses there. The first was the small farm associated with Strawberry Cottage at the north end of the land (south of The Limes). This had been run by the Thornton family from before World War 1. By 1963, John Thornton was the rate payer and he was 47. The second was Stairmand's market garden, with a house known as Park View, which had been a market garden since before 1847, as it is shown as one – probably an orchard – on the 1847 Ordnance Survey map. By 1963, Mabel Stairmand lived there, alone I believe, and she was 67. Bill and his land agent felt all this should be cleared and sold for housing.

**Bill Chaytor** remembers:

*"...there was another family who farmed the little bit of land which has the six houses as you drive south towards Northallerton on the left-hand side beyond Bridge House and Woodbine Cottage. Those six houses that are along there, between there and Waterside. That was a very scruffy farm with a bit of farmland, and the chap who was there called Mr Thornton used to drive his cattle over the A167 to the forty acres in front of Croft Hall, and he would drive them over and back and over and back twice a day to milk them. And even in that time, the road wasn't anything like as busy as it is now, but it was a nutty arrangement and most inconvenient. And so I said would he like to take on Pepperfield Farm, which is a small farm, a little bigger than what he had."*

Mr Thornton did not take on Pepperfield but moved to another small farm: Bay Horse. I'm not sure what happened to Mabel Stairmand. However, in December 1966 the Croft Estate put in plans to the RDC for permission to build a small residential housing estate. The houses were a mixture of larger and smaller dwellings, all with a consistent look.

The RDC rejected the outline plans quoting 'layout and density' as a concern. The plans were then revised to contain fewer houses. This time outline permission was conditionally given, but things did not progress. Maybe the Croft Estate felt it would be too difficult to get final permissions and they changed tack. However, as we all now know, the land was still sold, as 8 separate building plots. And individual buyers put up houses to their own taste, following planning permission granted for each separately. These are the eight, very different, detached houses set back from the main A167 Northallerton Road that we see today.

*Chapter 4 – Bust and Boom*

# An ancient mill

Two buildings that helped define Croft as a village for many years and which suffered major change, during the sixties and seventies were Croft Mill and Croft Rectory. The first was vacated, left to crumble and then sold and restored to a dwelling house. The second was converted into flats, its stables let as garages then an industrial unit, and finally its huge garden sold off for building plots. I'll start with the story of Croft Mill.

There are two mills in Croft parish: Jolby Mill and Croft Mill. Jolby is really a separate discussion and I haven't researched it, but I do know that Jolby was a significant medieval settlement at a time when Croft was not so much so, and that it deserves a study of its own. I have seen a transcript of a document dated 1295 that mentions 'John, son of Walter, the miller of Jolbie'. Another document dated a little later, talks about lands in Croft that 'abutt the Mill dam'.[10] So both of these water mills are very old. Clearly the buildings that stand today will be newer than medieval but it seems as though milling on the two sites went on for many hundreds of years. The earliest map we have of Croft – the one drawn for Sir Henry Chaytor in 1722 and included in Appendix B – shows Croft Mill on its current site.

The last people to run Croft Mill as a business were the Wilson Family – T.Wilson and Sons – but by 1930 their tenure was coming to an end. It was in 1932 that William Adamson arrived with his family. He described himself as 'farmer and self-taught miller'. He still produced flour for human consumption but much of his business was grinding grain for animal feed. He had horses, had some crops and was allowed to gather stones from the river bed or charge others to do the same. This was an ancient practice made possible by the route of the Tees before it was re-routed in the 1970s (see Chapter 5).

**One of the last pictures of the mill before it was sold, showing its dilapidated state.**

The mill field went in a huge arc to the rear of Monkend Terrace. It can be seen clearly in the aerial shots of Croft in Appendix B.

Mr Adamson's family consisted of himself (he was born in 1889 at Picton near Yarm), his wife Selina and their children Thomas Vasey, Florence Muriel (known as Muriel, see Chapter 3 on the war) and son Stephen. Thomas Adamson died in 1950. Selina died in 1964 and Muriel had married a Canadian and emigrated to Quebec after the war. Stephen lived until 1980 but seems to have moved to Hurworth. So Mr Adamson was left on his own at the mill, and by 1972 at the latest it was empty. Mr Adamson died in 1978, having lived his last years at Linden Court in Hurworth Place. He, Selina and Thomas are all buried in St Peters Churchyard.

**Heavy horses graze in the 'mill field' to the north of Croft Mill itself. Probably early sixties.**

In 1972 the Croft Estate – which had always owned the mill – made it known that they were looking for a buyer. Bill Chaytor said at the time that 'I don't want to see it spoiled or demolished but I would be sorry if it wasn't turned into a decent dwelling'.[11] He mentioned that negotiations were taking place with Gerald Kirkwood from Hurworth. However, in July 1978, a photographer from English Heritage was in Croft and took photographs of Monkend Hall and then the mill. Monkend Hall is listed, but the mill isn't, perhaps there was a discussion then about whether it should be. However the photograph on p121, shows that the mill was in a semi derelict state in 1978, so I am not sure when Mr Kirkwood actually bought it.

Nick Kirkwood, Gerald's son, could not remember when his parents moved into the mill – he thought it would be the 1980s. Nick himself was at university from 1977 and then away from home a lot. However, he does remember something of the state the mill was in:

**Nick Kirkwood**:

*"I'm not sure I ever met Mr. Adamson. But I know that that there were no mains services in his time here. I'm not sure how long he lived here on his own but but, you know, there was a two hole closet. And that was filled up and dragged out and emptied with sawdust and human excrement. I think water was all from a pump. I remember vaguely a pump. I suppose but I don't know whether that was not uncommon but it would be intriguing as to where that water came from."*

I can comment here that in the 1941 Ministry of Agriculture farm survey the mill is listed, like all the rest of the farms, as having no electricity and water from a well for the house, plus water for buildings and fields from a stream, presumably the mill stream. Whether the pump was from the well or stream I don't know. By the 1970's most of the farms had piped water and electricity, but perhaps the mill was not considered to be worth the expense of conversion when the rest of the parish was done in the fifties and sixties.

Nick's recollection was that the mill was a listed building when his father bought it and that was something of a hurdle:

**Nick Kirkwood**:

*"I do remember* [the listed status] *made the planning process quite hard work for my father. And then at the end of it, they did decide that the work that they had permitted was so extensive that they were going to delist it. Yeah. They sort of worked through on the basis – yeah, you can do that. And that's okay. And then at the end, they sort of reviewed it and said, 'that's too radically different'.* [...] *the house bit was the bit that that got demolished. And then the mill was converted. The far end room in the garden, I think was the dairy. And then then the middle room over the water over the bridge, I think that was a back kitchen. I do remember a couple of ranges in there, when the building work, or before we got moved in properly, I think they were ripped out. I think some were pinched. Whether it was the scrap or for anything else, I don't know. So yeah, the use of the building was that layout was rather different."*

I'm not sure it is the case that the mill was listed. I consulted Jane Hatcher, a notable local architectural historian, on the topic. Jane knows a lot about watermills and surveyed the Croft mill in 1978. Jane Hatcher's personal notes record:

*Very derelict buildings in decayed red sandstone & brick. Dam at Monk End collapsed c1950, and mill ceased working. High breastshot wheel, in quite good condition, in lean-to wheelhouse. Two grey millstones lying about, also part of a wire flour dresser. Cottages adjacent to the mill. River Tees has been re-channelled in front of the mill, which has altered the land levels.*

Jane was involved in the national re-survey of buildings commissioned by the then Secretary of State for the Environment, Michael Heseltine, in 1980. She told me that by that time she did the re-survey of Richmondshire the mill had been converted to a house, so was not considered for the new list that emerged from the re-survey

But it is definitely the case that the Historic Buildings and Monuments Commission – which became English Heritage in 1984 – sent their photographer to photograph the mill on 11 July 1978, the same day they photographed Monkend Hall. Their archive contains 9 pictures of the mill and 15 of Monkend Hall, taken on the same day. Monkend Hall *is* listed. But the mill is not. So it seems that Nick's account is right. Negotiations on sale of the mill probably coincided with conversations about listing it, and the commitment that would result in listing was just a bit too much.

There is a section on the operational history of the mill and its place in the agricultural history of Croft parish in Chapter 5.

# Wonderland

Another building, which is listed, and that underwent radical change in the 1970s, was Croft Rectory. The Rectory is one of Croft's most notable buildings. The current structure shows evidence of an early eighteenth century origin.[12] But it's fame is largely because it was the home of the Reverend Charles Dodgson and his family from 1843 to 1868. His son Charles Lutwidge Dodgson, who took the pen name Lewis Carroll, was the author of *Alice in Wonderland, Alice Through The Looking Glass, Jabberwocky* and the *Hunting of the Snark*, amongst other works. This association has brought people from all over the world to Croft. You can spot them peering down the Rectory drive in order to get a glimpse of the building that appears in so many of Lewis Carroll's own photographs of his family, imagining how it might have been when the extensive Dodgson family lived there. Reverend Dodgson died in 1868. He and his wife Frances are buried in St Peters Churchyard, just to the north of the church. After Archdeacon Dodgson's death the remaining family had to move, which they did, to Guildford.

During the twentieth century the fortunes of the Church of England declined steeply and after World War 2 economising became a big issue. In 1936 the Tithe Act abolished the system of tithe payments to the clergy, a process that had been trickling towards this conclusion for over a hundred years. Congregations were also falling. In addition, the Church of England also had a huge portfolio of old property that needed restoration and investment.

The first Rector of Croft within our timeframe was Reverend Harry Tompkins who lived in the Rectory from 1929 to 1949. During his tenure of the post it was apparent that the Rectory needed some repairs, and the Church Commissioners were struggling to find the money for them. The Rectory at that time was, like many others, no longer in step with the status and conduct of the church in a community. It belonged to the period when a vicar was second only to the titled gentry in the social hierarchy of his parish, and when he might have significant leisure time to read and pursue other interests, largely because he could afford to hire a curate, or maybe two, to do a lot of the parish work. In the case of James Dalton (1764 to 1843, Rector of Croft from 1805), Reverend Dodgson's predecessor, the other interest was botany. He was well known with connections to several famous botanists. The most eminent was Joseph Dalton Hooker, his godson and the founder of Kew Gardens. James Dalton might be one reason why the Rectory developed such a large and various garden. The Rectory was also greatly extended by the Dodgsons to house their large family. After Reverend Dodgson, Frederick Henry Law built the high wall along Rectory Lane and put in a large, heated, T-shaped glasshouse. He also built the Coach House at the back, about 1870. It is clear from censuses and other sources that the Rectory always had at least one gardener from Rev Dodgson up to the 1930s. The last gardener I am aware of was David Fyfe who lived at Rectory Cottages and then, later, Monk End Bungalow. He may not have been gardener to the Rectory at the end, he may have worked at Monkend Hall, I'm not sure. He died in 1938.

In 1949 Harry Tompkins retired and Gerald Edward Charlesworth was appointed Rector. Shortly after his appointment, the decision was taken to split the Rectory into flats and let off the stables as garages, as a way of making the parish finances more stable.

## Chapter 4 – Bust and Boom

The Charlesworth family moved to 1 Richmond Terrace while the renovation and alteration work was going on. The Rector was to have the bottom flat and there were two flats above him. Mary Bossinger, the third child of Edward Charlesworth, was a toddler when the family lived there and remembers little about Richmond Terrace, but she does have very clear memories of the Rectory garden and the bottom flat of the Rectory, which was for the Rector and his family.

**Mary Charlesworth**:

*"And we moved into the Rectory, but I was a teeny tot. We weren't very long in Richmond Terrace. I think it was just while they were busy renovating. But mum told us that she used to wheel me in the pram down to the Rectory and she used to garden there. And my two older brothers used to play in the gardens before we actually were living there. And so I don't remember much about Richmond Terrace. I must have been a baby. Maybe I was one when they moved.*

*[Living at the Rectory] was the most wonderful experience that you could ever have. My mother used to have a school bell, which she used to ring to call us in because there was no way that she we would be heard. We couldn't hear her. So the front garden had a big lawn and had this wonderful acacia tree in the middle. We always used to say, you know, 'we are the owners of Wonderland'. It was a children's paradise. There was a huge, great big, what we call the umbrella tree in the garden, which became our riding horses. We used to climb up and sit on the branches and we used to stand on these things and slid to the ground. So at the front there was what we call the garden of remembrance, which as you came in through the big gate was on the left, and it was very overgrown, wild, shady and mum planted all sorts of things in there.It was quite a well kept garden at the front and then on the side that was the side lawn. Lots of trees. Dad put up a swing in there. And then right at the very end of of the garden before you went into the orchard, there was this yew hedge and I was very envious of my brothers because they used to walk along the yew hedge. They used to walk almost inside the hedge, and this was great, great fun. And that led through to the orchard at the back and and then there were a couple of allotments which were rented to people in the village. And halfway down the wall, there was a door and people who had these allotments, they could come in through that door. And they grew strawberries and everything. We used to go on our hands and knees like Indians again, and go and snaffle some of the strawberries. So that's the section that they've now built on.*

*There were all the trees you could think of, apple trees. There were gooseberry bushes all the way along just before this back wall, and we would hide in the gooseberry bushes, scratchy gooseberries and, no, they' were made beautiful. They seemed to make great bushes and we used to crawl underneath these very, very old gooseberry bushes, and then along the back wall. There were rose hips. And we gathered rose hips and I remember this clearly gathering rose hips because the rose hips would be sent to make rosehip syrup. And so we gathered all the way along the back all the wild roses, which were absolutely magnificent. The allotments were along there, I don't know how far along the door would have been. It was quite far along. It was a big black door and then you went in and there were the allotments probably just behind the beginning of the orchard. On the other side of the orchard dividing the orchard from where I think the coach house and the bonds are, there was a wall running along there. And there were all sorts of fruit trees along there and blackberries and brambles whatever. And on behind that was was a stable yard and pigs. Billy Warne had his pigs there. And we got into big big trouble because my brothers were rather wicked and they decided to see whether I was fit to play with them and could I ride a pig. So they put me on a pig.*

*You know about the railway game with Lewis Carroll? He invented a game for his brothers and sisters which was called the railway game and he constructed out of apple boxes I assume crates, that's all mum told us. And they used to use the pathways in there were lots of pathways in the in the orchard and in the middle was the sundial which they have saved and then I saw it was outside in the garden near where my parents bedroom was. So that's still there. But it was at the crossroads of all these pathways in in the in the orchard and he invented this game called the railway game where the train would stop at various stations. But as far as my recollection, there were no tracks as such it was very much an imaginary child's game."*

The Charlesworths left Croft in 1959 because Edward Charlesworth had been asked to take on the depressed parish of Liverton Mines, where the mines had recently been closed and there was economic distress. They then, in the early 1960s, moved to Johannesburg, again because Edward had been asked to help build up the church around the township of Kimberley.

The flat arrangement seemed to work well and improved the parish cash-flow considerably. However, when Reverend Charlesworth left in 1959 the Rectory was again a difficulty. It was not attractive to a potential vicar. Eventually, the churchwardens interviewed a man called Mr Wylie whose existing position was at St. Chad's church in Headingley, Leeds. As Croft was a Crown Living, the churchwardens could not appoint anyone, they could only express their preference. It was up to 10 Downing St to recommend an appointment to the reigning monarch. But, in effect, the opinion of the churchwardens was highly influential in the appointment. Things went well at the interview and the churchwardens – Captain Parlour and Kit Chaytor in the main – felt that Mr Wylie was the man for the job, so they wrote to ask if he would accept, if they were to recommend him. His letter of response, dated 15 October 1958, was a bit of a surprise:

*Very unwillingly I have decided to withdraw from Croft. I like the Church and I like the Parish but every time I see it, the Rectory and its garden fill me with such depression that I think it would be unwise to take it.* [13]

It was a little while before Reverend Littleton (known as Arthur Littleton or, later, Canon Littleton) arrived. He too found the garden a challenge and he came up with a proposal. He put his proposal in a document addressed to the Church Commissioners on 31 October 1968. The first paragraph said this:

## Chapter 4 – Bust and Boom

> *The Rectory garden is too vast, and attempts to keep it in some sort of order take up too much of my time and energy. Although 7 tenants have plots in the kitchen garden I still have a large area to care for. Too many people have access to the premises, which results in a loss of privacy. We produce too much fruit and vegetables for our own needs and the disposal of it involves more work to no profit, because we give it away.*[14]

The 'seven tenants' were the villagers who had allotments in the rectory garden. In the second paragraph he points out that he receives £90 by renting out garages converted from the stables, but that the stables are becoming dilapidated. He notes that in a normal season the orchard produces a ton of apples. The additional two flats in the Rectory bring in £356 per annum. The solution, to him, was clear: 'I propose that the area indicated on my plan should be sold as housing sites, with the possibility of placing some restrictions on the number and type of houses to be built'.

Canon Littleton felt that the current accommodation at the Rectory was adequate for the Rector and he was not in favour of building a new rectory at that point. After a while his plan was approved. The garden would be sold for housing. But the Rectory itself would also eventually be sold, the parishes of Croft and Middleton Tyas would be served by one vicar and that person would live in a new house in Middleton Tyas. This went further than the Parochial Church Council of Croft was anticipating, but in 1978 the Rectory was put up for sale. It was bought by Mr and Mrs Atkinson who spend a great deal of time, and money, on restoring the building to a single dwelling. Canon Littleton retired in 1978 and died in 1985. He was replaced by Nicholas Horton, up to 1981. Then Richard Cooper became Rector of Croft up until 1990. But he, of course, never lived in Croft.

When the plan for selling the Rectory was announced people in Croft were very uncomfortable that there would no longer be a Rector in Croft. The churchwardens proposed a new Rectory in the old Rectory garden. That didn't work. They then, after the new primary school opened, proposed that the old school building be knocked down

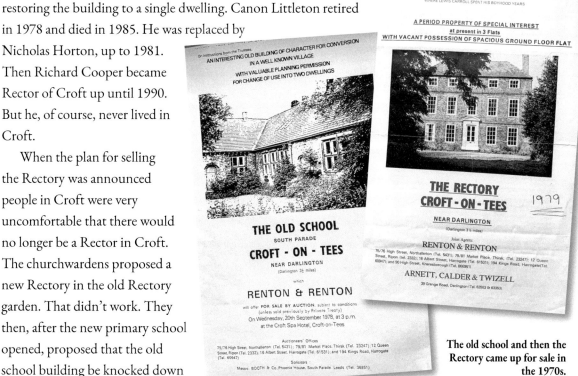

**The old school and then the Rectory came up for sale in the 1970s.**

and a new Rectory built there, but destroying the old school was not to be considered. What about the old school garden? No. Finally, last gasp, a proposal that a new rectory be built at the end of Monkend Terrace, where the Mill Race development is now, was suggested. Again no. The Church Commissioners were having none of it.

Arnett, Calder & Twizell were appointed to handle the sale of three plots of land situated in the rectory garden – the Charlesworth children's 'Wonderland' – to be sold for housing. The first buyers were for the middle plot, Mr & Mrs Matthews, on 15 December 1969.

The plot bordering The Gable and the old Rectory Wall went to Mike and Cath Wood. They set about building a new dwelling house – Alice House – on the plot, but later also wanted to convert the stable and coach house into a light industrial unit for manufacturing electronic equipment. Mike was an inventor, and his inventions sold. Much of what he invented was specialist equipment for laboratory or engineering use but he also invented an early breathalyser and a speed gun amongst other things. Unfortunately for Mike, Croft didn't do industry. There were howls of protest and a special parish meeting to discuss Mike's planning application was held on 12 March 1975. Minutes made it quite clear that parishioners felt 'this is a purely residential area'. But Richmondshire District Council overruled the parish on this one and the stable and coach house was converted. This did not go down well with the Parish Council who accused Richmondshire of being out of touch and throwing their weight around. However, this is Mike's account of his purchase and purpose:

**Mike Wood**:

*"The rector was coming up to retirement, Canon Littleton. And he was the last rector* [in the Rectory]. *Incidentally, Croft Church was considered to be the richest stipend in Britain, which was quite something. Also, it had claim to fame with the author of Alice in Wonderland, spent his early days there. And in the garden they had a railway which consisted of a cinder path, which they used to roll a couple of barrels and a plank* [laughs]. *And they had station names and he used to push his sister around on this, on this so-called train. We bought the site of where the the Carroll* [Dodgson] *children must have played. And where, in fact, we built Alice House. It was one of three. There were three plots sold. And the site for Alice House was unique in that behind it there was a dividing wall separating it from what used to be the coach house for the rectory. And that was not part of the sale of the land on which Alice House was built. And the vendors phoned me up one day, and said, 'There's a plot of land behind the part you've just bought. Would you like it?' So I said, 'Well, it wouldn't be a bad idea. What's the asking price?' They were asking £1,500 for it. And I said, 'Would you be prepared to take an offer?' And they said, 'Yes, make us an offer.' So I said, 'Would £1,200 be reasonable.' And they said, 'Yes.' They thought that was very reasonable. And it was accepted. I later found out that Captain Parlour, who lived in the Hall on the other side of the lane, had offered £300 for it and he had been rejected* [laughs], *sent away with a flea in his ear. And one of the people who were renting the lock-up garages which had been built in the area we're talking about, he offered £600, and that had also been rejected. So I came along, and my offer was grabbed, I think."*

*Chapter 4 – Bust and Boom*

# The death of Halnaby Hall and a rich man's folly

Beyond the domestic architecture described above, and the grand old buildings that saw oblivion or change, there are also some big stories to tell about the destruction of two grand and significant houses.

People in Croft get misty-eyed about Halnaby Hall. They talk about the beautiful gardens and treelined avenue, the magnificence of the architecture and its history. Particularly the Milbank family, notably the marriage of Annabella Milbank to Lord Byron, and the latter's 'honeymoon from hell' at the Hall in 1815. It was certainly true that the Milbank association put Halnaby Hall in touch with the most elite Georgian circles, but by the time we get to 1930, the starting year for this book, the Hall was in the hands of an ageing Lady Catherine Wilson-Todd. Her death was to precipitate not only the end of the hall but also the dispersal of the 2,000 acre estate that went with it.

I tell the full story of the estate dispersal in the next chapter – Living on the Land- because the event had a significant effect on the agricultural community of Croft parish. In this chapter I will talk about the Hall, and Lady Wilson-Todd, whose death precipitated its fall.

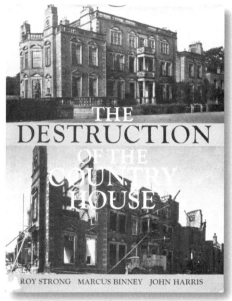

This book edited by Roy Strong charted the demise of hundreds of country houses in the mid twentieth century. The cover shows the 'before' and 'after' pictures of Halnaby Hall - a testament to the shock felt at its destruction.

**Mr George Gregory poses for the camera in the doorway to Byron's bedroom at Halnaby Hall. 1950.**

**Doris Cameron** had specific memories of Halnaby: *"Of course, yes, I remember Halnaby Hall. It was beautiful. And the tennis court they had. I remember Lady Wilson-Todd, she was a very good woman. I don't remember her husband. But she had the shakes. And my aunt and uncle lived over at Halnaby Grange and it belonged to the estate, and she was so kind when my aunty was poorly, you know, she bothered to send something over for her. She was a very kind woman. But her son died of pneumonia when he was young. There's a window in memory of him in Croft Church. It's a west window. And she was broken-hearted. And then when she went her nephew got the hall and he turned it into a blooming hotel or something, and they sold it."*

An RAF aerial shot of the area around Halnaby.

*Chapter 4 – Bust and Boom*

# The story of Catherine Wilson-Todd

Catherine James Crawford Russel was born on 7 September 1860 into a very wealthy family. Her father was James Russel of Blackbraes, near Falkirk, a Coal and Iron Master.

The infant Catherine was born at Arnotdale, still a substantial house today, then a Falkirk residence of note, built by her grandfather in 1830. As well as being a lawyer and investor, her grandfather had been prominent in Falkirk civic life. Catherine's father James was the eldest son and inherited his father's estate but when he himself died suddenly just a few months after her birth everything passed to his son, Catherine's older brother James. However, James was only 2 at the time, and the James Russel Trust, a group of uncles on both his mother's and father's sides plus his mother herself, was set up to manage his inherited assets until he reached majority. Baby James's mother was born Eliza Curle and she came from a legal family in Melrose. She had been married little more than 5 years. On her husband's death, the family removed from Arnotdale it seems and in 1871 they were living at Moray Place in Edinburgh's fashionable New Town. Catherine, James and their older sister Isabella were all educated at home by a governess. The household kept six servants.

Before her marriage two other significant events affected Catherine Russel. First, in 1873, her mother Eliza remarried to a military man, Captain George Bliss McQueen. Then, in 1875, the James Russel Trust bought Dundas Castle near South Queensferry, just outside Edinburgh, for the sum of £185,500 (the equivalent of £16.5 million in 2022).[15] The family moved to the Mansion House.

Both Isabella and Catherine also had Trusts set up after their father's untimely death. Documents I have seen show that Catherine's Trust had investments of nearly £100,000 (£9.5m in 2022 terms). She seems to have signed over at least a portion of the interest from these investments to her mother. The Trust was administered by the Curle family legal firm in Melrose, Curle & Erskine.[16]

Catherine had lived at Dundas Castle at least ten years when she met William Pierrepont Wilson-Todd (1857-1925), son of William Wilson-Todd of Halnaby Hall, then a Captain in the Fourth Queen's Own Hussars. How they came to meet is unknown, but a military connection could perhaps have been the opportunity. Not only was Catherine's stepfather, who was born in Limerick, a former army officer with nearly 15 years experience, he had served much of his time in England and the rest in India with the 51st Regiment of Foot and then the Yorkshire Light Infantry. Her sister Isabella married another military man at Dundas Castle in April 1879 – Charles Maitland Pelham Burn, Lieutenant of the 71st Highlanders. Isabella had six children, one of whom, Catherine Wilson-Todd's niece, was Kathleen Pelham-Burn later Kathleen Moore, Countess of Drogheda, a well known socialite in the 1920s and 30s and a significant woman aviator. She does not, however, make an appearance in Lady Wilson-Todd's will.

On the occasion of their marriage, on 20 July 1887, William and Catherine received the Halnaby Estate as a wedding gift from the groom's father, William Wilson-Todd. This, of course, was a matter of tax efficiency. I believe that inheritance tax would not have been payable on transfer of an estate if the transfer was a wedding gift during the donor's lifetime.

William Wilson-Todd senior (1828-1910) was not a baronet when William and Catherine married in 1877. In fact he had only recently become a Wilson-Todd. His family name was Wilson, and he was from County Wexford. His family house, Roseville, was built in the early nineteenth century by his father Colonel Joshua Wilson. William was sent to Sandhurst, and took up a commission in the 39th Regiment of Foot, although his military career was not a long one. William became a solicitor then Conservative MP for Howdenshire from 1892 until he stepped down in 1906. Hansard records that he made 6 contributions to parliamentary debate in his 14 years as an MP. He was given a baronetcy in 1903.

In 1855 William Wilson had married Jane Marian Rutherford Todd. Jane was the only child of John Todd MP, who had purchased the Halnaby Estate from the Milbank family in 1843. John Todd did not want his estate to pass out of his family, so it was an agreement that on marriage his daughter and her husband would be both be known as Wilson-Todd and that they would own the estate via a trust. William Wilson changed his name by royal licence. John Todd died 6 June 1854. He is buried in Croft St Peter's churchyard in the 'Todd tomb' which is a large tomb to the south east of the church

The younger Wilson-Todds, including Catherine, are nearby,[17] but Sir William and Jane are buried at North Ferriby, where the Todd family originated..

When they were first married, although the Halnaby Estate had been gifted to them, William and Catherine lived instead at Leases Hall near Bedale, because William's parents were still alive and resident at the Hall with his two as yet unmarried sisters, Elizabeth and Evelyn. Although William's mother Jane died in 1909 and his father William died in 1910, William and Catherine were still living in Leases Hall at the time of the 1911 census.

They were living at Halnaby Hall in 1919 though, when their only child James died. James Henry Wilson-Todd was born at the Roxburgh Hotel in Edinburgh in November 1891. One imagines his appearance was unexpected and that his parents were on a visit to see Catherine's family, but this is conjecture. James lived most of his life at Leases Hall and died young. An obituary in the Yorkshire Post reported he:

> ... served for a short time during the war in the Queen's Own Hussars, his father's old regiment holding the rank of Captain, but was obliged to resign due to the state of his health. He died from heart failure following an attack of influenza. He was of a retiring disposition and never took any part in public affairs.[18]

There is an unusual request in Catherine Wilson-Todd's very detailed will, which she initially made in 1945. She writes 'I specially direct my trustees on my death to destroy the picture of my son James with a dog, by Slocum'. That is her first specific request in a will of many requests. Later she bequeaths another portrait of James to a great-niece. James was a collector of stamps and coins, and on his death Lady Wilson-Todd gave the collection as a bequest to the British Library where the collection bears his name. In her will she also intimates that he collected china and glass. He died on 3 March 1919 during the Spanish Flu epidemic, leaving his parents without children.

There is a lot more to be said about the Wilson-Todds but what is related here is the background to

## Chapter 4 – Bust and Boom

the critical situation that arose when Catherine Wilson-Todd reached her final illness in 1948. By this time she was an old lady of 88. She died at 153 Morningside Drive, Edinburgh on 9 December that year. When and why she was there I do not yet know. Maybe she still had family there, but both of her siblings had long since died. She seems to have been at Halnaby up until July 1948 as a codicil to her will was made at this time and signed and witnessed in Darlington. On her death certificate it says her 'usual residence' was Halnaby Hall and that the cause of death was Pneumonia and Senility. What happened next saw the end of Halnaby Hall and its estate and changed the parish of Croft forever.

Given that she was predeceased by her son, her husband and both of her siblings, Catherine Wilson-Todd had to consider carefully what would happen to Halnaby after her death. She had a number of nieces and nephews. On the Russel side her sister's marriage to Charles Maitland Pelham-Burn had yielded six children. On her husband's side there were 3 children from his sister Elizabeth's marriage to Marmaduke Wyvill. None of these people inherited Halnaby, and not all of them received anything in her will. Her will is clear that she had the power to settle the estate on an heir as the lead Trustee but she did not do so. It was the estate Trustees who would decide what to do after she had died. Her will is detailed and is testament to the many valuable objects the Hall contained – portraits by Lely, valuable sporting prints, Chippendale furniture. But she was generous to many people, not so much family, more so to Halnaby associates, tenant farmers and servants. Every servant and associate was left some money and her favourites, those she felt were loyal to her, were left significant sums. She thanks her physician, Sir William Errington Hume, for his care and attention leaving him £300. Favourite servants Frederick Scarth Beadon (her land agent), Harry Dimmock (her gamekeeper), Johan Lindboe (her chauffeur) were all left decent sums. Her personal estate was valued at over £149,000, out of which £96,000 in death taxes were paid.

The Trustees for the Halnaby Estate at the point of Catherine's death were two: Alexander Ormiston Curle and Patrick Cecil Smythe. The latter was a solicitor, the former was a retired solicitor and second cousin of Lady Wilson-Todd's. Alexander Curle was also a Fellow of the Society of Antiquaries in Scotland, a Commissioner for the Royal Commission for the Ancient Monuments in Scotland and a Director of the Royal Scottish Museum. These two men do not seem to have spent much time looking for solutions to Halnaby's lack of an immediate heir. Lady Wilson-Todd died in Edinburgh on 9 December and she is buried with her husband and son in Croft churchyard. Probate was granted on 2nd June 1949 to Curle and Smyth. On 1st July they sold the whole Halnaby Estate to D.J.Place & Company Ltd of London, for £62,000.[19] I'm not sure what the terms of the sale were but no conveyancing took place. Place & Co immediately set up an auction of the Estate and this took place on Thursday 13 October 1949 at the Croft Spa Hotel. Almost every farm tenant and estate worker attended and there are many copies of the sale catalogue to be seen in Croft parish today. They have been retained by the farming families almost as a talisman, a record of what they once were, of a way of life which has been lost, each with the hammer price carefully written against each lot. Conveyances from the Trustees to the buyers were effected after the auction, but all monies went to Place & Co.[20]

The dispersal of the estate proper is dealt with in Chapter 5, as its impact on the agricultural aspect of Croft parish is significant. What I will deal with here is the sale of Lot 1 – Halnaby Hall with land amounting to 15 acres 2 roods and 7 perches including a drive and avenue, a tennis court, garden, walks and nearly 8 acres of woodland. The house itself dated from the 17th century and was said to have been designed by Inigo Jones or perhaps by one of his pupils. Country Life magazine ran two articles about the hall in 1933, in which it published over a dozen photographs of the interior with detailed description.

Lot 1 was sold to Tunnicliffe (Timber) Ltd of Silsden, near Bradford, via a conveyance dated 6 May 1950. A newspaper article gives the price as £4,100.[21] Tunnicliffe would have been interested in the large amount of woodland around the hall which is visible in the aerial picture on p130. Timber was scarce and attracting premium prices after the war.

There now occurs a diverting interlude in proceedings. Enter Mr George Norris Gregory, 33, of Leeds. A few months after Tunnicliffe took ownership of Lot 1, it seems they sold it again to Mr Gregory, for about £4000. Mr Gregory saw potential to use the Hall as a film set. The conveyance dated 26 October 1950 does not name a price. But it looks from subsequent documents that Tunnicliffe gave Gregory a mortgage to make the purchase. And I can't help thinking that they laughed all the way to the bank, because the conveyance writes in Tunnicliffe's retention of 'all timber and timber like trees'. So they had their asset, but none of the liability for the hall and its grounds ...

George Gregory, who was recorded as living at Oakwell Mount, Leeds, was, at this point, embarking on a career in the film industry. He had just bought his way into a film – *Ha'penny Breeze* – that had been released with modest success. His partners in this enterprise were D'arcy Conyers (31) and Frank Worth (26). D'arcy Conyers actually appears in the film as himself. The plot is about a an ex-serviceman who has hit on hard times, buys a boat and enters a yacht race. Flushed with success, Gregory was keen to interest Conyers and Worth in a project to make a film about Byron's 'honeymoon from hell', shot at Halnaby.

A report in the *Yorkshire Post* dated 29 December 1950 notes that Gregory has already spent money on the Hall which is converting to a residential country club. Unfortunately the film did not get made. Even more unfortunately, the country club just didn't take off. In December 1951 he complained 'I ran Halnaby Hall as a country club for 12 months. I sat there five days a week and no-one crossed the threshold'.[22]

Mr Gregory's ideas would have been entirely reasonable if the date had been 1960 and Halnaby had been located in the Home Counties. Unfortunately, they were not suited to the rural north-east corner of Yorkshire in the early 1950s. Rationing was still in place and very few people had a car, or even access to one. In addition, much of the estate was in the process of being stripped of its woodland by purchasers of the plantations who felt no obligation to remove any stumps or craters they might have created. By the autumn of 1951 Gregory despaired of his venture and sought to have the building demolished. The RDC rate book shows that the Hall required £87 to be paid annually in rates. As an empty property the sum would be £36. In addition, Gregory had the mortgage on the property to pay. Hereafter began the whole debate as to whether Halnaby Hall should be saved, conserved, preserved for future generations.

*Country Life* magazine was in the vanguard in raising interest in Halnaby Hall. In April 1933 they had run extensive articles about the house in consecutive issues, written by Christopher Hussey, a leading writer on English architecture. The photographs of the interiors taken for those articles are superb, and are now held by Historic England. You can browse these photos online.[23]

Local papers – the *Northern Echo* and *Darlington & Stockton Times* – covered the proposal to demolish the Hall and the debate around its preservation. The D&S was keen to report the debates at the RDC. For example, on 28 January 1950 they reported the first debate on the future of Halnaby Hall because the council had received notice that it had been put on a list of Buildings of Special Architectural Interest. This was before Mr Gregory bought it. A Councillor Nelson said at this meeting that 'historically the value of the hall is nothing but it could be used for flats.' Apparently NRCC had been asked about their attitude to conversion for flats and had said they wouldn't oppose such a thing.

But a wider audience was also becoming engaged and this report from the *Yorkshire Post* of 19 December 1951 sums it all up:

> [...] *A Ministry of Local Government and Housing inquiry at Northallerton in support of Mr Gregory's request for permission to demolish the Hall was told that he had made every effort to sell it, so it could be occupied by someone. And that he has spent 551 pounds in advertising* [the country club], *but without success. Much damage had been done by beetles, woodworm and wet rot. A watchman cost 200 pounds a year, and there had been several burglaries. He paid £4400 for the Hall, and had spent £2000 on it.* [...] *The North Riding County Council, who are the planning authority for the area, refused to make a building preservation order for the Hall and the former Minister of Local Government and Planning made the order direct. If permission to demolish the Hall is not given the owner can require the planning authority to buy it.*
> *Mr. Gregory's request is supported by the North Riding County Council and Croft Rural Council. It is opposed by the York Georgian Society, the London Georgian Group, the Yorkshire Archaeological Society and the Society for the Preservation of Ancient Buildings. Mr. W. A Harrison for the County Council, said there was no national historical or historical architectural interest in the hall and there was no public amenity, as it was three quarters of a mile from the nearest road. The chairman of the Croft Rural Council, Mr. CWD Chaytor Croft Hall, Darlington said a building which the public could not see and were mainly unaware of, should not be preserved at public expense.*
>
> *Mr. CWC Needham, York representing the opponents of the proposed demolition, was asked by Mr. Gregory 'what will they contribute towards its maintenance'? 'Nothing at all', replied Mr. Needham. The inquiry was conducted by Mr. Shirley Knight, who said an advisory committee claimed the building was an outstanding example of an 18th century interior applied to a domestic building of the 17th century and considered that everything possible should be done to preserve it. A decision will be announced later.*

In the end it was money that did for Halnaby. There wasn't any to maintain it. It's clear that Croft RDC opposed its preservation. Kit Chaytor probably put it in a nutshell when he said 'If no-one has any money for its upkeep, what is the alternative?'.

On 2 May 1952 the front page of the Yorkshire Post reported:

*A nine month controversy over the future of Halnaby Hall, near Darlington [...] ended yesterday when the owner, Mr G N Gregory, a Leeds auctioneer, received a telegram from the Ministry of Housing and Local Government. The telegram gives permission for the Hall to be demolished".*

A last ditch attempt by the Society for the Protection of Ancient Buildings appeared on the correspondence page of Country Life on May 23rd 1952, when they made the case for its survival and pleaded for a private individual to buy it, failed. By September 1952 the hall was sold to Warnegate Products Ltd, a Halifax firm. They promptly arranged for everything of worth in the interior to be stripped out and sold. Fireplaces, cornicing, bannisters, staircases, doors, windows, along with the land the Hall stood on, and the outbuildings. Eva Banner, in her privately published book *Halnaby People*, notes that this sale provided furnishings for the recently burned Wycliffe Hall and that Middleton Lodge and the Bridge Inn, Walshford were also beneficiaries.[24]

An indenture dated 12 Aug 1960 shows that she bought the bundle of land (15.543 acres), that was Lot 1 in the estate sale, the one that included the Hall, from Mr Ernest Sharp, then living in Darlington, for £400. Eva's address is given as Home Farm. Her husband Lawrence started a business on the new land, supplying specialist machinery to farmers. Eva recalls the destruction of the hall in her book.

*When the building had been stripped bare of its treasures the* coup de gras *was delivered by explosive and all that remained was a pile of brick rubble, used for hardcore with giant oak beans incongruously pointing at varying angles to the sky. There were half demolished outbuildings with their jagged steps clinging to the remaining eighteenth century west wing which was soon to be populated by Mr Sharp's deep litter hens and a saw bench.*[25]

This latter remaining land and outbuildings was sold by Warnegate Products to a man called Ernest Sharp in a conveyance dated 23 January 1953 for £600.[26] Mr Sharp then eventually sold this on to Eva Banner of Home Farm, Halnaby. The conveyance is dated 12 August 1960 and the stated price is £400. Eva Banner was born and brought up in Moulton but she had a real feeling for Halnaby. She and her husband Laurence made considerable investments to develop the remaining stable and out buildings as they are seen today. Eva notes in her book that many people tried to maintain something of the dignity of the old estate, herself included, but, little by little, it became something else, and the big house became just a ghost. Eva herself died in July 2000.

Whatever the considerations, the Hall was gone. Just a shell left. It was a common story across England at that time but many mourned its loss.

**Mary Andrew**:
*"... before the estate was broken up, you know, anybody could go just anywhere and went anywhere because the roads were just free for all, very different to what it is now. [...] But it was, When the*

*hall was, was demolished, it was just really sad. And the whole estate was* [*sad*]. *You know, when the woods were all chopped down. And we used to love to go down to the North Lodge, the lovely drive down there, covered in snowdrops and primroses. It just all went. Really sad."*

It took a while for Halnaby Hall to die. However, the end for the unloved Clervaux Castle came more swiftly and more privately.

Clervaux Castle was very much the brainchild of Sir William Chaytor, 1st baronet of Croft and Witton Castle. As early as 1824 Sir William felt that Croft Hall was not a suitable gentleman's residence. The Hall was old and not so very grand. It was also in the middle of the Spa tourism that he himself had promoted. Footpaths allowed visitors to cross his land daily. And he himself was beginning to lobby for his baronetcy, which was granted in 1831. So he let the Hall to two women in which to run a girls' school. Sir William removed himself to Witton Castle and then Newbus Grange near Neasham in 1839. He found Newbus unsatisfactory and moved to Hurworth House as a stop gap until his castle was ready. In 1838 he engaged his favourite architect, Ignatius Bonomi, to design and have build a home suitable for a baronet. It was to be a little further from the village than Croft Hall, between the Jolby and Middleton Tyas roads, north west of the Old Spa Farm. In May 1842 advertisements for masons and labourers to work on the castle appeared in the press. No expense was to be spared, and Sir William's correspondence with Bonomi up until the time of his death demonstrates his meticulous demands.

I have not been able to find out exactly how much Sir William spent on Clervaux Castle but what I do know is that it was unfinished at the time of his death, that he lived in it unfinished from 1844 and that it was not lived in by any other Chaytor baronet, as far as I can see. The second baronet (Sir William

**A mid-century postcard of Clervaux Castle.**

Richard Carter Chaytor) seems to have preferred Spennithorne Hall. The third baronet and his heirs lived at Croft Hall and then Witton Castle. (The last active Chaytor baronet – the seventh – died in 1976. The baronetcy still exists, but is unclaimed.)

Sir William died on 28 January 1847. His will was the subject of an epic legal battle which went from the county courts to the Court of Chancery. But Chancery could not resolve the matter. Consequently, resolution came with a private act of parliament passed by an empowered private committee who had to make a final judgement. It was debated and passed on 20 August 1853 and *Hansard* styles it as 'An Act for raising by Sale or Mortgage of the Real Estates devised by the Will of *Sir William Chaytor* Baronet, deceased, Monies for Payment of his Debts and Legacies, in aid of his Personal Estate, and for other Purposes, and of which the Short Title is *Chaytor's Estate Act, 1853*'. (The same system is in place to day for cases that have met stalemate in the courts.) I have yet to get to the detail of all this but I have seen the pile – and it is a large pile – of documentation for the Chancery case, and within it is a statement from Sir William's wife, Isabella. In it she states that not only was the castle unfinished at Sir William's death but that she herself had completed the interiors 'at considerable expense' and that her sons had paid for landscaping of the park. She also alluded to the range and extent of Sir William's debts.[27]

It was Isabella who lived on at Clervaux and she did so up to her death in 1854. Then her unmarried daughter Harriet lived there until her death in 1901 when the Castle was let to George May, a colliery owner and mining engineer from South Shields who was also an enthusiast for country sports. May died in June 1914 and the Castle was empty again. The sixth baronet, Sir Edmund Chaytor, tried to sell the castle in 1918 but clearly did not succeed.[28]

But in December 1922, Sir Edmund sold the whole Croft Estate to his second cousin Alfred Henry Chaytor[29] and he – Alfred – decided that he and his family should live in the Castle. He hadn't, actually, wanted to buy it. The correspondence about the sale shows that he quite wanted the estate without the expense of the Castle. But he ended up having it.

It's not that the Castle was hideous. The exterior was a little austere but not unlike some other castles. To me it looks a bit like a grandiose Bolton Castle, seat of the Scrope family. The interior was very grand. And it was huge. However, amongst the correspondence on the estate sale of 1922 is an assessment of the Castle by the surveyors. The opinion was:

> *The approaches to Clervaux Castle are in a very poor state, owing, presumably, to the fact that it has been untenanted for some years. We are agreeably surprised that the structure appeared to be in a good state of repair, but as there has been no caretaker there, any damage which has arisen by reason of the blockage of down pipes by birds nests, or other causes, has been magnified on account of their not being attended to at once. [...] at present time the kitchen is some distance from the Dining Room which is a great disadvantage [...] there is Central Heating but this would want thoroughly overhauling [...] There is no light, therefore electric light plant would have to be installed [...] the kitchen boilers would have to be entirely renovated.*[30]

The surveyors summed up by saying that a considerable amount of money would need to be invested to make the Castle liveable in, and they recommended a price of £2000.

So one assumes that Alfred made those changes for his family's comfort. But Alfred himself was not well. He was a distinguished man of the law and an expert fisherman. He owned lands in Sussex (where he had previously lived) and at Riding Mill near Corbridge where he loved to fish for salmon in the Tyne. He was an author of a classic book on salmon fishing called 'Letters to a Salmon Fisher's Sons'. He had insisted on going to the front in World War 1 when he was not really well enough to do so and came back in a fragile state. Perhaps he felt pressured to join his family's tradition as two of his brothers were distinguished military men and his eldest brother, Sir EWC Chaytor, was Commander of the Anzac forces in World War 1. A plaque in Croft Church is testimony to Alfred's sacrifice and sense of duty. On coming to Croft in 1923 he lead a retired life but his health did not completely recover from his war experience and on 12 July 1931 he died.

Alfred's widow Dorothy and her grown-up children moved from the Castle fairly soon after Alfred's death and Croft Hall was a Chaytor home once more, after some 20 years of occupation by land agents. Clervaux Castle was never lived in again. Several attempts to let it at minimal rent failed.

**Doris Cameron**:

*"I can remember Clervaux Castle. The soldiers were there. And I remember before the soldiers were there. When I was at Croft School, they were living at the castle and the school used to go up to the castle for a treat. Now, I don't know how we got up 'cos we must have got lifts, but I don't know whether we did. And they used to take the children boating on the lake. And it's a most beautiful lake. They used to row the children on the lake."*

It's generally known that soldiers were at Clervaux during the war, but I haven't been able to find anything at all about who or when. After World War 2 ended, the Castle was empty again. Kit Chaytor, as owner, decided to demolish it and it was done. No inquiries, no questions it seems. A short article on the front page of the Yorkshire Post for 31 October 1950 announced the demolition. Kit Chaytor said the army had left the building structurally sound but that thieves had taken lead from the roof and panelling, which had exposed the building to further decay.

One tower of the castle – the one you can see in this picture – remains and is part of an accommodation for the Croft Estate gamekeeper. The ornamental lake is still there and the park is maintained. But Clervaux Castle's life was not a rich one, and its demise was not much lamented.

I came across an article in the *Northern Despatch* for 10 September 1947. Titled 'A Castle After All Is But A House', and signed only by 'D.P.', it asks questions about the redundancy of such a building. It begins: 'Curiosity awakened by the fact that while 2,400 wait for houses in Darlington, the offer of a large mansion not five miles out of the town for housing accommodation has been turned down by the Croft Rural District Council, yesterday I paid a visit to Clervaux Castle'

The author further relates the story of his (or her) cycle ride: 'In the shelter of the neglected woods the going was easier. A little army sentry box was a reminder of the fact that the mansion, like so many of

Britain's stately homes, until recently had been occupied by the British Army. Almost unaware I rushed out of the trees beneath the proud towers of the castle itself around which unsightly Nissen huts nestled cheekily'.

The author corroborates the impact of military occupation. Then he (or she) ruminates on the facilities that could be afforded for any conversion to accommodation, and the derelict condition of some the grandest rooms. He concludes 'To an admittedly inexperienced observer, it seems absurd that this fine old building should be allowed to slip into decay when it might at least be Squatters' Castle.'

But it never was for squatters. If it had been, the Squatters Tale would have taken a different turn.

# The essence of Croft: Croft Spa station, the Old Spa and the New Spa

The final demolitions of this chapter, are important as far as the village's moniker as 'Croft Spa' is concerned. I discuss the whole business of 'Croft Spa' and the some time tradition of calling the village by that name in Chapter 1.

Croft Spa station, which probably started the whole 'Croft Spa' thing, was blown up in March 1969, having opened on 4 January 1841, and for 130 years served the Darlington to Richmond branch line and also excursions direct to cities like Middlesbrough, Sheffield and even London. Mike and Cath Wood lived in Banks Terrace, which is in Hurworth Place, just opposite where the old stationmaster's house is now, from 1966.

**Mike Wood** had a specific memory:

*"When we were first there, there was a Croft Station. And you could get into Darlington on the train. Well, while we were still at Banks Terrace, they blew up the platform.*

*In fact, we have a picture of a brick that went through Cath's shop window [on Hurworth Road] and another one through our roof at number six. We were woken up at three o'clock in the morning with this massive explosion and they literally just put charges everywhere and blew it all up.*

*I remember going down to the railway the following day and going down onto the railway line because you could go out the back of Banks Terrace down some steps and onto the railway platform. So if we wanted to go to Darlington or anywhere else by rail it was so easy. `But the Beeching review decided to close it."*

A number of our Croft voices reported going to school in Richmond by train. You could always get a bus into Darlington, although many people used the train, but there were no service buses to Richmond. Once secondary education became separate, and you couldn't attend Croft School until you left, Richmond had the default schools: Richmond Grammar, Richmond High and Richmond County Modern. But it was always a bit of hike from Richmond station: up the hill and onwards was a good walk, especially for the County Modern and High School pupils who had to go to Darlington Road.

## Chapter 4 – Bust and Boom

**This picture of the Old Spa bath-house – which was situated by the Spa Beck near what is now Old Spa Farm – dates from the last years of the 19th century I would guess. It is already looking dilapidated and by 1970 it had completely gone.**

After the station closed, everyone had an easier but longer journey by bus.

I do not know when the Old Spa was demolished. It was built in the mid nineteenth century to provide bathing access to the oldest of the springs in Croft, the one by what is now Old Spa Farm. It is clearly marked on the 1857 OS map. There appears to be something on the same site on the 1951 map, though not the full building. By 1972 there is nothing.

The story of the New Spa, built in 1829, is somewhat different. Located close to the village centre, and within a mile of the Croft Spa station when it opened in 1841, the New Spa was what made Croft's Spa trade kick off. It spawned the new improved Croft Spa Hotel (formerly a coaching inn on the Great North Road) and many lodging houses, first at The Terrace, as built by Sir William Chaytor, and then also in South Parade and Monkend Terrace. It was a popular day trip for people living in and around Darlington and it was known in the towns of County Durham – Sunderland, Hartlepool, Stockton – and beyond. There are hundreds of postcards still in circulation on the collectors' market, mostly dating from 1900 to 1930, depicting 'The Spa'. However, after World War 1 the spa trade declined and by the time we get to 1930, the start of the period we are looking at in this book, the Spa was really of marginal interest to most people. Arthur Riseborough, the last bath-house keeper, was tragically killed on the road outside the Spa in 1927. He had been turning right on his bicycle off the Northallerton Road to the Spa and was hit from behind by a motorcyclist. He was a parish councillor and a popular man in the village: people were shocked and saddened by his death. Stoically, his widow carried on at the baths for some years but it was never the same. The spa water was still available to drink, but there didn't seem to be much bathing going on. However, quite a few people had memories of Mrs Riseborough and the final years of the Spa. For some years the Croft Tennis Club was in front of the bath-house and the Spa tearoom was used for refreshments.

**Margaret Horseman**:

*When I was little* [early 50s] *it wasn't running as a spa. It was open as a tea room. And the tennis courts were open. And the members of the tennis club, I was in the junior tennis club, we would meet regularly down there. And I don't know whether the spa was still open. But I know when I was little, on a Sunday or a Saturday my parents and my brother and I would go for a walk and we'd go to the spa rooms. It reminded me of an Indian bungalow. You know, the big heavy rooms that come down and a veranda running round and glass doors. It was a bit like that. And you'd go in – it was all wooden floors. And I think if I remember rightly sort of like cane seated chairs and little tables. There's a big counter here with glass jars behind. I think it's called a Nickelodeon or something – a big wooden thing with around copper disks that you'd put a penny in it would play. And we'd go in there and have a cup of tea or lemonade.* [...]

*And I think there might have been sweets there. And you could sit on the lawn at the front and there were seats to sit. Or you could go for a walk along the spa beck. Now that's what we did.* [...] *It was a proper little Cinder path. And there were little bridges went over and back again. And you could go over the bridges and go along. And if I remember rightly running along beside the path, you could see the pipes, the lead pipes, bringing the spa water in. They've all gone now.*

**Sandra Veerman**:

*And when we were younger, as young girls* [early 1950s], *it was spooky. It was spooky because the old baths were still there. And they used to creak, but as a very small girl I remember Mrs. Riseborough. Yeah, she had the pumps and could pump it[the spa water] out by the gallon. John used to drink it a lot. But she also had jars of little sweets, and I couldn't remember were was they called? The violets, Parma Violets. And Mum used to, I can still remember being in the pushchair, she would take Trevor and me down. And there was the water to the beck at the bottom. And we would sit there and she said, now if you're good, we'll go and get some violets. From Mrs. Riseborough.*

**John Green**:

*The old baths were there. At the back. Yeah. When you went into the back, they were there. Yeah. And she sold the water from in there. I used to go and get a glass and I used to drink it.* [...] *It smelled. It smelled like rotten eggs. Yeah, but it had very little taste. And they always said that if he bottled it and put it in a fridge the smell will go off as well.*

Mary Riseborough died on 26 April 1958 and the Croft Estate did not attempt to re-let the building. By this time it was in need of a great deal of work. It stood empty and thieves stripped the lead from the roof and then the whole building started to deteriorate.

**Bill Chaytor**:

*"When I came* [1965] *it was a wreck because nobody was using it, and I was really concerned what to do with it, and I remember begging the district council, couldn't I turn it into a dwelling, and they said, 'Oh, no, no, absolutely not.' So, you know, I was stymied because that was the one way to save it that I saw. And while I was dithering we had burglars who pulled out all the lead valley*

## Chapter 4 – Bust and Boom

The New Spa Bath-house in the late 1970's, before demolition. Major roof damage made the building difficult to repair.

*gutters, and the water was pouring into it. So I took a deep breath and I said, 'We'll demolish it,'."*

Bill was clear when he spoke to me that he did what he could to preserve the building but, as with Halnaby and Clervaux, he saw no economic case for preservation. I believe people objected to the demolition, and to this day people say 'it shouldn't have been knocked down'. But at the time there didn't seem to be an obvious remedy.

In 1979 the spa bath-house was bulldozed. Only the spa cottages – three small cottages that had originally been a coach house and were then converted and used for workers – remained. The village rallied to save these and Richmondshire District Council was engaged. They agreed the cottages should be saved. At their meeting in September 1983 they reported that the Dept for the Environment had added 1-3 Spa Cottages to the List of Buildings of Special Architectural Interest. After a while these were bought and renovated by Mike and Cath Wood in 1983. They are now one dwelling.

**Mike Wood** remembered:

*"I had settled in at Alice House, and we'd been there probably something like eight years.* [Mike spent some years building the property.] *And then Bill phoned up this Sunday morning, and said, 'Mike, if you want*

The old plunge bath at the New Spa, available to those who wanted submersion in Spa water, not just a drink! This picture was taken in the late seventies.

**Postcard from around 1920 showing the location of the New Spa bath-house and Spa Cottages, on the left.**

*the spa, it's available. See my agent.' So from then on we considered the sale of Alice House but not until we'd refurbished the spa cottages. There were three cottages. In fact, originally, it had been a spa keeper's house, plus some arched entrances to places where they, presumably, kept their buggies, on inclement – in bad weather. They'd come and take the spa water, but they didn't want their seat to get wet. So these were very nice, arched – still, the arches are still visible. Because what we did is, we made these into windows and doors. And they were sort of very fancy French doors, you know, looking onto the garden. When we took it over, the garden area, which included the spa well, had been bulldozed and the actual spa building had been just demolished with a bulldozer, and the whole lot had been levelled. And the well, which was still running, but it had been filled in, there was a trickle of water running across this muddy area, running down to the beck. And that was all that was left of the well, the spa well. And one of the first things we did is to get a JCB and clean it up, excavate the footings of the – where the building had been. And, of course, they were brick footings. We excavated the areas underneath and we came across a plunge bath, which had been lined with concrete. And we found what was left of a pulley. So presumably they'd had like a bosun's chair thing, where people sat in and they were swung round from the overhead pivotable pulley wheel, over the plunge bath. And then they were lowered into the plunge bath. Because you couldn't get out of it. Well, there were steps to it, but it would have been difficult for somebody with gammy legs to get out of it."*

With both Spa bath houses gone, and then the station, the reason to refer to the Spa in the village name diminished. It never was really 'Croft Spa' again.

*Chapter 4 – Bust and Boom*

# Conservation and reflection

Change and development are inevitable and often beneficial. However, there was a feeling in Croft, and the country generally, that too much might have been lost. In those post-war years, particularly the sixties and seventies, the push was to clear away the old stuff and be modern. As the eighties approached the mood changed an amount of concern for the antique and ancient started to prevail. Conservation ... of both the natural and built environment ... was now A Thing. An opinion piece in the *Northern Echo* on 6 March 1979 declared in its header 'So we are all conservationists now', going on to note that ' ... from Prince Philip and President Nixon to the Prime Minister and the Leader of the Opposition, conservation and ecology (hitherto an unknown word) are suddenly fashionable.' However, long before this the people of Croft decided they needed to act to preserve their village from unwanted development and destruction, and that the local council was not to be trusted to do the job. In February 1973 a Croft Residents Association was set up following a meeting at the Scout Hut (which served then as the village hall). Bill Smith, Maurice Baker and Howard Godfrey were the leading lights. Residents were concerned that the field on which the Scout Hut stood was going to be made over for housing. 60 houses were mentioned. They didn't want Croft to become a commuter town for Darlington. They didn't want to become 'another Hurworth'. They wanted the village to be unspoilt, for the streets to be free of traffic so that children could play without danger and for there to a be a plan for preserving the character of the village.[31] A Mr Hugh Larcombe spoke to support the formation of the Association: 'These [planning] decisions seem to be taken behind closed doors. If changes must occur in Croft because of the rising population I would like to feel that at least the villagers are consulted and an amicable arrangement reached". The chairman, Mr Baker, noted that there had been a *'mass of rumours, half-rumours, lies and half-truths'* about planning proposals. The 40 people at the meeting voted unanimously to form the Residents Association.

The Residents Association did not mention the fact that, in 1971, the North Riding County Council began discussions with Croft Rural District Council about a village settlement plan that would lay down agreed principles for the development of the villages under the latter's control. They were not able to come to an agreement before the discussions were overtaken by the wider one of local government reform. Perhaps this was the 'behind closed doors' that Mr Larcombe mentioned. However, the Local Government Act of 1974 abolished Croft Rural District Council and established Richmondshire District Council. And one of the first things Richmondshire did after formation was to draw up plans for rural development place by place. The Croft Village Development Plan was published in 1974 and established the Conservation Area and its rules of development continue to inform development in the village. The plan noted that:

> *Croft is a fragmented settlement small in scale, but with a very individual and attractive character. Its special value lies in the fact that although situated within an area subjected*

*in recent years to the spillover of housing pressure from Darlington, it has remained a quiet backwater. Moreover, in a Richmondshire context, the village, with its pervading Victorian flavour and dominance of warm red brick as a material is quite unique. It is these particular qualities the village plan sets out to conserve.*

The plan made the area around The Terrace a 'landscape area' not for development. It designated 'infill only' and identified two areas for development. First, the area to the north of Monkend Terrace which became The Mill Race development in the 1990s. Secondly, the area between the school and the Hotel which became Lewis Close in the 1980s. The boundary for the Conservation Area remains today.

To finish this section I would ask … should we be sorry or upset that so much of Croft's history was swept away in the three decades after World War 2? Do we now think this was all wrong? I had an interesting discussion with Mary Andrew and her son Richard about how things have changed since Mary was a child. Richard now farms Home Farm at Halnaby, which was his parents' farm. Part of the conversation went like this:

**Richard Andrew**:
*"You know, it is really sad when you see the photographs of what* [Halnaby] *was and it's gone. But there is an article, the county council, I'm sure you've seen it, where they described it having 'no architectural interest'? And that's just a reflection of the time I'm sure. I suppose also, maybe the politics of the time, post war, people were wanting to sweep away the aristocracy. And if that makes any sense, there was absolutely no incentive for the political elite at the time to want to try and save it because the idea was to sweep away the old guard, wasn't it?"*

**Me**:
*"I think that is a very astute way of looking at it, actually. If you look at Croft parish as a whole in the in the 50s and 60s, and later in the 70s, there's a whole lot of stuff that got swept away. There's Halnaby, there was Clervaux. The Rectory got broken up. The Mill closed and was sold off. The Spa bath house was knocked down. A whole lot of things that had been really important to the village before the Second World War. And I think you're right, that the way people felt about things after the Second War was that they just wanted to move on."*

**Richard**:
*"You've got to be very careful you don't judge people's decisions by the current climate if that makes any sense. And, you know, we're in a completely different era, and, people wanting, understandably, different things. But these are what drives decisions, in the same way that decisions were made by people selling the Halnaby estate. I know we all think if we were sat in their seat today, we wouldn't make the same decisions, but we weren't faced with the same challenges."*

Those are all fair points. I tend to think that history is about trying to understand the past more than to judge it. The factors at play in any situation are usually complicated, not black and white. Some of

## Chapter 4 – Bust and Boom

those factors driving change in Croft parish have been outlined in this chapter. But we've been discussing buildings, the 'built environment' as it is also called. There are other things to understand, that have been mentioned in previous chapters. Things to do with our relationship to land and landscape. And that is where we are going next.

**Endnotes**

1. Andrew Marr, *A History of Modern Britain*, Chapter 1 p73.
2. Recorded in minutes of the Development Committee of Richmondshire District Council for September 1983
3. Andrew Marr, *A History of Modern Britain*, Chapter 1, p71-73.
4. You can view this newsreel online at: https://www.britishpathe.com/video/chalfont-st-giles
5. All letters from TNA, HLG 101/522.
6. RDC Minutes, October 1952, item 182. Subsequent discussions with Darlington Borough Council responding with an offer of six houses from those they were building. This must have changed later on as Peter said neighbours at Cockleberry had been housed in Darlington in the later fifties.
7. RoP, #10. It's interesting to note that Albert Oates built himself a nice house in Richmond in the early 1920s and subsequently worked on the development of the Westfields estate on the north west side of the town.
8. All based on the Croft Rural District Register of Plans (RoP) at NYRO (Ref DC/CRO/1/1)
9. RoD, Vol 714 (1937), p 748 and Vol 957(1947), p 108
10. "Documents at Burton Agnes" transcribed by Reverend C.V. Collier in *Transactions of the East Riding Antiquarian Society* vol XXVIII (1911)/ The Jolby reference is document 131 on p96 and the Croft reference is document 135 on p97.
11. Evening Despatch, 30 September 1972.
12. See Jane Hatcher, Richmondshire Architecture
13. NYRO, PR/CRO 3/9/14.
14. NYRO, Croft Parish Records PR/CRO 5/6/2.
15. The 1871 Census for Scotland gives the details for the Russel household in Moray Place.
*The Glasgow Herald*, 18 February 1875 reported the sale of Dundas Castle to the James Russel Trust. The solicitors were Curle & Erskine of Melrose.
16. Evidence from the Russel of Blackbraes papers held by Falkirk Archives
17. See Ann Fell, "St. Peter's Croft-on-Tees Monumental Inscriptions", 1990. Privately published for Croft Parochial Church Council.
18. *Yorkshire Post & Leeds Intelligencer*, 5 March 1919, p12.
19. I'm grateful to Juliet Hill for allowing me to see the extensive deeds for her house at North Lodges, Halnaby. These relate the details of the sale to DJ Place.
20. There is more about the Halnaby sale including lots and buyers in Chapter 5.
21. NRRoD, Vol 1052 p 1039
22. *Yorkshire Post*, 19 December 1951 p4.
23. There are 84 photos online relating to Croft-on-Tees.on the Historic England 'England's Places' website. There are a lot of Halnaby Hall, but also some of Clervaux Castle, the Church and some others. You can find them here: https://historicengland.org.uk/images-books/photos/englands-places. Just put "croft on Tees" in the search box.
24. See NYRO, 'Papers of Sir William Chaytor 1771 – 1847: a list with extracts edited by M Y Ashcroft', 1993, notably the Introduction
25. Eva Banner *Halnaby People*, p35. I've seen a copy of this work but it is not available in any library. The Banner family are the best people to
26. NRRoD, vol 1155, p382
27. TNA, C14/959, Chaytor vs Chaytor. Affidavit of Isabella Chaytor.
28. Press advertisement in the *Yorkshire Post*, 31 July 1918.
29. Alfred Henry Chaytor, KC. Born 1869, Marshlands, New Zealand and died Croft-on-Tees 12 July 1931.
30. Report of Daniel Witney & Son to Alfred Henry Chaytor via Farrer & Co, 24 July 1922, NYCRO ZQH 15
31. *Evening Despatch*, 8 February 1973

*Chapter 5 – Living on the Land*

# CHAPTER 5

# LIVING ON THE LAND

he civil parish of Croft contains some 4600 acres. Of these, at least 4000 are agricultural land. Farming, estate management and country sports are thus the business of over 80% of the parish. That is pretty much true today, and it was even more the case in the years covered by this book.

*What if, by some miracle, a farmer's son, killed at Waterloo in 1815, at the end of the Napoleonic Wars, had been resurrected and sent to work on a small farm in September 1939, just in time for the Second World War, he would have known what to do. The horses and their harness would have been familiar to him and the plough that they pulled, although perhaps a little lighter and stronger than those with which he had been brought up, was essentially the same. He would have known how to stack sheaves of corn on the waggon and how to make them into a rick in the farmyard before they were thrashed. If he had no personal experience of them, he would at least have heard about seed drills and machines that thrashed out the corn and milking the cows by hand would be a familiar task.*

*But if he had been resurrected in time to take part in the Falklands War, in 1982, he would have been completely baffled. Where were the horses? How are the cows milked by some strange device attached to their udders? And how could they possibly produce so much milk? Why were there no pigs or chickens or geese wandering around the farmyard and no ricks of corn waiting to be thrashed? What were those noisy smelly metal things that appeared to move on their own without any horses to pull them? And where was everybody? How could those enormous cereal crops that he could see in the field be harvested when hardly anybody appear to work on the farm?*[1]

The extract above seeks to illustrate the huge changes in agricultural practice between the pre-World War 2 years and the later twentieth century. The book it appears in argues the case that this period saw more revolutionary change in the way human beings made their living from the land than any other period in history. The authors know that is a moot point, but they demonstrate the extent of the change in the pages that follow, and all of it was visible in Croft parish. The way people went about agricultural production, their approach to the use of land, for work and for leisure, changed a great deal during the mid twentieth century, and that is what this chapter is about. Living on the land meant something different in 1990 to what it meant in 1930, and we are going to look at that story from a range of perspectives. First, the farmers. Secondly, the estate owners. And, lastly, the country sports people.

In 1941 there were 24 working farms and 3 market gardens in Croft parish, and the totals would have been the same in 1930. Fast forward to 1990 and that total comes down somewhat, I reckon to 20 working farms and no market gardens. Today, in 2023, the total of working farms has gone down to less than a dozen. Some farmhouses have been knocked down, but mostly they've gone for residential dwellings. The land however, carries on. It's farmed but more acres are farmed by fewer farmers. And market gardens are just a thing of the past.

## Farming and fruitfulness

If you go back a couple of hundred years in Croft's history, there isn't much in the parish that isn't to do with farming. In 1823 there were cottages around the main road and the hotel. Sir William Chaytor was starting to build up the spa trade. There was the church and the three halls – Croft, Halnaby and Monkend. Everything else was about farming. Not even the market gardens had come about by then. The many farmhouses in the parish in 1930 were mostly already built in 1823, at least in some form.

In 1941, during World War 2, the Ministry of Agriculture conducted a thorough national survey of the nation's farms, market gardens and other forms of growing or food production. It was a necessity to know how Britain, with its heavy reliance on imported food, was going to survive now those imports had become practically impossible to obtain. We are lucky that the surveys for Croft still exist in their entirety at the National Archives.

What we see in this survey is a group of farms following historic practice. Today we would say they were small farms doing a bit of everything. Some cattle, some sheep, plenty of pasture and hay fields, barley and oats, some wheat, turnips and potatoes, hens and ducks, often pigs. Work was done by men with horses and a few machines for specialist tasks like thrashing and baling. None of the farms had mains electricity or water. Toilets were outdoor privies with dug trenches below. Light was from lamps, often paraffin, maybe candles.

This would have been a similar picture in 1930 with the added issue that farm wages were at rock bottom and farm labourers lived in rudimentary tied cottages, or 'hind houses' as they are often called in North Yorkshire. I talk a little bit about this in the discussion on evacuees in Chapter 3. In the thirties, farm labouring tended to run in families and there was a ready succession of new workers. Not so later on. After the war opportunities opened up for young people to do new things – to train, to work in industry, or an office. If you have read Ronald Blythe's classic book *Akenfield* you will have come across the changes in attitude to working on the land narrated first hand. People had transport, and could work further afield. The national move to create a new breed of farmers, versed in modern techniques and practices, through college education meant that even farmer's sons got to look carefully at the life before committing to running a farm, and people who had been brought up in towns could now [2] be successful in agriculture. But there was that other feeling, that we've come across before in this book: after the war people wanted something different. Deference to the farmer or estate owner was no longer *gratis*. Young people wanted a future and a future that was modern, progressive, varied, and, at least in part, fun.

A number of our Croft voices remember farming in the period from 1930 to 1950.

**Doris Cameron**:

*"My father and mother had a car. And then there used to be hirings day. I don't know whether you've heard of hirings day have you? And they used to go to Darlington and pick a maid or a farm worker. And the poor things used to stand there waiting to be picked. My father used to go to the market day to hirings. And he brought Little Benny back. And he must have worked so hard in the pits poor thing.* [Doris said a lot of the labourers at that time came from Sunderland and/or the coal pits.] *He was short, but he was the most intelligent man. And when I went to college, he was still here. And really, he was just a wonderful person, you know, and he used to live here and sit with us. And I can also remember that was the kitchen through there. This was just the where we used to wash the clothes and everything. And Little Benny, when we had some people in, and I remember – felt so ashamed – Mother was setting this table out in the other room. You know, to sit at and for people to come, friends to come. So 'listen, Benny', she says, 'Do you mind if you sit on a separate table because you're the worker'. But that was life wasn't it?*

**Gladys and Doris Hobson (Cameron) help their father Thomas load bales. Mid 1950s.**

*I would only be small about 10 or 11 [1937]. But he was really what you call most marvellous with the animals because we didn't have any modern milking machines we just had cows that you milk by hand. We got them in twice a day, milk them by hand. And I used to milk them by hand as well. And we had a bull, and Benny could look after that bull. And it was an absolute... it was naughty... but we had a bull that used serve all the cows. My father took the bull to market to the Auction Mart which was up by the [Darlington] station. I remember, he came back in the car he was driving, he could hardly drive. And the bull had a ring through the nose and they used to lead it with a stick. And the stick broke when he was leading it round the ring. And fortunately somebody pulled him through the railings and the bull attacked him. And so he was in bed for ages because he'd been bruised. [...] That's how you manage on the farm. You hand milk cows, feed the calves. I was still feeding calves when I was going to work.*

*Darlington was our market place. And mother used to take the butter and everything she made to the Darlington market. Father used to take the car and he used to go to the market and then go to the pub. And I remember we used to go in the market you know where there were stalls inside and she used to have a stall to sell the butter and homemade bread and she'd stand there all day you know, selling the stuff, and that was her money to go shopping with because she used to go to the Co-op shop. We used to go to every Monday market day and we used to stand there all day. Then she used to go Fridays, selling round Croft, eggs and things. And she worked hard because she was only 66 year old when she died."*

**Peter Metcalfe** was born at Pepperfield Farm in 1930. It was a small mixed farm with pigs, and seven cows:

"*[My father] was one of 11, born in 1896. And he always wanted a farm of his own. But he rented that farm, and he had these horses, work horses. He used to plough with them. Well, with a couple. He was a fairly good horseman. And he used to go buying horses and selling them with Benjamin Stevenson from Crawleys Farm, Rushyford. And he was father of Arthur Stevenson who was big in winning point-to-points. [...] Then, in 1939, the aerodrome come and I watched them build the aerodrome.*

Peter was involved in the daily business of farming. For example, fertilising, he remembers how that was done at Pepperfield just before the war.

"*They used to get the horse and cart and it had sideboards on, only about that deep. With two legs at each side. And then he pulled one out, laid across the back and then pulled out a galvanised housing on there. Tip his bag of pellets in there. And then set the horse going. They were trained, they would go straight. Or I would be driving, or one of my brothers. And you'd stand in the back of the cart and scoop it out like that.*

*And harvesting, we didn't have much, there would be a couple of fields of corn. And the thrasher, the steam thrasher I remember come once, and that would be in the 40s. And they had to get the steam up, at four o'clock in the morning. I think some times it was the same fella, Jack Hall they called him. He would come at four o'clock if he didn't stop on the farm, if there wasn't a bed for him. And get up at four o'clock and fire the engine up to get the steam up for eight o'clock to start with the thrashing. And I remember once we put some stones in them ruts of the last bit [of the farm track] from the [railway] bridge to the farm so the big iron wheels can squash them, squash the bricks and stuff. And I also remember my younger brother, when you when you got to the bottom of the stack there was often some rats. And mice. And I remember, my younger brother Alan having a go at killing these lumps with a stick.*"

Peter remembered that things were hard before the war and some farms were not kept well. There were fields full of thistles and not ploughed. But people couldn't afford machinery and labour to put things right.

Bert Walker came to Birch Springs Farm in 1942 when he was 14. He had been brought up on East

## Chapter 5 – Living on the Land

This picture of Laurie Walker with two heavy horses was taken, probably, in the early fifties. By the 1960s the number of heavy horses used on farms had plummeted to zero.

Thorpe Farm near Barningham, where his father John Walker was the farmer. He was 'a sheep farmer, a dales farmer' Bert said. But after the war started the Ministry of Agriculture identified that land as suitable for conversion to forestry. Bert's dad did not want to be part of the Forestry Commission and they had to find another farm. Mr Wearmouth, who had been the farmer at Birch Springs up until then, was moving, so that is how they came to the Croft area. John Walker had to change his approach to farming and it was Bert and his brother Laurie who adapted better to mixed farming as young men.

**Bert Walker**:
*"I thought it was quite good, 'cos it was a different type of farming, and tractors which, you know, interested us. And from there on the machinery took over and you know – corn growing – we'd never grown corn before. And the cattle was just more or less the same. Actually, probably a bit different breed, but it was similar. [...] We had horses when we first came. And we bought our first tractor when we came here, a Fordson tractor, and it's just progressed from there.*

*We didn't have much to do with Croft, at all. I had left school and I never went to school at Croft. So, I didn't know a lot of people at Croft. I just knew the local people round here, such as Doris Cameron and her father, and Biglins, And I knew most of the farms around about. 'Cos we used to you know, when there were thrashing days, you know, the corn was all stacked and the thresher used to come. And we used to help each other, borrowed hands we called them. And when they came to our place, we went back to their place when they were thrashing."*

This wooden cottage was built for Doris Cameron's grandparents at Vince Moor West, then occupied by her parents. It has no running water or electricity which was standard for pre 1950s farm buildings. The picture here shows the cottage's last occupant John Middlemiss, an itinerant slaughterman who serviced many farms in the parish. The cottage is now derelict.

It should be noted that at this time, before the Halnaby sale, almost all of these farms were rented from the landowner. An exception was Vince Moor West, which was bought from the Halnaby estate in 1920 by Doris Cameron's grandfather, Thomas Hobson. Doris told me that her grandfather came from Crakehall and that he drove his stock from there to Vince Moor West in the 1890s. On the indenture for the sale, dated 5 August 1920, the farm is specified as having 120 acres. It was bought from the trustees of the Halnaby Estate – William Pierrepont Wilson-Todd, James Russel and William Hodgson. The sale was freehold but the indenture contains a clause that says that Sir William Wilson-Todd kept 'rights over game, rabbits and fish' and 'the right to hunt, shoot, fish and course'. There's no sign of any mortgage.

Doris's family have remained at Vince Moor West ever since. Her father Thomas Harold Hobson continued the line, Doris stayed on the farm with her husband Eric Cameron although neither were farmers. Doris was a teacher and Eric had a job at the Catterick NAAFI. Certainly he was able to acquire

**This picture, from the early fifties, shows Doris's father and Eric with what I believe to be a Fordson tractor.**

## Chapter 5 – Living on the Land

A break during threshing at Portobello Farm. Second on the left, standing, is Wilf Biglin from North Walmire, seated is Hughie Nattress from Middle Walmire, Bert Walker is seated on the right with the dark hair. Date would have been around 1950.

stocks of beer because Bert Walker told me that when they didn't have the energy to walk to Dalton or Croft they would go to the farmhouse at Vince Moor, and that it was known locally as the 'Cameron Arms'. Eric and Doris, who married in 1950, managed the farm and they worked on it too, but they must have hired others. It was a small farm, probably without a lot of machinery. In the 1941 farm survey it's reported that the only vehicle at Vince Moor was a converted Morris car, an option that was utilised if you couldn't afford a tractor, as many farmers couldn't.

I couldn't find any reference to planning applications for building improvements at Vince Moor West before the seventies (although that doesn't mean that changes weren't made). In 1973 Doris asked for planning permission to build three houses on the farm site and these now house members of her family.

Jean and Bert Walker remembered that they saw very few people at Birch Springs. It is an isolated farm with the nearest farms being North Walmire (now demolished), Vince Moor West and Portobello Farm. Bert's father bought Portobello and Birch Springs at the Halnaby estate sale. Bert eventually took over Birch Springs and Laurie Walker was in charge at Portobello. So the two families had a lot to do with each other. Brian Walker remembers his cousins being his main playmates.

**Jean Walker** was born in Darlington and married Bert in 1953. She found the isolation hard:
*"I never met Doris until I'd had my second child. You never saw people. Before, when we first married Bert, showed me enough of driving to take the car over and get the bus to Darlington. To Darlington, to my parents. So, you never saw anybody. Anne was a baby before people even knew I had a baby. Just no one mixed."*

Jean met Bert when he used to go to dances in Darlington in the late forties and early fifties. He would walk – a long walk – to Croft Spa Station get the train and then do the same in reverse, until he later got a motorbike. Other farm people had similar struggles to get a social life.

**Doris Cameron** mentioned Mrs Minns, who she called 'the angel of Croft':

*"Mrs Minns lived in The Limes. 'Cos there were two lime trees there, which have gone. And she had a shed at the back and a nice big garden. And all the people of Halnaby would never have been able to get the bus to Darlington if it hadn't been for Mrs Minns. She let us all, and you talk to people, take our bikes round the side of her house and put them in the shed, and then go over the bridge and get the bus. What would we have done if we hadn't got Mrs Minns? I mean people like that are wonderful aren't they? And her shed used to be full, and she never got a penny or anything.*

*Mother and I used to go to the pictures, which was along Skinnergate* [in Darlington]. *What was it called along Skinnergate? It'll come to me. Anyway, my mother and I used to do the same, cycle to Croft, leave our bikes at Mrs Minns. Anyway, go over the bridge,* [get the bus], *go along Skinnergate to the pictures. But we always had to come out before the end 'cos the last bus was before the end."*

However, although the farming families were a little bit removed from the centre of the village there was no doubt that life in Croft ran to the rhythm of agricultural life. For example a good number of children at Croft School would be farm children as we've discussed in Chapter 2. Attendance at school was sporadic by today's standards. Sometimes the weather meant that children did not make it to school,

**The rogation service had been part of the christian calendar since medieval times and occurred about a month after Easter. The purpose was to ask God to bless the land and deliver crops from disease. In this picture Reverend Charlesworth (Back to camera) leads a service in the field below The Terrace. The date would be mid fifties.**

particularly from the farms, and sometimes there were childhood diseases like measles that meant the school had to shut for several weeks to prevent transmission. But sometimes also farm children were just 'kept back' because their parents wanted them to work. And in addition – on top of the normal school holidays – there was always a one week closure for hay-making in June and a fortnight in October for potato picking. When the North Riding Education Committee took over the school as Voluntary Controlled, after the war, agricultural holidays were acknowledged but not so indulged. There were long weekends for potato-picking but no more and by the 1960s these sorts of breaks were thing of the past.

The focus on farming continued at Church. In the 1930's Harvest Festival lasted almost a week and attendance on the Sunday was over 400. The church also celebrated other occasions in the agricultural year such as Rogation Sunday. On Rogation Sunday, celebrated after Easter, God is asked to bless a community in the coming growing season and this was a feature of church life in Croft during Rev Charlesworth's time. By 1990 Harvest Festival was still a major celebration, even allowing for a drastic drop in church attendance.

# Wartime Improvement

And so farm life in Croft went on, with the seasons, from one year to another, some years of harsh weather, some much kinder. The farming families hardly changed: some people died and others were born. The land agents for the estate owners – people like Captain Beadon or Colonel Newton-Taylor – kept a check on what was happening but were mostly happy if rents came in on time and expenditure was not too high.

However, the war brought an urgency to farming in England that had scarcely been seen. England was under siege, and food was vital to survival. We'd been used to relying on imports from the colonies and now we had to feed ourselves. Farming was on the front line. I discuss some of this in Chapter 3.

As mentioned above, in 1941 the Ministry of Agriculture conducted a farm survey that went down to the nth detail for every farm, or area of growing land (this included market gardens and gardens and large houses as well) in the country.

Croft's farms were primitive. They had no electricity or running water and earth closets were the usual sanitation. The odd farm had a generator and many had wells for water. Most relied on captured surface water for fields and animals. Every farm had horses and horsemen while, at this stage, only a handful had a tractor. In terms of what they did, most farms were one to four hundred acres in size. They had cows, usually some pigs, usually some sheep. They grew some corn, a bit more barley and oats and had a lot of land laid down to pasture. The majority had chickens and some had ducks and geese. As these were family farms, the family did most of the work, and there weren't large numbers of farm labourers but most farms had one or two. It was a model for farming that was age-old. If you look at the first Ordnance Survey map for Croft, surveyed in the late 1840s, all but one of the farms in the 1941 survey were on that map, so you can say that, at the time of the 1941 survey, the main part of the farm was probably at least 100 years old. And a look at the Croft Parish Registers will show that some farms have been in the same place for many more hundreds. I saw a reference to Birch Springs dated 1620. I saw an indenture dated 1559 with the same field names around Halnaby as were used in the sale catalogue of 1952.

But, whatever the traditions, the war was an emergency and farmers were about to get firm instructions on what to do, and how to do it, by an empowered committee called the North Riding County War Agricultural Executive Committee (CWAEC).

The CWAECs or 'War Ag' was charged with implementing agricultural policy at a local level during the World War 2. I have already mentioned them in Chapter 3. For years Britain had relied on imports, many from the countries of the Empire. That policy led us to the imposition of rationing as soon as World War 2 broke out, but the country somehow had to make up the shortfall in national production. The CWAECs were famous for getting farmers to plough out their large stocks of grassland and plant food crops. But they also controlled the Women's Land Army and the allocation of POWs to different farms, because lack of labour was a major obstacle to productivity in the war years. The plough-out campaign was backed up by legislation: the Agricultural Development Act of 1939. This provided for a grant of £2 per acre for farmers who ploughed up grassland to plant food, and also provided a national market for output because the Ministry of Food bought everything. It also controlled prices.[3] One result was that imports were halved and the calorie consumption of the average Brit during wartime was 95% of the pre-war diet. It's just that the calories tended to come from cereals, vegetables and dairy products rather than meat. A further feature was the concept of the 'national farm' providing for the nation. Central policy making and monitoring became a fixture.

Croft parish came under the North Riding CWAEC but it's not clear what local group it belonged to. There was no Croft representative on this county committee or any of the local ones.. However it was at this county level that all of the instructions to farmers on ploughing-out or, in some cases, keeping fields fallow for future planting, occurred. Every instruction is catalogued in the minutes of the committee and it would be possible to construct a full picture of instructions to Croft farms across the whole of the war and beyond (because the instructions did not stop until rationing stopped in 1953). Here are just some examples that show that we aren't talking about whole farms being dug over, just a portion of many.

| # | Farmer/Farm | Field # from 1914 OS | Acreage |
|---|---|---|---|
| 10 | Haughan/Lodge Farm | 179;146 | 17.141 |
| 11 | Turnbull/Waterloo Farm | 252;Pt 263 | 28.235 |
| 12 | Biglin/North Walmire Farm | Pt 130;Pt 127 | 23.000 |
| 30 | Hobson/Vince Moor West | Pt 170 | 14.000 |
| 930 | Thurlbeck/Paradise Farm | 352 | 12.870 |
| 931 | Raper/Standalone Farm | Pt.430 | 9.000 |
| 932 | Parlour/Dobbs Hall Farm | Pt 538;Pt 599 | 15.000 |
| 935 | Metcalfe/Pepperfield Farm | 438 | 5.025 |
| 1037 | Fell/Monk End Farm | 580; 582; 583 | 18.525 |
| 1038 | Kirk/Bullmire Farm | Pt 277; Pt 296; Pt 287; Pt 279 | 19.000 |

## Chapter 5 – Living on the Land

The control exerted by the CWAECs was not popular and there were sad stories about farmers that had been 'put off' their land. This was via the issue of a Compulsory Order by the CWAEC when a farmer would not comply with instructions. I'm not sure how often this happened but I came across a booklet published by The Farmers' Rights Association around 1943-45. It was called *Living Casualties (The Dispossessed Farmer)*. It gives cases of hardship amongst farmers as a result of CWAEC activity. It argues that the Ministry of Agriculture have 'the most far-reaching powers, against the abuse of which there are no safeguards, and no appeal to the Court of Justice'. The author says the pamphlet was published to raise public awareness of the problem. It finishes with an account of the case of

**Bert Walker is accompanied by several unidentified local children on his tractor at Birch Springs, early fifties.**

George Raymond Walden, a Hampshire farmer of mature years who refused to leave his farm on issue of a Compulsory Order to do so. He ended up having an all-night gun battle with police, was shot, and died. This happened in July 1940 and there were plenty of newspaper reports on it. On 3 August that year an inquest found that Mr Walden's death was justifiable homicide. This must have been an extreme case. I'm sure there was resentment in some places, but I'm not aware of any in the Croft area.

The CWAECs were not loved but they saved the nation from starving during the war and after the war they definitely presided over improvements in farm practice and yields. Farmers don't like filling in forms and surveys but the returns helped the CWAECs make decisions that helped us all. We now look down on the mechanisation of farm work but in the lean years it improved productivity and availability of machinery made all the difference. Food rationing did not cease until 1953. Supplies did not magically reappear after war ended and Britain was bust anyway in those years. What farms were able to achieve on the home front was essential to our national recovery.

**Mary Andrew:**

*"as far as I remember we would get a tractor just about when the war finished. And then of course we had a lot of grassland to plough out, you know that after the war, because we had no food. And I would think that was when we got a tractor because this had been really heavy land, you know, difficult to work."*

At this point we should perhaps also quickly discuss the impact of Croft Aerodrome on the farmers of Croft. Many had land requisitioned, and in the early forties the agreements for requisition would have been made with the landowners. However, those requisitions were only legal in times of emergency. After the war, the Air Ministry had to regularise their landholdings by becoming owners of the land themselves.

There are a number of deeds in the North Riding Register of Deeds that demonstrate that process to some extent. However, after the aerodrome was cleared of people in the early sixties (see 'The Squatters' Tale' in Chapter 4) they started to release the land back to the farming community.

After World War 2 there were huge changes in farming. The national trend was towards more use of machines, driving bigger fields, advances in agricultural science and big changes in the skills required of farmers and farm workers. The result was much higher yields, greater specialisation, fewer and bigger farms, more use of insecticides and fertilisers and a decrease in the number of labourers. Earning your living by muscle and sweat was no longer quite what it was about. Understanding basic agricultural science and skilled operation of machinery was at least as important as slog-power if not more so.

How this traces through to individual farms in Croft is not easy to ascertain. We have a farm level survey for 1941, but that is a one-off. Despite the fact that surveys happened most years in the period covered by this book, the individual returns are lost for the North Riding. However, there are many summaries of the surveys at parish level. I've taken some parish surveys across the timespan and put them into a table. Surveys tend to differ, according to the interests of the day, but the figures I give are roughly right for the consistent items. The table illustrates everything we've just highlighted above, and there's no evidence that Croft was going a different way to everyone else – it looks consistent with the big trends of the time.[4] Please note that all the figures for crops are in acres and the total amount of agricultural land in the civil parish is around 4200 acres (slight variances from survey to survey, I suspect because some farms straddled the parish boundary and are treated differently in different years).

|      | # Holdings | Working Horses | Labourers | Wheat | Oats | Barley | Grass | Fruit & Veg | Other Crops | Dairy Cows | Beef Cattle | Sheep | Poultry | Pigs |
|------|------------|----------------|-----------|-------|------|--------|-------|-------------|-------------|------------|-------------|-------|---------|------|
| 1930 | 34 | 102 | 68 | 153 | 275 | 118 | 3544 | 157 | 13 | 210 | 579 | 2372 | 5104 | 132 |
| 1941 | 34 | 86 | 50 | 314 | 239 | 138 | 2283 | 45 | 425 | 327 | 817 | 1710 | 2476 | 185 |
| 1951 | 34 | 36 | 77 | 348 | 358 | 420 | 2212 | 69 | 253 | 305 | 951 | 1895 | 4970 | 288 |
| 1976 | 20 | 0 | 48 | 655 | 57 | 1280 | 2090 | 118 | 99 | 684 | 1178 | 2351 | 1138 | 398 |
| 1988 | 17 | 0 | 42 | 1341 | 12 | 1161 | 1311 | 56 | 618 | 414 | 978 | 2542 | 200 | 4137 |

If this table tells us about what people farmed, it does nothing to reveal how they farmed or much they produced. The latter are the areas of biggest change – productivity between 1950 and 1980 soared while technology – machines and agricultural science – came to dominate how things were done.

Nationally the sort of farming done in 1930, 1941 and 1951 was the same as in Croft: small farms doing a bit of everything. 'Up to the 1960s many farms were mixed to some degree or other. Mixed farming was seen as the traditional system. But it was more than that. It was held to be the right system, a system that maintained both soil fertility and employment on the land.'[5] After the war the small mixed farm came in for harsh criticism. Farming to that date had been a struggle. To be truly prosperous and to achieve food security for the nation, the way forward was specialisation. Those of a mixed farming persuasion argued that doing something of everything was the least risky approach, and that specialisation was putting all your eggs in one basket, prone to disaster. But the cost and power of mechanised farming

## Chapter 5 – Living on the Land

**Brian Walker drives a Massey Ferguson combine harvester: early 70s.**

drove expansion of field size in order to get the full benefit of technology, and with that expansion, it was argued, came specialisation.

An example was the advent of the mechanised milking parlour and the collection of milk by tankers. Both of these drove better hygiene and bigger yields of milk, which benefitted the customer in terms of confidence in the product and lower prices. It also resulted in the end of milk collection from churns in the 1970s. By 1979, the whole country was converted to collection by tanker. This meant the dairy farmer had to have their own tanks from which tankers could collect the milk, and also farm lanes that could accommodate a tanker. For those with a small dairy herd the cost of conversion was not viable. Larger herds were the norm, to cover the farmers fixed costs. A farm might keep a 'pet' cow or two for their own milk, or they might diversify into dairy products – cheese or yogurt for example – but small dairy farming was no longer attractive to most farmers and many farms either just got rid of their herds or made a decision to increase the herd size. Birch Springs decided to give up on cows in the early 1990s I believe, specialising in beef cattle.

So, the cost of investment in machines and biotechnology drive bigger fields and herds, and bigger farms. Bigger farms with more machinery drove more specialisation. This was the pattern that had emerged nationally by 1990 although the full extent of it was yet to come. On 1 January 1973 Britain joined the European Community and this heralded the start of the era in British farming where the Common Agricultural Policy created the incentives, disincentives and regulations of production rather than our own Ministry of Agriculture and its successors. British newspapers were quick to poke fun at the CAP and one joke was that it was 'the greatest creator of lakes and mountains since God'. However, British productivity continued to expand into the 1980s. Again, how this played out in Croft, and what legacy it left for the area's ecology, is another an investigation waiting to be done.

# Market gardens and Croft Mill

An important part of living on the land in Croft was Market Gardening. Market gardens are small farms where the focus is on growing fruit and vegetables for sale at market. Sometimes these could be wholesale, sometimes retail. Market gardens often kept chickens and pigs as well. There were four market gardens in Croft in the mid twentieth century. The oldest was what was known as 'Stairmand's'. Certainly it belonged to the Stairmand family in 1930, and probably ceased as a market garden in the 1960s. George Stairmand died in 1947 but his daughter Mabel lived on at their cottage until the mid 1960s. The evidence of Ordnance Survey maps is that this garden was in operation in the mid-nineteenth century. It was situated along the Northallerton or Dalton Road. I can't say that I know about what it grew but the OS implies there were fruit trees there. The site would have been turned over and any plants removed when the Croft Estate sold the land for housing in 1969. I don't *know* where the Stairmands sold their produce but I had heard they had a shop in Cockerton, on the outskirts of Darlington.

The other three were all on the area called Monkend Gardens which in the mid-nineteenth century was the whole of the west end of what is now South Parade. I calculate from maps that they covered about 18 acres. The market gardens seem to have been there from the late nineteenth century, then as one garden I believe, rented by John Allison and Robert Beswick. From 1905, the portion of these gardens that was south of the Croft to Stapleton bridleway was run by Ada and Henry Inness. Ada also owned the other bit of land to the north, but I believe her tenant was still Robert Beswick. Some of this land, as we've seen, became housing, and in the thirties Gerry Andrew became the tenant. Mr Andrew had a stall at the covered market in Darlington and most of his produce went there. From the war onwards he got more and more into keeping pigs and this was not at all popular with local people due to the smell. Eventually the Council granted him permission to have large scale piggeries further along the bridleway, and you'll see in the next chapter that after Mr Andrew left the area these were considered for conversion to the Village Hall! I believe Mr Andrew ceased in the 1960s. The Croft Allotments are on his old land and so are the new houses at the north part of Monk End. I believe the Croft Estate bought his land when he left.

The Innesses garden was mostly orchard. However, In 1937, Ada Inness sold part of her land at Monkend Gardens to her son Fred. Fred built a small bungalow called High Thorn, and he ran that end of the market garden as a separate concern. In 1947 he sold it on to the Titchmarshes as a market garden. They seem to have finished in the fifties. The Inness garden and house called Monkend Gardens was sold to Wilfred and Elsie Hauxwell in 1954. The Hauxwells ran it as a garden at a low level for a while but when they became elderly they sold much of the land, in about 2002, for housing.

Market gardening flourished when transport was slow and localised markets were essential for the supply of perishable fruit and vegetables. As soon as motor transport became the predominant form of transport more people could go further to sell. As horses on farms and for transport became scarcer, horse manure, a staple for the market gardener as a fertiliser, became more difficult to get. And then with the trend towards larger-scale and more mechanised production it became harder and harder for small local producers to survive. Ironically, it is exactly their model that is advocated today as we try to limit the effect

## Chapter 5 – Living on the Land

**The front of Monkend Hall as it looked during the Parlour's time there (1925-78).**

of 'factory' production on the environment.

In the early horse-powered era of farming Croft mill was an essential part of the eco system. It simply wasn't economic for individual farms to maintain the means of grinding their own corn. Grain was taken to the mill and either sold to the miller who would grind it and sell it on, or give it back to the farmer to use on the farm. The Wilson family were the last commercial millers at the Mill, and from 1932 it was Mr Adamson, who I talked about in Chapter 4. He was from Picton, near Yarm, and had been a farm worker before coming to the mill. He had big shire horses which you can see in the picture below, and in the MAF 1941 Farm Survey he describes himself as a part-time farmer. Bert Walker remembered going to the Mill very early in his days at Birch Springs, but a little later they did their own milling using an attachment you could fix to a tractor motor. Mary Andrew also remember that they had the means to grind their own corn at Waterloo Farm after the war, she thinks powered by a tractor. She also had a more specific memory:

**Mary Andrew**:

*"I remember going to Croft mill with corn with the horse and cart and you hooked the bag at the bottom and then he hauled it up to the top to grind it. I remember Mr. Adamson. I remember going there. And then if we were selling corn or barley, you had to go to the station at Croft to get the railway sacks to put the corn in. And it went on the train. Often a wagon came for it. Because I seem to vaguely remember putting the sacks on to like a lift and then you had to wind the handle to get the sack up onto the wagon, you know, because they were 16 and 18 stone in those days. Wheat went in 18 stone and barley was 16. Yeah, we had this lift, you put the sack on the bottom and then you wound this handle and chain lifted it up onto the level of the wagon."*

**John Green** also had a very clear memory of the mill:

*"And when we came [1946] the old mill was working. Fella called Adamson used to run it. And*

*the farmers used to bring some of the corn and that, and he would grind it and then they came and picked it up. Because the mill race came down way on the other side of the market garden from the beck... of course its all filled in now. But he had to walk all the way up there to where the Clow Beck came and it branched off and he used to open the sluice gate so the water came down to drive the wheel. And then of course he had to go back up to shut it again. But he always knew when there was a flood coming. And he moved everything upstairs in his house that was connected to the mill.*

*And also the farmers used to come with a horse and cart, or tractors and trailers and go through past the mill and on to the gravel bed and get gravel off. From the river. Where that gravel is now, where those trees are rooted up again now, they used to keep that gravel cleared out and the take it to the farms to put on the roads and the tracks things like that and that was long before the flood bank was there."*

An article in the *Northern Echo* dated 11 May 1968 contained an interview with Mr Adamson himself. He was still living at the mill then (he ended his life at Linden Court) but the mill wheel had stopped. One of the things that had stopped the mill from continuing was ever larger bills for repairing the mill dam, or race, which ran from the Clow Beck across the flat fields parallel to the river that were once part of Monkend, now owned by the Croft Estate. Whenever the Tees flooded those fields, and the dam, were prone to a battering. As the demand for milling decreased, the bills became uneconomic and Kit Chaytor decided enough was enough. The mill wheel was retired. The article confirms Mary's account of hauling the sacks from a cart to the upper door for grinding. When he'd finished Mr Adamson would set the sacks in rows across the floor with the owner's name on a board above the row, so the farmer could help himself if there was no-one about.[6]

What happened to Croft mill happened to thousands of others. It was something that milling of some sort continued at Croft after World War 2. All across Britain, small wind and water driven mills started to disappear from the late nineteenth century, when large steam driven mills could process imported grain at the ports, straight after unloading from ships. This created cheaper flour which was in demand. Wheat growing also started to diminish in Britain, and the small mills with it. They were soon reduced to milling for animal feed and some services to local farmers. Over the twentieth century, an industry that existed even before the Norman conquest vanished from the countryside.

Mr Adamson, the last miller at Croft, mentioned that swallows liked to nest at the mill and that he liked to watch them. Every farmer would have had stories about the wildlife they saw on their farms but I haven't collected any memories of that except Doris's mentions of badger setts along the perimeter of the aerodrome. The juxtaposition of human engineering and the flux of nature in the parish is important, and it is foremost in what we think about now, in the twenty-first century, as we count the cost of the huge improvements that were made in farm efficiency in the twentieth.

**Ian Dougill** had a memory of how earlier farming practice affected the sort of wildlife you could see and hear:

*"My father pointed out to me that, on the top field, which was normally a hay meadow, there were*

## Chapter 5 – Living on the Land

*corncrakes in there. And they have very distinctive call. And I'm hoping I'm not on a fantasy trip here but I'm sure I did hear corncrakes in the thirties, up in that top field* [this is the field that runs behind South Terrace, on the corner of Jolby Lane]. *And when you consider that 97% of English meadows have disappeared since the thirties, it's a horrendous figure. A hay meadow is just the sort of place where they would come to nest. Now that is a real indication of the change in agriculture because that would be an unimproved meadow probably there for a long long time. And I believe it was part of the old Croft racecourse. We've almost lost all our traditional hay meadows. And they were hay meadows year after year after year so they built up a very rich flora and it was ideal for corncrakes. Because by the time they came the cut them, the chicks had left the nest. So, you see, the old fashioned agriculture was very friendly to wildlife."*

Sandra Veerman explained that in the 1950s the top field to the west of Monkend Hall, south of the old mill dam, was also a hay meadow year on year. *"And I used to love picking the wild flowers, they were so pretty, Hundreds of wild flowers and dozens of different types. I liked to gather them up."* This was the hay meadow where they liked to play among the stooks after her father and Mr Adamson had gathered them up. Her father would get angry if they messed things up – see the hide and seek memory in Chapter 2!

**Richard Andrew** had a memory and a reflection:

*"Agriculture comes in for some stick, you know, rightly or wrongly. But interestingly, because my*

**This picture was taken in summer 1950 during a break in haymaking in the back field at Monkend Hall when Sandra Green/ Veerman was around one (she's the baby). Sandra is sitting on her father John Green's knee and her mother Gladys is at the front. William Adamson – the last miller at Croft - is at the back.**

*mother in law had just been moving a a couple of years before, we found a lot of pamphlets. She's always been involved in farming. And one of these pamphlets was from 1937. It was issued by the government of the day. And it was titled 'The efficient removal of hedgerows'. And it told you how to. Because everybody could get hold of dynamite. Yeah, you know, and how to fasten chains together between boulders to remove hedgerows. And, of course, this was driven by government policy, they wanted farms to be more efficient. And so you're kind of left with that legacy of all the hedges being removed, nobody can deny that. But that was what was politically demanded at the time."*

The history of the agricultural community in Croft parish is a huge subject and an important one. We've scratched the surface here. But I hope I've given the reader some ideas about what was happening between 1930 and 1990. It's an important subject in itself, and also as background to the following sections.

# The influence of estate management

As we have already seen, there are two estates in Croft parish that had a number of farms: Halnaby and the Croft Estate. In general terms, Halnaby occupies the south west half of the parish while the Croft, or Chaytor estate occupies much of the north west. Boundaries are far more jagged than that of course. Halnaby, when it existed, was the larger of the estates at 2,200 acres. But both ran cheek-by-jowl along the the road from Croft to Middleton Tyas chiefly. And anyone who has explored the country along those gentle hills, featured by copses and rows of deciduous woodland, will understand that land there is as green and pleasant as England can be.

**Chapman Pincher** evokes the essence of it:
*"There was a wonderful, quiet road connecting Croft with the next village, Middleton Tyas, which was so rich in wild flowers, birds, butterflies and other insects that I called it Omnology Lane – because everything could be studied there. When it was a ribbon of moonlight I would stride it with my dog listening for owls and vixen."* [7]

At one end of this road, nearer the village, were Old Spa Farm, Clervaux Castle, Paradise and Standalone Farms and the collection of cottages and wood yard called Newtown, all key parts of the Croft Estate. At the other end was Bullmire, Moor House, Waterloo, Lodge and Home Farms, key parts of Halnaby. But the progress of these estates from 1930 to 1990 has varied, because the management history of those estates has been different.

You already know, from the previous chapter, that the Halnaby Estate as such ceased to exist after the sale of 1949. We've talked about how this happened and we've considered the loss of the Hall and the estate structure in general. But what of the individual farms? All the farms were put up for sale, and many of them were sold to the sitting tenants. So that's why there are still Kirks at Bullmire and Walkers at Birch Springs, and why the Turnbulls and the Burdons continued on in their farms. What happened was that they were able to attract mortgage funding, and to buy their farms. Instead of paying rent to the Estate Office, they paid a mortgagor. Sometimes it was an organisation like the Midland Bank or the Darlington Equitable Building Society. Sometimes it was a private individual looking for return on their spare money. There were some families – notably the Banners at Home Farm – who did not get their farms. Home Farm, for example, was bought by someone from outside Croft, presumably just as an investment. Alan Kirk said that Kit Chaytor – then in charge of the Croft Estate – had declined to bid for the farms if the current tenant was bidding for them, and that he had told the farmers that was what he was going to do. But it has to be said that the Croft Estate did not buy any lots at all at the Halnaby sale. They later bought Dobbs Hall Farm and Lodge Farm and maybe some pieces of land, but not at the time of the estate sale.

The sale of the Halnaby Estate in October 1949 was a great occasion in Croft. The front page of the catalogue sets the scene.

Of course, paying a mortgage was not the same as the ritual of going to the Estate Office twice a year. Bert Walker remembers the few times his father went before the sale: *"earlier, and before the war, every rent day the farmers used to go to pay the rent at the Halnaby Hall. They used to have a beer and a tea party for them"*. It was a social event. And also when the estate was broken up the farms lost a rich benefactor who might help with a big expense, but also the scrutiny from the agent who was trying to ensure the value of the estate's assets:

**Mary Andrew**:

*"They used to come round you know the land agents of the estate, they used to come round and see what you were doing and if things weren't being kept. Cos you know, they could charge you dilapidation on your buildings in your house and everything if things weren't right. I can remember Captain Beadon he lived in Croft. Yeah, he was the estate agent for Halnaby. I can remember he used to call* [at Waterloo Farm] *and have a walk around. And then on on rent day twice a year, not that*

The list of lots, with acreage, defined for the Halnaby Estate Sale of 1949.

*I'd remember, but Mum said, Dad had to go down to the Home Farm to pay the rent.*

*I didn't really know Lady Wilson Todd but I think she was quite a fair person. And she would know Mum from when she lived at Lodge Farm. And she always called her Sally. Mum's name was Sarah. Why Lady Wilson-Todd called her Sally I've no idea. But I think she was quite a fair person, because Mum, after she got married* [to John Turnbull], *she decided they were going to have cows and sell milk. So she got quite a few cows together but they had only two small cow byres at Waterloo and they weren't together. And she was wanting to have a milking machine. Well, they couldn't. And the gamekeeper Mr. Dimmock had gone across one night to Waterloo. He often did go across and Mum was telling him that she'd got these cows gathered. So he'd gone to Lady Wilson-Todd and he said 'By, Turnbulls have got a lot of nice cows gathered up you know. They could do with a with a decent cow byre'. So she said to Mr. Dimmock, 'Well, if Sally wants a cow byre, she shall have to have a cow byre.' So Mum got her cow byre."*

But undoubtedly, after the estate sale, farmers became their own masters, up to the point of government regulation, and the trends of modern farming of course. Halnaby became democratised, and the owning families maintained their own longevity at farm level.

The following table tracks the fate of the Halnaby farms at the time of the estate sale:[8]

| Farm | Purchaser | Acres | Indenture date and (if given) price | Tenant before sale |
|---|---|---|---|---|
| Bullmire | G.Kirk & Sons | 210 | 13 Feb 1950/£4,785 | Kirk |
| Portobello | JW Walker & Sons | 178 | 13 Feb 1950/£7,428 | Walker |
| Birch Springs | JW Walker & Sons | 185 | Included in the above | Walker |
| Creaking Tree | Thompson | 345 | 14 Feb 1950/£6,241 | Thompson |
| Waterloo | Norman Gaze (Reading) | 338 | 9 Mar 1950/£3,350 | Turnbull |
| Lodge | Arthur Sidney Reason (Reading) | 270 | 9 Mar 1950 | Burdon |
| Halnaby Grange | Wright | 188 | 3 Mar 1950/£3,574 | Wright |
| Home | Ernest Sharp (Ferryhill) | 56 | 20 Mar 1950/£7,206 | Banner |
| Moor House | Myers | 114 | 13 Feb 1950/£4,184 | Myers |

Those farms that were bought by outsiders were bought as land assets, not for them to farm on. The reason two of the farms were bought by people in Reading was probably because the estate sale was handled by Nicholas, auctioneers based in Reading, and Tain Bainbridge from Darlington, so clearly there would have been some advertising beyond the North Riding. Most of the indentures for the transfer of ownership to a sitting tenant were accompanied with Mortgage Deeds for the same land. In addition there was separate sale of woodland – always to timber companies, usually from Durham or Yorkshire – and the estate lodges. Tracing the indentures through you can see that some of the buyers who were not local soon sold when they had taken assets from the land or the finances were right. This gave families like the Turnbulls the opportunity to buy their farm at a later date. The Turnbulls had previously bought one of the West Lodges at the sale (indenture 6 Feb 1950, price £1080) and in 1956 they bought Lot 17 – Richmond Road Plantation – after the sawmill that had bought it at the sale had done with it. They also bought Home Farm from Ernest Sharp via an indenture dated 14 September 1959, no sum of money disclosed. Mary Andrew and her husband farmed this after their marriage, as her son Richard does today.

The Banner family had been the tenants at Home Farm and I have been told that they had wanted to buy it but had lacked the funds to. They continued as tenants under Mr Sharp's ownership. The Turnbulls bought it after the parents of Laurence Banner died. Laurence and his wife Eva had wanted to buy it but at that time could not. Laurence and Eva were, later, able to buy the remains of Halnaby Hall from Mr Sharp and they put their resources and energy into transforming the stables and other remaining buildings that were still standing.

Arthur Reason also sold Lodge Farm, having received a few acres of land back from the Air Ministry, in 1951. He sold it to the Croft Estate for £6,300, which could well have been a profit. The Burdon family are still the tenants.

Although, post 1950, all of these farms were independent, and they all went slightly different ways in terms of their choices of what and how to farm, there was, when I interviewed, a distinct sense that they all felt they were Halnaby farms, not Chaytor farms. One farmer, who was born after the sale of the estate, said *"I'm glad I was Halnaby"*. I'm not completely sure what he meant but I think I know: if he'd been part of the Croft Estate decisions would have been different and not to his liking, so the next thing to do is to look at *how* they might have been different.

The Croft Estate made its own path through the challenges of mid twentieth century. In 1922, Alfred Henry Chaytor had bought the estate from the Chaytor baronet of the day, Sir Edmund Chaytor, his second cousin. Alfred's younger son – Christopher William Drewett (Kit) Chaytor – became the estate manager and 'squire'. Kit married late and did not have any children. And so, as with all landed families, the problem of succession arose. Kit's older brother – Alfred Drewett Chaytor – had three children, one a boy. Bill. And in the early 1960s Drew and Bill agreed that Bill, who was born in 1936, should take on the estate in succession to Kit.

**Bill's Chaytor**:

*"Well, my family have owned land in Croft for a long time and I, being the oldest son, I suppose might have lived here, but my father and grandfather didn't really get on very well* [laughs]*, and my father's younger brother, my Uncle Kit, was therefore the one who was passed on Croft. And he had no children sadly. He was a lovely man, and he decided to pass Croft onto me. So it didn't come from my father and I didn't spend my early childhood here. My early childhood was in the magic of Coverdale which is next to Wensleydale and was sort of wild and free and very few neighbours. We could have been lonely, but we were not because my sisters and I all had things to play with and it was a beautiful place. And when we came to Croft as children, there was a nervousness about it*

*in that there were lots of rules and aunts and things we could do and couldn't do, which we didn't think very reasonable. And so I can't say I understood Croft itself. It was ruled if anything by my grandmother, my grandfather having died five years before I was born, and my grandmother was living at Croft Hall with her son, said Kit Chaytor who at that stage was not married. [...] So, I didn't come here until Kit said he was going to leave the place to me in the early '60s. By that time I was travelling or I was about to go travelling, in '57 after national service, and my father said to my Uncle Kit – the two brothers got on very well despite one of them getting on with his father and the other one not – but my father said to Kit, 'If you are leaving this to Bill, you probably ought to tell him before he goes to Australia 'cos he might not come back.' He might have too much fun there, you know – so I suppose I must have been told, but I don't really remember being told or being suitably excited. It was obviously a wow situation as far as I was concerned and it's been dominant in my life ever since then, but at that stage I wasn't aware quite what it all meant."*

The Chaytors were quite serious about civic duty and genuinely felt a responsibility for the land they owned and the community living on it. Alfred wrote a set of essays published in 1930[9] and they are very revealing of his views on estates and the need for estate owners to provide an example of sacrifice and servitude. As a successful barrister, Alfred wrote several essays in this collection on the law, and one set of laws he had a tilt at were the laws concerning Death Duties and the rules of inheritance for landowning families. The essay is titled 'On Needless Breaking Up of Estates and Families'. He has a pop at the Administration of Estates Act 1925 and avows that, apart from the scale of Death Duties, 'no more deadly blows have been dealt for centuries at the old family estates on which the continuity of our English families really rests'. Interesting, given that Alfred and all his siblings were born in New Zealand, that he should feel strongly about the welfare of English landed families. However, clearly, the former saw themselves as being part of an 'English family' by dint of being Chaytors. Alfred had been in England since he was sent to boarding school here, and after World War 1 his two distinguished brothers – D'Arcy and Sir Edward Walter Clervaux – also came to live here.

Alfred's point in his essay – written before 1930 remember – was that legislation was making estates inoperable. And that was a bad thing for rural communities and the landscape. He is specifically against the abolition of the law of primogeniture – the law that requires an estate to pass to the heir of the current holder. By abolishing this, Alfred argues, and by imposing large Death Duties, the government has removed the conditions under which estates thrive because they get broken up and sold to satisfy the needs of various descendants of the owner, rather than a single heir. He argues for reform:

*not only because the owners serve England well by caring for the beauty of her countryside, nor because they and their families have always served her in peace and war, but above all because each family, so long as it can keep together, tends to maintain a high standard of honour and conduct for all its members, men and women alike, and that is a thing no country would willingly lose.* [10]

## Chapter 5 – Living on the Land

Not everyone would agree with that as a description of the ruling classes, but you can see what he means. And I think he, and many others, believed that landowners had a duty to set a standard and be involved in local life. Coupled with the deference of their underlings before the war, and, in rural communities until much later, this gave them a lot of power in local forums. But landed people were very often well-educated and worldly; they could certainly discharge public duties well if they were minded to. And no-one can deny that they had their influence on how the rural landscape and community evolved. You can see that in the evolution of the Croft Estate.

At the time of Alfred Chaytor's purchase of the estate he had a report from Daniel Watney and Sons to Farrer & Co, who were his solicitors, that assessed the condition of every asset. The general opinion was that most of the farm buildings were in poor repair, many damp and roofs dilapidated, and that investment would be needed. (It also said that many cottages, including the older ones along Northallerton Road which Bill later demolished, were not worth investing in.) The form of this report is about valuing the estate and it talks only of assets, value and investment liabilities. It's not really couched in the terms of 'serving England', more serving the estate owner. But I suppose that is what land agents do.

Throughout the period 1923 to 1965, with a suitable pause for his service during World War 2, Kit Chaytor was a regular applicant to the RDC for permission to alter buildings on the Croft estate. Often these were agricultural buildings: an 'Implement Shed' at Bay Horse Farm, drainage at Dobbs Hall, a new dairy and other improvements at Grange Farm, for example. What level of improvement he sought in agricultural practice I don't know, but that was most definitely a major concern for his nephew and heir.

Bill Chaytor, head of the Croft Estate up to his death in June 2023 and Alfred's grandson, wrote a memoir which he published privately. I feel honoured that he gave me a copy. It covers Bill's life as an individual, his role as the head of the Croft Estate and some of the broader involvements he had in his lifetime, notably in matters of the environment, that he felt passionate about. Bill took on the Croft Estate in 1965, shortly after his marriage to his first wife Sue, and moved to Croft where he lived in Woodbine Cottage at first, then Waterside. He was ambitious to modernise

**Kit Chaytor in shooting mode on the moors, with his dog Inky, 1950s.**

the estate and was full of ideas. His uncle Kit was a great support in his early years and it was Kit that encouraged Bill to take a wider role in Croft, just as he had. Bill was on the Parish Council, the Parochial Church Council and, briefly, North Yorkshire County Council (a role he did not relish). He also became a magistrate. Kit had told him that taking on these involvements was 'the squire's lot'.

Kit Chaytor died in 1969, and Bill was now very much the leader of the Estate. He says in his book that two questions were uppermost in his mind 'How should I be managing land; and what, if anything, was my wider role?' [11]

He set about his duties and he wanted to set the estate to rights, to make it sustainable for the immediate future.

**Bill Chaytor**:

*"Following suggestions from my Uncle Kit about getting onto the parish council, I remember I put my name forward for it, and my aunt who was actually on the parish council at the time retired, but so popular were they that people voted for me and I had far more votes to be on the parish council than anyone else. But it was no credit to me personally, it was because of the popularity of Aunt Ray and Uncle Kit. Everybody loved them and they were very special people. At the time, as you may have read in my memoirs, there were fourteen farms at Croft, and there was a great feeling of co-operation between farmers and farming, and Kit took enormous interest in them and knew them all. And it was a different scene, it was a very happy, call it a pre-War set up. It was the sort of thing that Doris has subsequently explained to me. And I admired this and liked it, but well, what happened – literally from the first year I got here – was that tenants were saying, 'You can't farm. This size of farm just doesn't work,' and they were about 120/130 acres. I think there were a lot that were elderly, almost nobody who was young, and so they were ready to either retire or go and do something else as a mid-life decision. And it was in a way sad to me to see this, but I had a guide and mentor who again was a great tower of strength. An agent who was a scholarly man, might well have worked for a university but he decided to be a land agent, called Tom Wrightson and he had his own firm. And he said, 'Well, what I think is going to happen, I would predict, is that farms are going to get bigger and bigger. The real price of food is going to go down and down', and that's what's happened because of the efficiencies of producing it with using particularly fertilizers and sprays, and also all the other efficiencies of science being applied to agriculture. And therefore, the price of food goes down and despite the fact that you're getting more food per acre, you need to farm more acres in order to make a livelihood. And Tom was saying, 'This I think is what is coming, and you could make this your job.' I hadn't assumed that I would necessarily work at farming, but he said, 'I think you'll find there is an awful lot to do,' in preparing land and working different farms together, some of them which are heavy and grow better crops or better grass, and some of which are lighter and grow certain vegetable crops say. And you balance this all up and do that and also, altering field sizes which at the time the average seven acres which is actually tiny.*

*I applied myself to that and I remember deciding that it seemed that about twenty-five acres which is ten hectares was a good size for fields. And so, I planned where there would be new hedges and I know I took out an awful lot of old hedges which sounds very destructive but I replaced them with seven miles of new hedges."*

Another thing that Bill, and Kit, set out to do was replace woodland. Sir Edmund Chaytor had sold off a lot of timber before he sold the estate to Kit's father, and had left stumps with no new planting. In 1950 Kit brought in Ron Fletcher to work as a woodsman and Ron worked on at the Croft Estate until he retired in the 1980s. He was involved in a lot of the planting that Kit and Bill did. Paul Fletcher, Ron's son, recalls:

**Paul Fletcher**:

*"Ron and Doreen moved to Croft in 1950 when Ron was employed by Kit Chaytor as woodman, looking after 200 acres of woodland. His job also included repairs to gates, barn doors, windows etc on the farms belonging to Croft Estate. Their first home was 2 Spa Cottages, opposite the Spa Baths. I was born there on 29th March 1952 which was also the day Dad's parents moved to Croft. George, my Grandad, was employed as a gardener in Croft Hall gardens. Initially they lived at Spa Road Cottage on the Northallerton road next door to Thornton's Farm/Dairy but soon moved to 1 Spa Cottages which was next door to Ron and Doreen. In 1955 we moved up to Newtown. I have no idea why it was called Newtown. The house looked like it had been built after cutting the plans meant for two semi-detached houses, in half. There were no windows at all on the Richmond Road side of the house. At the time of moving there was no electricity. That arrived a few years later. The plot of land belonging to the house consisted of a grassy paddock, a group of mature hard wood trees, an apple orchard near the house and various fruit trees and bushes scattered around the rest of the paddock with a flower and vegetable plot at the rear.*

*When we moved to Newtown there were various other buildings dotted around the acre or so of land. The most important was 'The Joiners Shop'. Basically this was just a large wooden workshop used by Ron. Inside one end of the shed was a big wooden workbench plus various hand or pedal powered stone sharpening wheels, drills, chisels etc., all used by Ron to make the farm gates and doors etc. There was also a big log burner stove. The other part of the building was a timber store which eventually acted as a garage when the estate provided a little Fordson tractor that Ron could use to pull timber out of the woods rather than having to hoist timber on to his shoulders. Next to the Joiners Shop were the remains of a stone building that had been demolished. Thirty yards father up the road were two attached cottages (Newtown Cottages) one of which was being lived in when we first moved there but they were knocked down in the early 60's. Between those cottages and the end of the Newtown garden there was a short track that lead to a large derelict building known as The Lime Shed. It had a small farm building attached which, together with another long farm building opposite, were used by Mr Pearson for rearing pigs."*

In another memory, Paul recalls that one of his favourite places in Croft was Spa Wood, to the west of Croft Hall, and that it was his father who had planted much of that.

This picture of Middle Walmire shows the collection of farm buildings before they were demolished in the 1960s.

**Bill Chaytor** recalls in his memoir:

> *I began a programme of planting small, four-acre game spinneys in the more treeless areas of the estate away from the centre of the castle remains. Ron Fletcher entered into the spirit of all this; we worked out variety mixes and planting patterns, most often using oak, spruce and European larch, as nurse trees to the oak, and some ornamental trees on the edges. Additionally, starting with Big Stranborough Wood and Blackwood, we followed Kit's lead in replanting the old woodland blocks which Edmund had felled off in World War 1, where there were only self-sewn trees and scrub."* [12]

We have already looked at some of the decisions facing Bill in relation to buildings in Croft village. But he had many decisions to make about the farms. His strategy, forged in association with Tom Wrightson, was to increase the size of the farms and introduce more scientific method. That's what most people were doing in the sixties and seventies. The farms on the Croft Estate had not changed much since that 1941 survey. There was still a lot of small scale stuff. Farms now had electricity and water, tractors and other machinery, maybe a combine. But there was still more room for modernisation. Also, in common with the estate's village property, much of the farm property needed investment.

Bill decided to get rid of some of the farm buildings and bring the acreage under the control of the Estate's main farm – Grange Farm. Middle Walmire had buildings that had not been functional since the

## Chapter 5 – *Living on the Land*

**An early picture of the Nattress family of Middle Walmire during a break from haymaking. I don't know the date but clothing suggests late 1920s or early thirties.**

war, so they were demolished. There was an ancient earthwork marked in the fields but no-one had ever found any relics there, so the fields were levelled and hedges taken out to produce a viable unit. North Walmire was also demolished and similar stuff was done with that land. Bill spent some time building up a 'Walmire' dairy herd on the land, but this did not involve the old buildings. Bay Horse and Pepperfield were tiny acreages: eventually they went for rent as domestic properties after their farmers retired. Bill had a lot of elderly farmers and farm workers and that gave him opportunities for rationalisation. That was the first wave of reform. Later on, from the 1980s the estate became arable only as dairy farming became less viable for the small to medium size herd. Bill continued to sell bits of land and property not least because a new owner would put in the investment to modernise and tidy them. Today, in 2023, to my knowledge, there are only two working farms on the Croft estate: Grange Farm, which is the largest one, and Lodge Farm which was a Halnaby farm which the Croft Estate bought a few years after the latter estate was sold. The remaining farm buildings are lived in, but not by farmers.

In 1996 Bill brought in his son-in-law, Trevor Chaytor-Norris, to manage most of the estate and the various farms and other property were split between him and his children James, Kate and Nick – he became more interested in long term sustainability and the environment. In the early twenty-first century he founded the Clervaux Trust.

*Crofts Crossing*

# Wade in the water

Although this chapter is called 'Living on the Land', it would be strange for a book about Croft-on-Tees not to look specifically at how the River Tees has shaped life in the parish and how it's propensity to flood has been tamed over the years.

The River Tees is one of England's major rivers and the ancient boundary between Yorkshire and County Durham. Rising in the High Pennines by Alston in Cumbria, it gathers water across those rainy moors all the way to the precipice of High Force and down into Teesdale. It then enters flatter lands to the west of Darlington. As it comes round the bend from Cleasby (on the Yorkshire side) and Blackwell (on the County Durham side) it comes to Croft. And just before the village of Croft it is joined by the River Skerne, that flows down through the town of Darlington. Then it widens and flows on, round the corner to Hurworth, out of sight from Croft Bridge and into its meander before widening again at the estuaries around Stockton and Middlesbrough. In summer you can wade to the middle of the Tees at Croft as the riverbed is flat stone. In winter it is dark, cold, swollen and swift-flowing.

As our period of examination begins, in 1930, there has just been a flood. The newspapers talk about pigs being drowned and cellars filled with water. That story repeated regularly over the years as the river flooded into the fields next to the riverbank, maybe into Monkend Terrace, the Church crypt and occasionally onto South Parade. Usually it was Hurworth Place that caught the brunt as the River made Darlington Road impassable. There were major floods again in 1939.

A particularly bad flood was in 1968. John Green and Sandra Veerman had strong memories of it. It was in March, and Sandra had arranged to go to the CB Inn at Arkengarthdale for the evening. She remembered she was learning to drive and a friend had let her drive his Hillman Imp.

**Two children paddle down a flooded South Parade. This is probably the flood described by John and Sandra, in 1968.**

**Sandra Veerman**:

"*[The CB Inn] was the place to go in the sixties. People came from all over and that little dance floor that was basically ... well ... afterwards I learned it was just propped up on beer crates. And a lot of us went from all this area it was a fun place to go. And you had to go over Grinton Bridge at Grinton to go there and of course I had friends because I was at Richmond School so it was that area. But the water was coming over Grinton Bridge when we got there and the brakes were starting to get dodgy so we said we're better go back and we came back into the village* [Croft]. *There were no streetlights then. And there was somebody at the at the corner here* [by The Moorings] *just by the school gates with a lantern. And it was Dad, and Dad shouted 'don't come any further' and the water was coming down South Parade.*"

**John Green**:

"*And I got out. And I walked through and there was about that much* [indicates about two feet] *clear next to the wall by the front gardens going up. And we had called for some fish and chips hadn't we? And we had those at our house. Then I put me wellies on and went to see if it was any different. And I couldn't get down that gap, it was right up to the front gates.*"

Sandra and John went on to talk about rescuing Mrs Wilkin and Mrs Thurlbeck from further down South Parade, and then their own father! Mr Green had gone to his pigeon loft which was where The Mill Race development is now and got stranded as the water rose. They had to call the police to rescue him, but the pigeon loft got swept away and all the pigeons died. The next morning was different.

**John Green**:

"*this was on the Friday night and I had to go to work on the Saturday. And I wondered if I could but by the time I went it was way down. It was clear along Darlington Road, quite a way along. And it was all just slurry and slush.*"

As early as 1355, concern about the impact of floods on Croft Bridge were expressed to the extent that the village was granted extra funds to repair it.[13] In the 1970s concern about the impact of the swollen River Tees on Croft Bridge was again at a height. There were fears a particularly violent flood would bring the bridge down at the Hurworth end, because that was where the main channel of the river was and where the water moved most quickly. This was caused by the extensive field and gravel bed belonging to Croft Mill. In 1976 the decision was taken by the Northumbrian River Authority (NRA) to move the course of the river so that the impact on the bridge would be evenly spread. This involved removing a lot of ground on the Croft side.

The first proposals from NRA were presented by the latter at a village meeting at the school (the old school) on Wednesday 22 January 1975. Mr Burnley and Mr Buttress from the Thornaby Division of NRA did the presentation to what was basically the parish council (Bert Coates, Edith Allen, Betty Chaytor, Mrs Headon, Ron Fletcher, Mr Huddleston and Mr Pearson and the clerk (Mrs Dobson)) plus one parishioner. Three plans were presented as options and it was unanimously agreed that 'Scheme D'

This aerial photograph from, probably, the mid 1960s, shows how the main channel of the river was all along the Hurworth bank, pushed out by the extensive mill field to the east of the old mill race. The water then swung across towards the wall around Bridge House (pictured top left). The front of the Croft Spa Hotel is top right.

## Chapter 5 – Living on the Land

was the one to go for. The cost of this was £73,500. The Parish Council were asked if they could make a contribution to this and they said they would consider giving £150 at the next PC meeting. The meeting lasted an hour.

Although this scheme improved the security of the bridge, Croft itself was still prone to floods. The last year in our period when there was an unusually high flood was 1986. On this occasion the Mill and Monkend Terrace were badly flooded and the water came across the field between South Parade and the riverbank and lapped up against the back doors of houses in South Parade in some cases. Mrs Pat Godfrey told us that number 7 (which we bought from her) had had the water at the back doorstep, but it didn't get into the houses. Mr and Mrs Kirkwood, however, had moved into the Mill a few years earlier and they were stuck.

All of this, plus another very high flood in 1995, kicked off more discussions with what was then the Environment Agency and eventually the 'levee' that we see today was built to keep the water back. The first flood defence of 1975 was metres high and there was an additional floodgate at Clow Beck to stop water backing up the Beck and across the fields at what was then Monk End Farm. It was necessary to raise the height in 2000. However, this levee has kept Croft dry, and another advantage is that the Croft Estate agreed a permissive footpath along the top of it which makes an enjoyable riverside work for both people and dogs.

However, the Tees at Croft could have been very different it wasn't for the resistance of the Parish Council, Croft's people and their neighbours in Neasham, Eryholme and Hurworth, and one man in particular – Bert Coates. There could have been a weir built across the river upstream from the Skerne, damming the water at that point, reducing the flow downstream and removing important dilution of the polluted River Skerne, which joins the Tees north of Croft Bridge. The argument about this took place in 1966. It entailed a public inquiry, and an appeal to the High Court before the scheme was abandoned.

This is the story. Imperial Chemical Industries (ICI) at Teesside were expanding and had contacted the Tees Valley and Cleveland Water Board (as it was then) to demand a much bigger supply of clean water to their site at Billingham. This was not something the water board could immediately respond to. They needed to make some major changes to comply with the wishes of what was then one of Britain's largest industrial companies, if not the largest. The drawing below shows the Water Board's intention. Not only would there be a weir, but also a pumping station on the Durham bank. They sought planning permission from NRCC.

Bert Coates was chair of the Croft Parish Council at this point. To begin with, the council followed

The hero of the Croft Weir saga, Bert Coates, is here receiving a presentation from George Chapman, on his retirement from Croft Tennis Club. His son David is in the centre of the picture, and to his left is Charlie Headon.

procedure by responding via the Rural District Council and NRCC planning committees. Imagine their horror when the outline planning permission was granted regardless of their concerns. This greatly enraged the great and the good in Croft, both Kit Chaytor and Captain Parlour were strongly opposed, as were many people in Hurworth and Neasham. Bert Coates set to work. They would not accept this decision.

ICI were adept at publicising the merits of the scheme and the importance to British prosperity that they get what they wanted to increase production. But Bert wrote letter after letter to gain support. He got together with the other 'downstream' parishes at Hurworth, Neasham and Middleton-one-Row. He lobbied influential people like Chapman Pincher who was supportive, but could not persuade his paper – *The Daily Express* – to run the story. The Darlington newspapers – the *Northern Echo* and the *Northern Despatch* – were engaged and sympathetic to the cause. Local opinion began to swell. The NRCC refused full planning permission for the building work to proceed.

The *Northern Echo* ran a series of articles under the title 'Fight to Save the Tees'. On 15 June 1966 it was moved to print the headline 'Croft Goes Militant':

> *Croft, centre of the storm, shows mounting militancy. Many people do not like the idea of the Tees being diminished in size by the proposed weir and the pumping station that will accompany it. And they have their supporters – in the four villages downstream that will also be affected by a smaller Tees.*

Bert expressed the view that Durham County Council and other local councils had let those other villages down. It is a mystery to me as to why there is no profile for Croft RDC in the fight, why it was the Parish Council that was left to battle on. Kit Chaytor was strongly opposed and he was a district councillor. Local people always felt that they were fighting a Goliath and that ICI's influence was being wrought in the corridors of power.

In its leader for Tuesday 26 July 1966, the *Northern Echo* pinned its colours to the mast:

> *There is already too little water in the Tees at Croft. The proposal to take out further water at a new weir can only make things worse. This is why the Minister of Housing and Local Government ought to reject the Croft weir plan, an inquiry into which opens today. [...] We in Britain have woken up slowly to our need of water. We are only beginning to look at schemes like the Morecambe Bay barrage for storing water in estuaries. We do not yet have a cheap method of taking the salt out of seawater to make it fit for industrial use. As a result we are still struggling with stop-gap schemes like the Croft weir. But it would be stupid, almost criminal, to allow a temporary expedient of this kind to destroy the attractiveness of the Tees at villages like Hurworth, Neasham and Middleton-One-Row. The weir must go to Worsall, not Croft. And one way of ensuring this will be for the people most concerned, the villagers, to make their views heard at today's enquiry.*

## Chapter 5 – Living on the Land

**Flooding of the Tees is a regular event but 21st century flood defences prevent scenes like this one: Gerald Kirkwood is rescued from Croft MIll, unsure of the date.**

The Echo gave detailed coverage of the inquiry. On day one, there is a picture of a bus-load of villagers who had turned up at County Hall, Northallerton, to show solidarity. The newspaper reports that much of the evidence was detailed and technical, so the former must have had a dull day. At the end of the three days the paper noted that no-one from ICI had bothered to turn up.

While awaiting the inquiry decision Bert felt the strain of responsibility on him to make the argument. On 31 October 1966 he wrote to Richard Crossman, the Minister of Housing and Local Government. He wrote that 'I have been troubled for some time because I feel that I did not adequately represent the residents of Croft … I hope therefore that I may be allowed at this late time to stress the points I should have made.' And he makes his points very articulately, noting that 'the people of Croft, rightly or wrongly, regard the River Tees as "ours", and resent most strongly any reduction in the flow of water'.

The *Northern Despatch* lead with the following, on 27 February 1967: 'The Croft weir decision has been taken: it is a wrong decision. A stretch of river from Croft to Yarm is to be destroyed.'

The inquiry decision had not gone Croft's way. The Despatch noted that the case for the decision was full of holes, and focussed on the plea from one of the Minister's own Inspectors that the weir should only go ahead if the case was overriding. They argued that it wasn't, rather 'It is a sad story of cynicism, ignorance and sheer incompetence: it is a terrible indictment of the planning machinery and a victory for "Big Brother knows best".'

However, the villagers were not giving in. An appeal was made to the High Court in Kit Chaytor's name as the local landowner. It was registered as *Chaytor v Minister of Housing & Local Government*. But the appeal was never heard. On 25 October 1967 the Tees Valley and Cleveland Water Board's solicitors wrote to those representing Croft: Latimer, Hines, Marsham and Little of Priestgate, Darlington. The Water Board had decided to withdraw the plan for a weir at Croft to avoid the expense of litigation. The villagers had won.

The weir was never built. And the water board learnt its lesson. In 1974 there was another scheme – Blackwell Pumping Station – that also aroused great concern in Croft. At that point the Northumbrian Water Board said that would not repeat the mistakes in communication and consultation of the past. Again Bert Coates attended a public inquiry on the Pumping Station and gave clear arguments about the despoliation of the river downstream. In his statement he quoted the foreword to a book called *Tomorrow's Countryside* by Garth Christian. The foreword was written by Prince Philip, Duke of Edinburgh: 'The process of development is virtually irreversible, which means that we cannot afford to let things happen by chance or accident, only to be regretted later'.

This time Croft was not successful. In May 1975, the order to proceed with Blackwell Pumping Station was given by the government.

The Croft weir story is a good example of what local people can do when they feel strongly enough about something. The people of Croft did indeed feel that the River Tees was 'ours'. They had a sense of the natural order of things and serving industrialists by tampering with the river's ecosystem didn't sit well with them. The River Tees is essential to Croft's identity, even though the river also wreaks its havoc from time to time. Establishing the name Croft-on-Tees was entirely apposite.

*Chapter 5 – Living on the Land*

# Field sports

> *My father was an enthusiastic and skilled shot and fisherman, as that was how he had spent his childhood at Riding Mill on the Tyne. On one occasion, his sister (my Aunt Clare) had poked fun at her brothers Kit and Drewett, who enjoyed much of their time fishing and shooting, commenting 'It's a lovely day today. Let's go out and kill something'.*
> [From Bill Chaytor's memoir, with permission]

As a rural parish, it is inevitable that 'country sports' or 'field sports' played a significant role in Croft, particularly in the earlier part of the twentieth century. Sometimes this was because Croft residents participated in those sports, sometimes because they depended on those sports for a living and often because those sports were a very visible and occasionally intrusive part of living on the land. Although I have lived in the country about half of my life, I write this section with some trepidation. I have no interest in field sports as a practitioner either actual or potential. Field sports interest me as part of social history. I know little about them other than what I have read in books or observed as an outsider. I'm aware that these sports have traditions and a language especially for them. I apologise in advance for any ignorance I display.

Anyone living in Croft in 1930, who was interested in field sports, had a wide range of wildlife to go after. Salmon had been known in the Tees before World War 1 but I'm unsure there were any later on in the century. There would certainly have been trout and coarse fish to catch. Hare hunting was still a thing, and you could follow the Croft Beagles, on foot, for that. There was a pack of otter hounds, the Croft Otter Hounds, in the Thirties. Pheasant were readily available to shoot throughout the period. I have not heard of any duck shooting but I guess that would have been possible on the lakes around Halnaby Hall and Clervaux Castle. If you were friends with Captain Parlour it would have been easy enough to set up a day on the grouse moors. Of course there was fox hunting. And these were just the main sports.

Most of the first hand accounts of field sports in Croft parish come from written sources. One such source is Chapman Pincher's autobiography *Pastoral Symphony*. We've met Mr Pincher in the previous sections. He does not write a great deal about Croft but it is clear that being in Croft as a youngster formed his love of the outdoors, natural history and country sports.

> *Going to live in Croft* [as a 10 year old] *was a mutation moment in my life. Most of us, probably all, can pinpoint a few moments which have proved decisive in changing the course of our existence. While the landlord* [of The Comet] *and his wife, my beloved parents, slaved long hours for scant reward, life as a landlord's son was one long round of pleasure with a continuous flow of invitations – 'Come on, ferreting!', 'Come on, rook shooting' There were sudden summonses* ▶

*to harvest shoots when the last quarter of an acre of a cornfield being reaped would be literally shaking with rabbits.*

*I confess that I followed the local otter hounds which, though shaming now, was quite 'natural' for a country boy when otters were common enough. The hounds never killed while I was there and I gave up following them after I watched a pair of otters repeatedly sliding down a mud path while I was fishing.*

*My greatest joy arose from an old man who was in charge of three miles of fishing starting almost at the pub [The Comet] doorstep. He gave me sole run of the river which was stuffed with trout and coarse fish.* [14]

I came across an undated, unsourced, newspaper article by a man called Stan Eden. It looks, from the typeface, to have been written in the 1960s or maybe 70s. It was an account of his life as a boy in Croft in the 1930s. He says:

*Where the Spa beck joins the Tees we watched otters playing in the river, and were relieved later to see these delightful creatures safe and sound after the otter hounds had passed. I suppose otters took their toll of fish – and I remember seeing the occasional salmon – but alas otters and salmon are no more.*

*Also hunting in the area were Croft Beagles, controlled by the Inness brothers. In their green jackets and cream breeches: a fine sight on a frosty winter morning. Somehow the ethics of hunting were rarely raised in those days. The Inness family ran a market garden at Monkend, where we picked gooseberries for a shilling a day. The stomach ache was free!*

On 16 April 1932, the *Yorkshire Post* reported:

*Mr Charles Peat, MP for Darlington, has accepted the presidency of the Croft Beagles, and Mr Charles Cayley, of Croft, is to continue as Master. Tom Watson, who has been whipper-in to the Northern Counties Otter Hounds, has been engaged as kennel huntsman. The Hunt has ten and a half couples of hounds, and it is hoped to start next season with twelve couples.*

The latest reference to the Croft Beagles I have seen was dated 3 August in the *Leeds Mercury*. It was reported that, at the Beagle Hound Show, Croft Beagles had won the award for best beagle.

I haven't been able to find out a great deal about the Croft Otter Hounds except that they existed in the thirties and that I have not seen a reference to them after World War 2. The otter hounds were followed on foot and the expectation was that followers would enter the river, so otter hunting usually took place in the summer months. Otter hunting was one of the field sports that declined very quickly in our period, not least because there was a growing public feeling that it was wrong. In 1949

## Chapter 5 – Living on the Land

a Parliamentary Bill was presented to the House of Commons proposing a ban on the hunting with dogs of deer, otter and badgers. It did not succeed, but from then on there was a great deal of scientific study on the effect of otters on fish stocks and the effect of hunting on them. Many concluded that otter hunting was both unnecessary and cruel. The Conservation of Wild Creatures and Wild Plants Act 1975 made otters a protected species and, in 1977, otter hunting was suspended.[15] And just to finish, Mr Eden was wrong when he said otters had gone from the Tees. Today, in 2023, they can be spotted from Croft Bridge, playing at the edges of one of the river islands.

*Country Life* ran an article on 29 December 1934 on the Croft Beagles. It was a jokey sort of piece and didn't tell you much about the Beagles at all, but there were two pictures of the Beagles – one of them at Newbus Grange near Neasham. The implication is that the dogs were kept at Gainford. The point of beagling is that the 'master' and other hunters follow the dogs on foot, and they are usually after hares (maybe rabbits). The sport is not the same as 'hare coursing' I believe. Green jackets and cream jodhpurs are the traditional outfit worn by the Master and other hunt officials and the beagle pack is not usually more than a couple of dozen dogs. Or so I have read. On 4 February 1938 the *Yorkshire Post* reported that the Croft Beagles were still in existence but that their future was rather uncertain. It said that the sporting artist Lionel Edwards was to paint them – this was the case, and you can still buy a print of the work online. However, I have not seen any mention of them post-World War 2.

The predominant sports pursued by the residents of Croft parish through our period were shooting and fishing.

Fishing on the River Tees at Croft was, and is, an established part of life for a great many people in the local area. Clubs like the Darlington Brown Trout Angling Association, Darlington Angling Club and the Thornaby Angling Association were regular features throughout the period covered by this book and they were able to secure specific fishing spots for their members by negotiation with the Croft Estate. Both held regular competitions at Croft. The Croft Estate owned (and owns) the whole of the Tees riverbank within Croft parish. They have also been at pains to preserve their rights over the riverbank whenever they have sold land on it. For example, when William Parlour Senior bought the land for Waterside in 1914, which includes the river bank, the indenture[16] stated that there were two reservations on tenure of the land. One was that the riverbed itself, out as far as the county boundary belonged to the Vendor (the Croft Estate); the second was that 'sole and exclusive right and liberty of fishing in the River Tees' also belongs to the Vendor. It was not at all uncommon in this period for estates to protect 'sporting rights' on any land they sold. However, when Bill Chaytor sold the plots north of Waterside, all along the river bank up to what is now Mole End, he did not put such reservations in the deeds about fishing: however he did put in that the river bed belonged to the Croft Estate.[17]

It is very clear from newspaper reports that salmon were available in the River Tees around Croft in Edwardian times and I saw a newspaper report about the flood of 1934 bringing a 16lb salmon onto the riverbank at Croft. But in our period of examination, as today, the major prize in the Tees was the brown trout.

It is worth mentioning at this point that Alfred Henry Chaytor was a renowned fisherman. He wrote a classic book called *Letters to a Salmon Fisher's Sons* published in 1910.[18] The book is addressed to Drewett and Kit and contains a wonderful photo of both as young boys with rods, straw hats and an array of their father's catch, on page 123. AH Chaytor also owned lands bordering the River Tyne at Riding Mill in Northumberland and that is where he liked to fish for salmon, as well as on the great salmon rivers in Scotland of course. In chapter 1 he explains that trout fishing is the basis from which you learn to fish for salmon:

> *We most of us begin as trout fishers, and after a season or two of salmon fishing we feel that we know all about it, and that there is really not much to be learnt by any decent trout fisher. But a large experience brings doubts. We find that in low waters and in the worst conditions some men can regularly catch fish, whilst everyone else on the river is doing nothing. [...] the difference between a merely ordinary fisher is just as great in salmon fishing as it is in trouting.*

I have seen no written evidence that Alfred fished for trout on the Tees at Croft. He was not in Croft long – less than nine years – but you would think that he must have done.

One issue that anglers always faced at Croft was pollution. Specifically, pollution below the Skerne which brought down sewage and industrial pollution on a scale that would never have entered the Tees naturally. The story about Croft Weir above explains all of this. But before the weir was thought about, anglers were complaining about pollution in the river. In fact, there were major enquiries on the topic of the Skerne polluting the Tees in the mid nineteenth century so the issue was not new. In July 1869 Reverend Frederick Henry Law, Rector of Croft, wrote to the Home Secretary complaining about the pollution and the smell from the 'noxious effluvia' of the Skerne, asking if Darlington could be compelled to send their sewage elsewhere.[19] Reverend Law's letter, along with similar complaints from worthies in Hurworth and Neasham, instigated a public enquiry into pollution coming from the Skerne. At this point in history there was great concern about human disease as Darlington had had a cholera outbreak in 1853 and isolated incidences of cholera were still being reported at this time. But it wasn't only that: the effect on river flora and fauna was also a great concern. It seems to have been a concern that persisted through the twentieth century. Even though Darlington put in measures to decrease the pollution in Victorian times, I found a report from 1958 of the Thornaby Angling Association's annual competition at Croft where it was stated: *Although there was little water in the river, it was dirty and weights were feared to be low.*[20] Fish were caught however, all roach.

I stumbled across a lovely piece by the Angling correspondent of the The Times.[21] It vividly evokes the joys of fishing at Croft. The author had been brought up near Darlington and had many childhood memories of fishing on the Tees. He had been exchanging memories with Chapman Pincher. The latter's first fish was a dab, the former's a gudgeon, both caught on the Hurworth side, just below the Skerne. Both agreed that fishing was never quite the same after the river was re-routed.

Bill Chaytor says in his memoir that the Clow Beck had also offered good trout fishing in his life time at Croft.

*Chapter 5 – Living on the Land*

**Fisherman clearing the Clow Beck of coarse fish (Hoping to catch trout). The picture is dated 1962.**

*Another fishing scene was playing out on the Clow Beck, which had been excellent fishing when I first came to Croft [in 1965]. Partly because of the increasing floods and low flows caused by land drainage upstream and also the increase of shady backside vegetation which was not cut back [...] the trout population plummeted and was replaced by various coarse fish.*[22]

By contrast, the land around Croft was copiously primed for pheasant shooting. Both Croft and Halnaby estates had gamekeepers who were primarily occupied in the rearing of chicks for the sport and the maintenance of whins and other land that made the sport doable and fun. They would have had labourers to help with that and a retinue of beaters, usually farmer's sons and other farm lads, for shooting days. The last gamekeeper at Halnaby was Harry Dimmock who had arrived at Halnaby at some point after 1921 (he's an unemployed gamekeeper at Dalton near Richmond in the 1921 census. Previous censuses show him employed at Dalton Hall where his father was the gamekeeper before him). He was able to buy Keeper's Cottage with Pheasantry (where he would have reared chicks) in the Halnaby estate sale and the indenture dated 6 March 1950 states that he paid £1250 for it. The picture of Lady Wilson-Todd's shooting party pictures Harry and his son George. George was born in 1912 and also became a gamekeeper. In the 1939 Register he was a 'Gamekeeper & Rabbit Catcher' living at Thimbleby near Northallerton. Harry, born at Dalton in 1887, died on 19 April 1982 and is buried in Croft churchyard. What happened with regard to shooting and hunting rights after the demise of the Halnaby estate I do not know.

I don't have a full record of the gamekeepers at the Croft Estate. In the the 1939 Register the gamekeeper is listed as John Davison, born 1898, and he is resident at Newtown. At that stage there were several cottages at Newtown and also a woodyard. Much of Newtown was demolished in the sixties

A shooting party on the Halnaby Estate 1939. L to R: George Hume (later Cardinal Basil Hume), Madeline Hume, Lady Catherine Wilson-Todd, Sir William Errington Hume (Lady Wilson-Todd's physician), Harry Dimmock (Halnaby gamekeeper), George Dimmock (Harry's son)).

I believe, during Bill Chaytor's rationalisation of the Croft Estate (see above). In 1967 John Stoddard arrived and at first he lived in a caravan at the then demolished Clervaux Castle. The remaining tower and associated building was converted a bit later to make a gamekeeper's cottage and it is the gamekeeper's residence to this day. The woods around Clervaux are out of bounds for the public and as such make a good place to rear pheasants. John Stoddard died in 2020 after a lifetime on the estate.

Both Kit Chaytor and Captain Parlour were keen shooting men, and of course they had a lot to do with one another in terms of affairs in the village. They were both churchwardens, both councillors at one time or another, and both on the school management committee. Their camaraderie around the sport of shooting was a bonus and it's clear that Kit was invited to shoot on Captain Parlour's Weardale and Swaledale moors and that Captain Parlour was invited to shoot on the Croft Estate.

Captain Will Parlour was a biggish cheese in the local world of shooting. He had built up his ownership of grouse moors over many years and he was a sociable host. He held shoots on many moors in England and Scotland but these were the moors he owned, as listed in 1971:

| | |
|---|---|
| Summer Lodge Moor, | Swaledale |
| Hunstanworth Moor, Co. | Durham |
| Nookton Moor, Co. | Durham |
| Newbiggin Moor, | Northumberland |

This listing also notes that 'Later on the moors are driven, and in 1971 over 2,000 brace of grouse were accounted for on his moors'.[23] I'm not quite sure what 'accounted for' means here. Does it mean

## Chapter 5 – Living on the Land

Captain Parlour had grouse moors in Weardale and also owned a summer house near Hamsterley. Here he is with Gladys Parlour (right) and Betty Town at that location. Date is early 1970s.

This picture from around 1951 appeared in the press after the latest successes for the champion Sharnberry Setters. Captain Parlour (right) is with Betty Knight (later Town) his dog trainer and handler. The dogs are clearly very happy.

'shot'? However, Captain Parlour's big love was gun dogs. English setters to be precise. He used his home at Monkend Hall to breed them and the strain became well known and sought after. The 'Sharnberry English Setters' they were known as. These were champion dogs with whom Captain Parlour was successful both at dog shows and setter trials up and down the country. He had a dog handler, Miss Betty Knight, (who became Betty Town on her marriage). The name 'Sharnberry' came from Sharnberry Gill and area near Hamsterley, Weardale, where Captain Parlour owned moors and also a summer cottage.

**Sandra Veerman** remembers the dogs when she was a child at Monkend Hall:'

*"I particularly was involved with the the setters, the English setters. From very little. If I went missing, I was usually in the kennels with the dogs. The kennels were at the top of the back drive. The old stables was where the whelping was – you know, when they have pups. They were taken in and Dad used to say to me, 'shh you can come and look but don't talk, be quiet, don't upset the mother'. And I used to peer over. So that was a really lovely time."*

## Chapter 5 – Living on the Land

It may be of interest that when The Mill Race development was built opposite the entrance to Monkend Hall in mid 1989, Richmondshire District Council proposed the name 'Sharnberry Court' for it. Presumably as a reference to to Captain Parlour's famous kennels. The Parish Council were not in favour, asking that it be called Monkend something.

Sandra also had a story about the relative priorities of shooting and babies in the summer of 1947, which was a very hot summer and a noted one for grouse shooting. Her mother, Mrs Gladys Green, was expecting her older brother but had been working all day at the Hall in that August.

**Sandra**:

John Green Senior holds the shotgun, John Green Jnr carries the game bag on the front drive at Monkend Hall. Ca 1950.

*"That morning when Trevor was on the way she was still separating milk because in middle of shooting season everything had got to be in cream and whatever. Then Mrs Parlour took her to the maternity hospital. So she had Trevor and obviously Dad had been away all day with the Captain and Mrs Town shooting. And Captain Parlour said, 'well, we can't go straight home, we have to go and see this baby'. And of course visiting was long over and the matron said 'you can't come in currently, visiting hours are over'. And Captain Parlour – mum said she was mortified, she wanted to go under the sheets – he was a loud, bustling man. He said 'We have to see this baby and nobody is going to stop us. Come on, Green' He never said Mr. Green. It was always 'Green' to Dad. And they marched onto the ward to see Trevor. And they'd had a bumper day and mum said they were all red and sweaty and Dad was mortified too because he wasn't a pushy man, Dad."*

When David Kellie-Smith became established in London in the 1960s he rarely came back to Croft. However, he said, if shooting was on the cards, it would be worth the long journey. It seems his enthusiasm was shared by a good many people then, and it still is.

**Bill Chaytor** was one person who was not so enthusiastic:

*"... my enthusiasm for environmental conservation grew steadily and as years passed, I found my enjoyment of shoots, particularly big bag ones, was fading so I let our shoot to a succession of two or three neighbours from the mid eighties to the mid nineties. John Stoddard ran the days with those gents and I think their rent covered most of his salary."*

# Fox Hunting

In the period before the first world war, the practice of fox hunting was completely endemic in English rural life. If you were of a certain class and were known as a good rider, you would expect to go hunting. The Croft Spa Hotel, right up to World War2, advertised itself as a place where you could stable your own hunters and enjoy riding with the Zetland or Hurworth Hunts several times a week. Such was the popularity of the sport that the *Yorkshire Post* carried weekly reports on the county's hunts. Croft featured from time to time and you would have been likely to read something like this (this one from 4 February 1939):

> *The Zetland had capital sport on Thursday after meeting at Barton. A fox found in Allen's Whin ran on a small circle to Jolby Farm and coming back to Allen's Whin was killed. The pack going straight on with another fox ran by Bullmire to the Croft road and hunting slowly back to Allen's Whin afresh, found the fox and ran nearly to the Black Plantation when scent failed after a hunt of an hour, fast at times. Finding at Clervaux Castle Wood the pack crossed the Jolby Lane and the Clow Beck and with Stapleton Whin on the left ran down to the river at Blackwell, and coming back across the Great North Road, hunted slowly nearly to High House and bending left handed to Cleasby Grange recrossed the Great North Road and we're run out of scent at Jolby Manor, after a hunt of 80 minutes. Finding the Bungalow Covert hounds ran fast with Inkle on the left through Middleton Lodge covert and parallel with the Great North Road with Barton and Allen's Whin both on the left and crossing the Croft road by the lodge at Halnaby ran with Forty Acres just on the right also Birch Carr and Walmire and Stranborough on the left re-crossed the Croft road. The pack, with Clervaux Castle Wood on the left went over Jolby Lane and the Clow Beck and running between Monkend and Stapleton Whin ran from scent to view near Stapleton Lodge and raced down the river at Blackwell. The fox crossing the river, some delay occurred and he was lost on the riverbanks on the other side. This was a very good hunt of an hour and 20 minutes.*

However, in 1924 the League Against Cruel Sports had been formed, to fight for the abolition of fox hunting, otter hunting and hare coursing, and any other activity that treated the pursuit and killing of wild animals as 'sport'. As our period progressed, public opinion nationally became more critical of these pursuits too and by the post-war period this had reached a height as part of the general questioning of the 'old order' and the drive for a new, modern, Britain. At the annual meeting of the Zetland Hunt subscribers in Darlington on 10 November 1947, Lord Zetland himself noted that 'We are living in times in which we cannot regard hunting as a pastime for pure enjoyment and health, but we can serve a useful purpose by killing foxes to help agriculture.' [24] The Hunt Saboteurs Association was formed in 1963. On 9 April 1964 the *Newcastle Journal* noted that the Zetland had been told they would be prosecuted if they were found on Durham County Council land under the headline 'A Warning for the Tally-ho Trespassers'. In 1972, the Queen was asked to step down as a president of the RSPCA after Princess Anne was found to have ridden with the Zetland on a visit to the North Riding, her first experience of fox-hunting.

However, there was still plenty of hunting in Croft parish throughout the twentieth century, with the same hunts, the Zetland and the Hurworth. The fox coverts still existed and the hunts paid rates on them for 'sporting rights', the preservation of land primarily for the purpose of field sports – sometimes for rearing game birds, sometimes for the maintenance of coverts that attracted foxes to make dens. This is shown in the council Rate Books. But there were no fox hunts *based* in Croft in 1930 and local people had limited involvement in it, as far as I can see. The Chaytors were not hunting people, although Kit Chaytor's wife Rachel, who had been a Pease before she married, had always been a keen hunter. Sir William Pierrepont Wilson-Todd, second baronet of Halnaby, rode with the Zetland Hunt until he died in 1925 and before that, when he lived at Leases Hall near Bedale, he became Master of the Bedale Hunt[25] Mary Andrew had a painting of the Zetland outside Aske Hall which includes Sir William. Lady Wilson-Todd mentions a painting of her and her husband 'on hunters' in her will. But I don't know of many others, I'm sure there were some. Only one person interviewed for this book talked about going hunting. Doris talked about the hunt crossing her land.

However, Ann Reed was a keen rider as a child in the 1940s. Her uncle was involved in Turnbull's Stud Farm which occupied the field at the side of the Croft Spa Hotel and the Terrace, and that's where she kept her black pony, Dolly. She rode with the Zetland Hunt many times although she pointed out that she was 'hoi polloi' in jeans and sweater where the master and other well-to-do riders would be in their 'glory'. But she started young, and was committed.

**Ann Reed (Carnelly):**

*"I became a proper huntswoman when I was blooded and that was the most horrific day for a child of anything. I was eight and my brother George was twelve. [So this was about 1948]. I believe the fox enjoys it as much as the hounds, outwitting them, and he was outwitting them on this day. And you know the bend as you go round, and there's the lodges for Halnaby Hall, well it appeared there just on the other side of the road and it had gone to earth in a drain.*

*And the hounds couldn't get it so they sent to the farm for the terriers. And they couldn't get it, so they sent for poles and poked it out and fed it to the hounds. And then they cut the pads off and rubbed them on our faces. That was blooding us."*

But it does not follow that every country person supports fox hunting. We'll leave the last word to Doris Cameron. This is from a conversation we had in her farmhouse kitchen:

**Doris:**

*"So you could walk from here* [Vince Moor West] *to Halnaby Hall because it was all estate land, and hunting land. 'Cos the hunt used to come around, you know, the hunt comes round now, but they get played tiddly-pom from me. They're frightened* [both laugh]. *Angela Vaux, I can remember she was coming up here with the* [Zetland] *hunt, and she came up this road with the hunt, you see it's a bridleway, and we had some bales over there. This is Angela, she's still there now,*

*and she still gives me a weak smile. And they chased the fox up into the bales. So I saw them, and my sons were down the pigs hiding 'cos they saw me fly out of the house. [...] And the hounds were there, they were all sitting, you know, and the horses watching, and the poor fox was in the bales. So I said,* [bangs table] *'Right, what are you doing?' She says* [putting on polite voice], *'Well the fox has had a very good run, and he's in the bales now, so we're going to leave him and let him have a rest.' So she went* [laughs]. *So I shifted, 'cos I don't believe in killing foxes"*

### Endnotes

1. From The Real Agricultural Revolution. *The transformation of English farming 1939 to 1985* by Paul Brassley, David Harvey, Matt Lobley and Michael Winter, page 1.
2. *Calendar of the Patent Rolls Preserved in the Public Record Office*, 1354-1358 Edward III v.10. p329. The entry for 29 December 1355 express concern that the bridge has been damaged by flood and grants pontage – a fee for crossing the bridge – to Croft to pay for repairs
3. Further analysis and references for yet further reading on the general success or failure of the CWAECs can be found in *The Real Agricultural Revolution*, 'Agricultural Policy 1939-45' p 92.
4. All surveys are in TNA under MAF/68 North Riding.Parish agricultural land = 4300 acres approx
   "Poultry" = chickens, turkeys, geese, ducks et al
   "Grass" = temporary and permanent, for mowing and for pasture
   "Fruit & Veg" includes vegetables and fruit for human consumption including potatoes (and orchards)
   "Other" = any other crop not already counted e.g. turnips, flax, corn
   All land use in acres
5. "Specialisation and Expansion" in *The Real Agricultural Revolution*, p 204.
6. There's another article on the Mill in the *Northern Despatch* on 23 August 1937, and coverage of the search for a buyer for the Mill – with more about Mr Adamson – in the *Evening Despatch* on 30 September 1972.
7. *Pastoral Symphony*, Chapter1 p15.
8. All Details from the NRRD
9. Alfred Henry Chaytor, *Essays Sporting and Serious*, Methuen, 1930.
10. *Essays Sporting and Serious*, p 135.
11. Bill Chaytor, *Coverdale to Croft*, privately published and distributed, 2020, p159.
12. *"Coverdale to Croft"*, p 138.
13. 29 December 1355, in *Calendar of the Patent Rolls Preserved in the Public Record Office, 1354-1358 Edward III*, volume 100 p 329. This work is available on the Hathi Trust website: https://babel.hathitrust.org
14. *Pastoral Symphony*, page 14-15
15. Charles Watkins, David Matless and Paul Merchant, "Science, sport and the otter, 1945-78" in *Our hunting fathers: field sports in England after 1850* edited by R.W. Hoyle, Carnegie, 2007
16. NRRD, Vol 260, p 827, #290
17. I have checked this in NRRD.
18. Alfred Henry Chaytor, *Letters to a Salmon Fisher's Sons*, Flyfishers' Classic Library, 1992. First published by John Murray in 1910.
19. TNA, MH 13/59/530 Folio 632
20. *Hartlepool Northern Daily Mail*, 16 July 1958
21. https://www.thetimes.co.uk/article/hooked-for-life-by-splendour-of-that-gudgeon-dripping-stardust-and-light-s6jms5pjfk2
22. *Coverdale to Croft*, p155.
23. Leaflet on the Sharnberry English Setters shown to me by Sandra Veerman.
24. *Yorkshire Post*, 11 November 1947, front page
25. See Eva Banner's *Halnaby People*

*Chapter 6 – Community Glue*

# CHAPTER 6

# COMMUNITY GLUE

**W**hat makes a place a community? Is it 'facilities', events, pubs, parks, things to do? Is it a bunch of people who support each other? Is it something formally defined and sustained by structures like councils and clubs and associations? It's probably a bit of all of those but also something a bit intangible. Georgie Sale once called that intangible 'community glue' and that's a brilliant way of putting it. It's the *je ne sais quoi* that makes it all come together. A combination of people, places, structures and events.

In this last chapter I'm celebrating community glue, listening to what our Croft voices have to say about it and telling the story of some of places and people that did the glueing. It's a joyous story, of people coming together, of others giving up time and energy to organise things and to care for neighbours who needed a hand. There are so many people who were community gluers, I can't mention them all. I hope everyone feels acknowledged by association.

## Meet you where?

The first thing a community needs is a meeting place, and Croft had several sorts of meeting places before it finally got a Village Hall in 1986.

In the earlier history of Croft these places would have been The Comet and the Croft Spa Hotel. The Comet dates from the 1840's, the hotel from long before that. For 100 years, from the building of the ballroom and extension and renaming of the 'Croft Spa Hotel' from having been a simple coaching inn, the Croft Spa Hotel was the place where many things happened in the village. Auction sales, wakes, hunts, balls and major community celebrations, like George V's Coronation in 1911, were all moments when the Hotel stood at the heart of community activity.

In the period 1930 to 1990 however, the Hotel fell from grace somewhat with local people. It's interesting to consider how. In 1930, the hotel had just been bought by Mr Ernest Hinde, a retiring director of Hinde's Brewery in Darlington. He'd bought it from Loris and Mary Dingle who had owned it since 1921. Hinde's itself was in the process of being bought by the larger brewery James Deuchars of Monkwearmouth near Sunderland. On 1 August 1935,[1] Ernest Hinde sold the hotel to Deuchars, and from then on in things changed between the hotel and the village.

Mr Hinde's hotel manager was Michael Joseph Du Gay. Sometimes known as Captain Du Gay.

**The outside of the Croft Spa Hotel probably late fifties. Note the sign for the Spa Garage, through the arch.**

When the parish council was busy organising George V's diamond jubilee in May 1935, Mr Du Gay was fulsome in his offer of the hotel for celebrations such as the evening dance with full dinner provided.[2] Unfortunately, after Deuchars took over later in 1935, Mr Du Gay suddenly disappeared leaving debts, and the parish council had to ask Deuchars to pay off his rate arrears, which they agreed to do.

George V may have enjoyed his diamond jubilee but his misfortune was that he died less than a year later in January 1936. Then on 12 May 1937 it was the Coronation of George VI. A point of horror for the organising committee for the village celebrations was that Deuchars did not offer use of the Hotel. A minute for their February meeting states 'It was resolved that a deputation of the Chairman [T.W. Middlemiss, a farm bailiff on the Halnaby Estate I believe], the Clerk [Mr Lawrence Arnett] and Mr CWD Chaytor should wait on Mr Deuchars to point out to him that the Parish had had use of the hotel on such occasions for generations & we hoped that the new owners would follow in footsteps of their predecessors and offer the village the same facilities they had had in the past.' The minutes for April hint at the reception the deputation might have received. It is noted that the tent Mr Deuchars had offered for use by the village would not be required, and that the best that could be done was to get him to give a subscription. (He did: 5 guineas.)

In 1935 the Hotel had ambitions somewhat beyond village Coronation celebrations. It was now in

*Chapter 6 – Community Glue*

**In 1936 the new owners of the Croft Spa Hotel - Deuchars brewery - invested a lot of money in modernisation. Including building the swimming pool. This full page newspaper feature describes the improvements.**

A well-known view of the Croft Spa Hotel swimming pool of the 1930s, from a postcard.

the AA book of hotels and better still, it had received planning permission to exchange the kitchen garden on the south side of the hotel for a swimming pool. And not just any old swimming pool, a very modern art deco 'feature' swimming pool.

The swimming pool opened in June 1936 in a blaze of glory. Unfortunately the glory became tarnished thereafter by practicalities. It was an outdoor swimming pool and could only be used for part of the year. But worse, they had difficulty keeping the water clean. The Rural District Council Sanitary Inspector had multiple trips to the hotel to sample the water and bar the pool's use until an expensive clean-up was performed. These problems become less surprising when you realise that the water for the swimming pool was pumped from the mill stream (not 'spa water' as the article reproduced as the article reproduced on p.197 claims). Nick Kirkwood has confirmed to me that some of the pumping equipment is still on the mill's land. Every year it seems, the hotel pool was closed in the autumn then reopened and relaunched the following summer. It continued with business as usual during 1939 and 1940. Thereafter, wartime seems to have kicked in and I don't think it was used after the war. The thirties buildings were knocked down and the pool was eventually filled in and concreted over.

We've already talked about the hotel's role during the war and the servicemen who would have frequented it in Chapter 3. The hotel continued to be a feature of local life even after this cooling of the relationship in the thirties. However, in 1955 the hotel was put up for sale again. It doesn't seem to have been sold and in 1959 Deuchars was absorbed into Newcastle Breweries, later Scottish and Newcastle

Breweries. In 1973 they set about about modernising – again – the hotel's image. The trouble with the hotel was that the local area did not provide quite enough trade to keep it in a profitable state. It needed to attract visitors from further afield. Before World War 1 the hotel lived off a strong interest in Croft Spa. After World War 1 successive owners targeted the big towns of Teesside and County Durham. The *Sunderland Echo* carried adverts for twice-weekly dinner dances and tea dances throughout the 30s. Excursions to Croft by rail were also a feature. But by the mid 1960s these sorts of things were old hat. So in 1973 Scottish & Newcastle (who owned Thistle Hotels) were marketing the hotel as 'The New Old World of Gracious Living for Gourmets'. Artfully trying to marry tradition with modernity, they offered 'The Hunt Bar', 'The Zetland Lounge' and 'The Hunting Lodge Restaurant'. In the latter 'Old oak beams, wood-panelled walls, silver wine goblets, music from the grand piano and waiters in hunting pink, set the scene for the hospitality of this exclusive restaurant'.[3] I don't now how successful this was but in 1977 S&N sold the hotel to a Mr Hutchinson who bought it for £150,000, and he offered it for sale again in 1983 when it was bought by a Mr & Mrs White-Sansom I believe.

The Hotel continued as a feature in village life, but the relationship was always slightly fractious during the various revamps the hotel underwent. Signage was often an issue. 'Unsuitable' signage, not 'in keeping' with the village, was a continuing complaint. For example, in June 1989, when 'Little Chef' signs appeared outside the front of the hotel to the horror of many. Croft had standards to keep up: they had to go.

## A succession of halls

**Bill Chaytor** remembered:

*"Well, I made the first village hall, Ron Fletcher and I built it. I mean, it was our land, it was family land, I owned it, and Ron said could he build what was really like a great big chicken-house, as the scoutmaster. He had the scoutmaster's one, and then that kind of fell to bits and there was a chap called Smith, Bill Smith, who took one of the new houses that I'd sold off to be built down the Northallerton Road, and he had contacts with the building industry, and he got a site hut. And certainly, it covered the purpose of Ron's scouts. Why we did it – I can't remember – I think there was a youth club there as well, I'm pretty sure they were the purposes, and I helped him with it, and we put that up."*

So this was the genesis of the Scout Hut. The Scout Hut was never a village hall but people remembered it being used for social events. Whist nights were once a week. Ron (Skip) and Doreen Fletcher organised it.

**Cath Wood** went regularly:

*"... we used to play whist or something on one night a week, and we played for about half a dozen eggs and you'd think we were playing for a gold clock, you know. 'Why did you put that down?' 'I don't know, I don't know, I'm just here to play'* [laughs]. [...], *and Doreen* [Fletcher] *was*

*marvellous 'cos she baked cakes for everything. She was one of these people that did trays and trays of cakes, whatever you did, you couldn't imagine anything without her cakes. And she was lovely, and they did very well and they ran this whist, I'm sure they ran other things but I went to the whist because I had a young son and I thought I was supporting the scouts, but in fact they were all grannies (because I was still young then, you know) or people my age playing whist."*

Before the Scout Hut, Croft people went to Hurworth Place for a lot of their social life. Because there was a 'village hall' in Hurworth Road. It is where the Christadelphian Hall is now. That hall was built as a reading room. That's not reading the paper, or magazines, it means reading the bible, but I'm sure other items were available. It was built by Mrs Backhouse of Hurworth Grange, certainly before World War 1 and possibly in the 1900s.[4] The hall was taken on by a private committee of trustees after it was gifted by the Backhouse family in 1950. It remained popular until the early sixties, whereafter Hurworth Grange Community Centre and a decline in general demand left it in an unsustainable state. It was sold in 1975.[5]

**Margaret Horseman** had this memory of that village hall in Hurworth Road:
*"Well, when I was quite young, that was the village hall. So that would be in the 60s 50s. Because when I was sort of 12,11, probably 13, we used to have dancing classes. And Mrs. Raisbeck, McDonald, and Little, they used to do this dancing class on a Friday night at 730. And there was this old gramophone. We were taught, you know, the dashing white sergeant, the waltz, the progressive waltz, those things. And it was in the upstairs room. And I remember Mrs. Raisbeck, she would take some time to show me, but she was such a tall lady, that my feet were off the ground. I've never really got to know the steps because my feet weren't touching the ground."*

By 1976 the Scout Hut wasn't in great repair, and there was a need, once again to look for something that could serve as a proper village hall. At the parish council meeting of 8 September 1976, attended a number of parishioners as well as the council, the dire need for a 'Parish Hall' was discussed. There was a vote on whether such a hall was needed, and the view was yes, and that a steering committee should be set up at the next meeting. The overwhelming favourite was that the Old School, soon to be vacated when the new primary school opened, and still the property of the Church, be used. Canon Littleton explained the costs involved, and these were deemed too expensive. Things went on into 1977 and and the options considered were quite interesting. The parish council had the job of sorting it all out. They considered three options : (1) Repair Dalton Village Hall and join with Dalton (2) Do something to keep the scout hut going (3) convert the disused piggeries, which used to belong to Gerry Andrew, and which were situated along the Stapleton bridleway on the way to Monk End Farm. Doris Cameron quoted £500 to repair Dalton. A quotation of £7,000 had been given to convert the piggeries. The preferred option was to get a grant to improve the scout hut. Something like the latter option must have been progressed as there were no further minutes for seven years and no appearance of any alternatives.

*Chapter 6 – Community Glue*

**In 1986 the bequest of Clare Kellie-Smith enabled Croft to open its own dedicated village hall.**

On 10 July 1985, the parish council minuted that Clare Kellie-Smith's estate would give the requisite amount of money to provide a new village hall for Croft and that the Scout Hut would be demolished. The village hall would be on the same ground already leased by the Croft Estate for the Scout Hut.[6]

**David Kellie-Smith** recalls:

*"If we go back to 1984, which was desperately sad, you probably know my mother killed herself. She was living at Bridge House. She thought she was going mad and hanged herself. And we felt that we had to do something... we didn't want a situation where people in the village felt obliged to cross themselves every time they went past the house. So we had – and it was tremendous fun – we had a sale of virtually everything in the house. Dear Francis Calder organised it. We had a gorgeous day, and we had a charity sale. And we were amazed how much money we raised. It was terrific fun, everybody came along. And I think it kind of it took the sort of ghastly mystique out of the house, where old Mrs. Kellie-Smith went off her nut. And we basically contributed the cost of building the [new village hall], Bill chipped in the land, and Francis Calder did most of the grunt work. And that turned out to be an extraordinary success. And various people including Bill I think recognised it was really necessary. But we were amazed how successful it was and indeed that it lasted at all until, you know, they replaced it last year [2019]."*

The new hall officially opened on 16 February 1986 and this was covered in all the local newspapers.

# Church and community

If you travel towards Darlington on the A167 you cannot miss Croft Church. It faces the road full on as you slow to turn right onto the bridge. It is a striking building of red sandstone with a square tower, largely fifteenth-century in outline but with a history that goes back to before the Norman Conquest. However, that is just a building. The Church as an influence on the social fabric of villages is a different thing. In our period of sixty years there was probably a bigger decline in that influence than at any time in previous history. The Church still had a pull, people wanted it to continue, it offered a stability and continuity with the past. But by 1990, few people saw that this might involve some personal commitment from them and attendance was at its lowest point up to that time.

It's quite difficult to track church attendance because the church attendance books – which are kept by the rector – are very erratic. However, I can tell you that in 1930, when the rector was Harry Tompkins, the average attendance on a Sunday was over 100 people. Every Sunday would have three services, and there were several in the week. For significant Sundays in the Christian calendar the attendance would double or treble. So on the first Sunday in Lent, 205 people, Easter Sunday, 247, Whitsunday 290, Christmas Day 120. The biggest attendance in the year was Harvest Festival. Harvest Festival lasted a full week but at the Sunday Harvest Thanksgiving in 1930, 527 people attended during the day, the majority at the evening service (the population of Croft parish at this time was similar to today, about 450 people). Because figures are missing I don't know what the average attendances in the 1980s were. But where they are recorded it is double figures, sometimes single. Harvest Festival was still a popular service. You'll see below that big occasions involved the church and church services. But a big change had taken place over the sixty years, a national change, where the church as a fixture in day-to-day life had become almost invisible in the popular imagination.

However, in the earlier part of our period it is completely clear that the Church was part of community glue, not just in terms of bringing people together socially but in providing a unity of purpose to help others in the community and take care of people.

Harry Tompkins was rector from 1925 to 1949, and he was not always well thought of. He was not a good administrator and both the school and the church had some work to do to put things right after he left. Ian Dougill described him as a 'Carry on Vicar' character, old-fashioned and slightly comical to a young man of that time. Reverend Tompkins was succeeded by Edward Charlesworth in 1949, a man who cast quite an influence in his ten years in the job. Reverend Charlesworth and his wife worked hard to build up social inclusion in the church. Rev Charlesworth started the Scouts and Mrs Charlesworth started the Young Wives Club. Sunday School was a feature of many lives and those to be married were invited to evenings of discussion about what married life should be. But the one thing the Charlesworths did not have at their disposal was any church hall or meeting place. There has never been one. But this did not stop Edward Charlesworth from encouraging people to 'come in' to the church with any issue they wanted help with. From his temporary home at 2 Richmond Terrace – temporary because the Rectory refurbishments were not finished – in November 1949, he wrote to his parishioners:

## Chapter 6 – Community Glue

**The Young Wives Club was started in the 1950s by Mrs Charlesworth. Here they are enjoying a day out.**

*My dear people, I hope you will all note the above address. Due to the kindness of Mr. CWD Chaytor it has been made possible for me to use this house as a temporary Rectory and I am indeed grateful to him for his thoughtfulness and generosity. For you now have a Rectory and I hope sincerely you are going to use it. It has always been in my mind that as the Parish Church is a spiritual home of the Parish, so the Rectory should be the 'open home' where members of the Parish can 'drop in' freely, not only to meet their Parish Priest and his family, but also their friends. The Rectory cannot be run like an office or a surgery be special times for business and appointments. And I think it would be rather stupid for any priest to try and run it on such lines. Rather it surely must be the 'resting house', the 'meeting house', the house which is open to all and I can assure you that all will be welcome at any time convenient to the caller. But it will be up to you to use the house and make it your duty to feel at liberty to call. I shall also now have a greater opportunity to perform my duties of visiting and to get to know more of you. It's a great blessing to be living on the spot.*

Rev Charlesworth's commitment to making the church inclusive for everyone extended to establishment of a church at the temporary housing site at Cockleberry – St Thomas's.

Parishioners remember participation in the Church as a key part of village life and Reverend Charlesworth was a well loved and well respected Rector. He worked hard to bring strong values of care and justice to everyone; he wanted to bring people together in community. I write about Sunday School in Chapter 2. But there were also Church fetes and Church outings. The Church fete was usually held at Monkend Hall and, of course, took place in high summer. Outings were more irregular, but popular. The Church Fete was an annual fixture that continued well into the 21st century. But perhaps these trips and social dos incentivised behaviour not entirely driven by interest in religiosity.

**Janet Mackenzie**:

*"You're going to think I'm awful. If there was a trip going from the church I went to the church. And if there was a trip going from the Methodist church* [in Hurworth Place] *I went to the Methodists. We just went to Redcar or somewhere like that."*

After Rev Charlesworth left in 1959, to take on the depressed parish of Liverton Mines, and then at Kimberley in South Africa there were two further rectors in our period: first, Richard Cooper and then Nick Horton.

# Shopping and stopping

Throughout this book we've come across the impact of the motor car on lives in the mid-twentieth century. The car is one of the biggest differentiators between the 1930s and the 1980s. There has always been public transport and many people interviewed were brought up using buses and trains. The upper middle and upper classes may have had cars in the 1930s or 40s. But the ownership of private cars by the average citizen only really started to happen in the 1950s, grew during the 60s and became the norm by 1990. Private travel in your own motor car undoubtedly meant that you could seek entertainment beyond your local community and also shop further afield. Shopping further afield meant more choice but also less possibility of meeting and talking with neighbours. Cars were a kind of solvent to community glue in these respects.

**A bus waits opposite The Comet Hotel on Tees View ca. 1960. Note the shops on the opposite side of the road.**

In the first half of our period, however, most people shopped locally in Hurworth Place. Croft did not have any shops after Richard Row's shop on Richmond Terrace closed, and I believe this was around the time of World War 1. There was a good variety of shops in Hurworth Place.

**Janet McKenzie** hand memories of 50s and 60s:

*"What is the paper shop now that was a sweet shop, at the left of it that was the post office. Where the club is on the corner of the office, that was a butcher's. Then there was the Undertaker's that was Bill and George Richardson [...] just before the houses. The first house was the hairdresser's, Bissell. And on the left, before you got up the bank was a shop on the right. Was it an off-licence? [...] On the left hand side before you go up the railway bridge, that was the grocery shop. The house opposite, next to the station, that was the off licence. Then you went halfway up the bank. And on the right, down some steps, was a woolshop, and embroidery. And then you went the top of the bank, next to that was it another little shop. I can't remember what was in that. Then there was Hardens the butchers. And then opposite Oxford Garage, where there's a hairdressers now, that was the Co-op."*

Margaret Chapman's memories concur with Janet's although hers were a decade previous and she noted that her mother rarely went to Darlington to shop. Maybe on a Saturday. And that only a handful of people on South Parade had cars. The grocer on the corner opposite the station was Richard Raw. The Co-op did deliveries. Milk was delivered by Thornton's who had the small dairy farm on Northallerton Road and John Thornton came round on a horse and cart. There was also a greengrocer came round with a horse and covered cart.

Cath Wood had a shop in Hurworth Place on Hurworth Road, where the Co-op was in Janet's description. She ran the downstairs as a hairdresser (hiring in hairdressers, not doing the work herself) and upstairs she had a baby clothes, wool, and lingerie shop. It put her in the most marvellous position to know what was going on, and a wide range of people shopped there. Cath had this reflection on why the shops disappeared:

**Cath Wood**:

*"Well I think the problem was most people by then [1960s] ... supermarkets were here, more people had cars, and you know, this is what did for my shop really, that they could go into Darlington Market. Of course I lived opposite the bus stop. I mean it was marvellous, I just had to go out the back door and I was on the bus, you know, and this sort of thing, so I used to go to Darlington nearly every other day, because I had a pushchair and a little one, so I could only manage to carry a basket. I had to get it all on and off the bus, so I could only carry enough for a couple of days at a time, and then we started, Mike started, taking me [in the car] on a Saturday, and we used to go to [Safeway's at] Cockerton first, that was about the first supermarket I think."*

Chris Lloyd has written a full article on the shops of Hurworth Place in his Echo Memories column.[7] By the 1980s there were few shops in Hurworth Place. There was still a Post Office on Tees View, but if you wanted anything serious you got in your car.

# For Crown and Country

Croft was no different to any other village in the country when it came to royal occasions and national celebrations. They were keen to celebrate, not least because, for royal occasions, they usually had a day's extra holiday.

I have already talked about George V's Silver Jubilee in the section on the hotel above. On 22 February 1935 a special committee of the Parish Council met to plan the celebrations which were to take place on 6 May. The cost of the celebrations would be met by 'subscriptions', I.e. contributions from those who were wiling and/or able to contribute. Hurworth Place and Dalton had been invited to participate but were doing their own thing. Lady Wilson-Todd offered to buy a jubilee mug for every child at the school. Captain Du Gay offered a tea and a dance at the Hotel. Monkend Hall was offered for sports and prize-giving. CWD Chaytor would pay for tea for all children. After a church service at 10.30 am the events would begin. In the late afternoon there would be a Whist Drive. Cliff Smith's band was booked for an evening dance at the hotel. £8 5/4 profit was made and was split between the Prince of Wales Jubilee Trust and the Croft & Hurworth Nursing Association.

The Celebration Committee for George VI's coronation was formed February 1937. Events were similar to those planned for the Jubilee just two years previous. The school was used for teas, with the WI organising. Tea was ham & tongue sandwiches. Mr Arnett was the main organiser.

There wasn't a lot of scope for big celebrations in the war years. Strangely I cannot find anything about VE or VJ Day in Croft. What I did find was the various 'National Savings' events for the armed forces. These were week long events that gave people something to get together for but which raised money for

**The Croft WI started in 1925. I'm not sure who these women are. I think Gladys Parlour was chairwoman during the war and she might be the tall woman at the front here. Here the WI celebrate their 25th birthday in 1947.**

*Chapter 6 – Community Glue*

**I believe this is a mock coronation procession, passing the Croft Spa Hotel, in 1953.**

each of the services. Your entry fee included an investment in National Savings, on the promise of a decent premium when the war was over. There was one day for the Airforce, one for the Navy.

The next big occasion was 12 December 1952 when a committee formed to plan celebrations for the coronation of Queen Elizabeth II on 2 June 1953. This was a major event involving many people, the first big celebration since the war and a very distinct memory for most people who lived through it.

The organising sub-committee was formed on 19 January, and further sub-committees formed below that. It had been expected that people from the Cockleberry site would join in, but they too preferred their own 'do'. The parish council donated £10 to their celebrations. The committee also decided to invite the children from Oakwood Nursery School.

The Coronation celebration was a great example of everyone in the village working together to create a special day. It was community super-glue. Despite the awful weather, a good and memorable time was had by all. Plus the committee had £23 16/6 surplus at the end. A sum went for a present for Master Neil Burdon who had been ill in hospital on the day. The rest was split between the Bus Shelter Fund (£10) and the Children's Sports Fund (£13) although this was contentious. Bert Coates, then Chair, filed this report:

> *It rained almost continuously throughout coronation day. The celebrations started with a communion service in St. Peter's Church Croft by the Rector of Croft, the Reverend G. E. Charlesworth. After the service, it was decided to postpone the sports owing to the wet condition of Monkend Park. A slight break in the weather enabled a children's fancy dress parade to be* ▶

It rained almost all day for the Coronation of Queen Elizabeth II in 1953. Here, the Croft fancy dress parade does it best during a brief dry spell.

*held, which under the circumstances was very well done. Lunch for the children followed in the school room, and was thoroughly enjoyed. Everyone then departed to listen to the broadcast of the coronation on the radio or to view the proceedings on television. Owners of television sets were most generous in their invitation to view it was practically 'open home' throughout the village and all sets had capacity viewers. At 4.30 a very good high tea in the schools was served to all parishioners, children and adults alike. Boiled ham, beef, salad, trifles, jellies, creamed ices, tea, cakes, and chocolate biscuits. After which souvenir mugs were presented to the children. Much praise went to the catering committee and many trays were sent out to elderly or sick people unable to attend. The celebrations for the day ended with a whist drive in the schools, which was very popular and many prizes were given. After several postponements owing to the weather the programme of sports was eventually carried out in Monkend Park. The official programme and the minutes of meeting held are filed in the following pages the final meeting was the most contentious for some years, as will be seen from the number of amendments required to dispose of the balance of the fund. The final solution was not popular, and was probably reached out of sheer exhaustion.*

By the time the Queen's Silver Jubilee came up in 1977, organising people were getting blasé about these royal occasions. 'Mr Headon proposed we do what was done for Her Majesty's Coronation. Fancy Dress Parade, tea then Sports and presentation of mugs with dance at night in the Spa Hotel ballroom. Celebrations to commence at 1.30 pm. The committee appointed were Mr Headon, Mr Wrightson, Miss Allen.' The parish council also agreed to fund the planting of a beech tree in commemoration of the Jubilee, in the school grounds. Bill Chaytor and Ron Fletcher agreed to sort this out. And so it was.

There are some more memories of the event in Chapter 2.

An extensive write up of this enjoyable day, on which the sun deigned to shine, is available. Here are some of the highlights:

> *It has been popularly acclaimed that the day was so well planned that there was something provided for every section of the community, a day made more pleasurable by the preceding Flower Festival (Sat to Tues) in the Church. This Festival set the scene for the celebrations ahead, giving the Interdenominational Service a beauty much appreciated by the huge congregation which filled every seat in the church. Christian unity was the theme for the day: friendship and goodwill was the result, a feeling extended through the presence of Canon Littleton, Mr Alford, Brother Benet the preacher, to friends from the neighbouring villages of Hurworth Place, Dalton and Eryholme. [...] The Jubilee Tea was a signal success, catering for all, from our oldest resident, 93 year old Mr Middlemiss to the youngest child; a tribute to Mrs Mary Headon's[8] organisation as she and her helpers [a list of 10 village women] provided tea for everyone, which included delivering teas to those who were unwell. [...] The evening's entertainment continued at 7 pm with a Disco for the under 18s at the Croft Spa Hotel. Here 48 tickets sold in advance to teenagers and their friends from Dalton and Eryholme. This event was arranged by Mr Headon. [...] At 8.00 pea bonfire, behind the Scout Hut, with firework display and barbecue, was enjoyed in the field provided by Mr Chaytor, who with his helpers Mr Wrightson and Mr Fletcher gave everyone a spectacular show. Finally, the Jubilee Queen, Miss Kathlyn Nichol, and her attendants, presided over the Jubilee Dance at the Croft Spa Hotel for which 185 tickets were sold. Here Mr Headon, Mr Ibbotson, Mr Crawley and Mr Pearson provided entertainment that wiled away the last hours of the celebrations.*

The final royal event in our period was the Royal Wedding. Or, the wedding of HRH Prince Charles to Lady Diana Spencer, on 29 July 1981. The event committee for this really pushed the boat out, literally! A series of boat races on the River Tees was the feature event. Alison Kennedy recalls the races in Chapter 2.

# A Bit of a Do

> *... my memories of Croft I suppose are of the do's, we seemed to have a lot of do's, processions, and fancy dress parade, and this sort of thing, which I'm sure you've heard about from Charlie.*
> Cath Wood

At this point I am going to showcase the talents of a man who was Croft's chief purveyor of community glue for a very long time. All through the seventies, eighties, nineties and beyond the millennium. This was Charlie Headon. We've met Charlie already in this book. He was born at number 2 South Parade in 1932 and lived most of his life in Croft. After leaving school he trained as a coach builder for United buses in Darlington. Then, in the early 1950s Charlie did National Service in London. He enjoyed it.

**Charlie Headon**:

*"I did two years in that, in the Pier Corps, PNCO. I was in charge of a hospital pier, Woolwich Arsenal in London. And at the time in me life, if I could go back tomorrow, I'd go, do it again. Because it was a hospital and we used to go dancing regular, and they were all nurses and so forth. Oh, the world was your oyster.*

*I came out of the Army the week the Queen was crowned."*

Charlie also had a period living away from Croft when he was a transport controller and then a transport manager. When he returned in 1971 – age 40 – he bought the Quaker Coffee House situated in Mechanics' Yard in Darlington which was his business up until he retired in 1988. This was very much Charlie's domain – he was supremely talented at creating a place where people loved to go. He liked chatting, was expert at making people feel at ease, made people laugh and also had an acute sense of what people wanted for food and entertainment. And there you have it. He repeated all of that in Croft, in the hotel, in the village hall and – after he moved to The Moorings in 1975 – in his own home. He lived at The Moorings with his mother Ada up until she died in 1980. Stories of having fun at a Charlie-organised event are many. His friend Ian Calvert summed up: 'Charlie was the king pin. Well, nothing would have happened without him, on both sides of the village'.

I should say at this point that Charlie was not just about fun and games, although that was the bit

**Charlie Headon loved dressing up and organised frequent 'fashion parades'. Here he shows of his legs with someone called Ethel.**

## Chapter 6 – Community Glue

**Charlie Headon stands outside Croft Church, 1980s. Charlie was an extraordinary purveyor of 'community glue'.**

he liked best. He took commitment to other aspects of community glue seriously too. He was on the Parish Council for twenty years. He was active in organising the tennis club and chair of the village hall committee.

But it was Charlie's talent and energy for organising social events that people remember. He set up bus trips, whist drives, fish-and-chip lunches, parties, charity events, galas. He was always keen to include everyone and the events he organised are one of the main things Croft people remember from the seventies and eighties. In an interview in the *Evening Despatch* published 24 April 1990, Charlie cited a major change in his lifetime as the advent of television, drawing people indoors. He saw the village hall as essential to maintaining a community spirit.

Ian was able to recount how dedicated Charlie was to giving people in the village a good time. He was always organising. Charlie himself reported 'every [August] Bank Holiday for twenty years I ran a fancy dress ball at the Croft Spa [Hotel]'. Another example was the annual Christmas Party for pensioners. This was held in the hall at St John of God's Hospital, Rockliffe Park:

**Ian Calvert**:

*"Yeah, it was a big Christmas party. It was always in the hospital. St John of God's. Rockliffe. It used to be St John of God's hospital. They built on a chapel and a hall as an extension of it. And Charlie used to hire the hall at Christmas. And that was a mix that was Croft both sides of the river. 60 or 80 people. It was a proper party, with lots laid on. And me, dressed up as some bloody fool. He'd put on a show. I can't remember what I was the last time. I remember being dressed as a gorilla once, in a gorilla costume. And he would have a sing-song on the stage at Rockliffe. Like a little comic show, and a charade, and people used to sing. But the old folks loved it. And he used*

*to get everybody back again. He was organised. Then he used to have us all organised with the teas and the washing up and everything. Everyone looked forward to it. I mean, I think the first year he didn't do it everybody was really upset. 'We're not having a Christmas party!' I don't know the reason why, there must've been a reason for it."*

I've picked out Charlie as a great exemplar, but there have been so many people across the years who have given generously of their time to build and sustain community. We've seen some in this book – all the councillors, the decision makers, the organisers of dos, the carers, the church wardens and lay readers, the people who visit others when they are in trouble, the crafters and the grafters, the litter-pickers and the gardeners, the performers and the musicians. All types of people and all types of contribution make community glue.

And it continues. **Martyn** and **Sue Coates** came to Croft in 1986, at the end of our period, but soon established themselves as key people for maintaining the village community. They have been committed to it, both through the village hall committee, organising events, doing jobs and generally looking out for people. Sue was also on the Parish Council for years. At first it wasn't easy: *A lot of people here were either born and bred here or certainly been here a long time. So you had to wait your time as newcomers. We had to tread carefully. Which we did.* Sue and Martyn's commitment to the village was also instilled in their children, two of whom now live in Croft. Martyn said *I'm glad they're taking over, you know, in our tradition.* The tradition of community glue. It's always been there, in one form or another.

So what is community glue, and why is it a good thing? Is it just the shared endeavour and laughter that holds us together? Is about about finding and celebrating what unites us rather than what divides us? It's probably all of that, and we've seen it in operation in this book, listening to the Croft voices and from other sources too. I hope I've done a good tour, and that something of Croft's community spirit has shone through. Life is complicated: there are so many things I haven't covered but I hope this book contains some small testimony to lives lived and decisions made. These are the core of our piece of village history, and we have come to the end.

**Endnotes**
1. NRRD, Vol 659, p 205, # 66
2. Croft Parish Council minutes 21 March 1935.
3. Full page feature with glorious seventies illustrations in The Northern Echo, April 10 1973, p5.
4. Mrs Backhouse was Elizabeth Barclay Backhouse, wife of James Edward Backhouse, a devout Quaker and an early example of the intermarriage of the Backhouse and Barclay families. You can read more about her in Chris Lloyd, *The Road to Rockliffe*, *Northern Echo*, 2010, pp. 82-84.
5. *Evening Despatch*, 27 November 1974
6. The history of this is in the Parish Council minutes, NYRO, PC/CRO 1/2.
7. *Northern Echo*, 28 May 2022 and, at the time of writing, online.
8. Charlie and Margaret's sister-in-law; Dave Headon's mother.

# Epilogue

When you come to Croft, you will come to St Peter's church, and the churchyard. Whether in your car or, in an earlier time, in your coach, or maybe on your horse, or cart. The church and churchyard are just by the river. The enduring, strong river and old stone bridge are just to the side of the church. This is the seven arched bridge by which the flood is measured. Sometimes the water is way, way below, brookish and ambling, scarcely speaking above the summer's breeze and susurrous trees. You can lean over a parapet of the bridge to look at the river below, the weeds streaming seawards, the water lapping stones in the shallows. Sometimes though the water is high, almost to the top the arches, roaring above the howl of a winter gale, icy cold, dark and swirling, racing onwards and outwards beyond the border of its banks. You watch in awe, and keep your distance.

The church stands here by Croft's crossing. It is not disturbed by nature's changes, although it is surrounded by them. It keeps its moorings here on the bank of the river. In the churchyard there are high ancient trees, abundant, then bare, but always above, lived in by robins and rooks. There is much grass,. In winter it is just brown, damp tussocks but spring brings a green carpet with celandines and clovers. There is the summer pink rambling rose over the doorway that people like, planted in a child's memory, posing behind brides and grooms like a shy but decorative guest. And there is always ivy, deep green, edging across the paths and walls and over the stones. The head stones, crafted and placed to defy change, to keep the names of the loved and familiar seen forever.

When you come into the churchyard you will see big stones and little stones. Stones that call themselves tombs or family graves. Stones that have been formed into crosses and urns and sometimes angels. But others are an ellipse, with just a short story about who lies under them. There have been stones placed here for hundreds of years and they represent the people of Croft, a great many of them. Walking among these stones can feel like a connection.

In January 2022 I had started writing this book. I wanted to look at the 'Todd tomb' to see what dates it had on it. So I had a walk up to the churchyard one afternoon, and I ended up staying quite a while because I suddenly felt very at home there. I was enjoying walking round, listening to the rooks kicking up in the bare trees, feeling the freshening wind, looking at the graves and the stones and feeling quite at peace. Not least because the churchyard was full of people I recognised. There was a family grave for the Chaytors, a bit overgrown, but I knew all of the names and how they were related, and in some cases how they had died. Then another family grave. And then the Parlours and the Arnetts all in one place, just as in life. And Adamson, and Turnbull, and Coates, and other Parlours and Hobsons, brought to this centre from their farms. The churchyard was full of familiar names. I could connect, in my imagination, because now I felt I knew something of this place. I had learned from others who had known this village, the living and the dead. I was immersed in thinking about it and finding out about it.

What I am hoping is that you, the reader, might also now feel more connected with the recent history of Croft, that you feel you know more, and that that has made you think about how things change, and what remains. What was, and what should continue. What Croft used to be like and what it could be in the future.

I have been asked, in the recent past, to comment on what Croft is, what characterises it, what is good and bad about it.  If you look at what is in this book, there are so many angles to cover, and a blanket opinion is difficult to reach. We've looked at formative childhood experiences, the disruption of the war, how the built fabric of the village has change and why, how decisions were made that changed Croft for ever, the big changes in the agricultural landscape and the way people come together to make a community.  Most of my interviewees were happy to talk about being children, and houses, village do's and memories of the war. But there were some things that were not mentioned much. Only two or three people knew anything about wartime evacuees and knowledge of the camp at Cockleberry was very scanty. Oakwood School was referred to a couple of times. There were few reports about any problems or incidents of tragedy. Maybe that is what memory does to us : we tend to accentuate the good, push away the sad or difficult if we can. What I've presented in this book may have similar nostalgic bias as a result.

But certainly there *are* things that characterise Croft. I do think that there is an undertow, even today, of tradition and connection to the past in Croft. A tradition long established and seen in many other rural places I'm sure, based on connection to the land, respect for authoritative structures like church and estate, and a common life within the community, all doing similar things together. To an outsider this undertow is felt but not openly acknowledged or  is maybe not noticed by those familiar with it. To a newcomer it can feel exclusive, at least at first., but it is comforting to be welcomed in.  Maybe Croft is also a bit resistant to new ideas and ways of doing things. But strong tradition and a sense of identity have seen it through, across many  imposed changes., and creates a fierce loyalty in many people. Honouring an enduring way of doing things lays down long roots that are not easily torn away. Today, however, we face a new period of change, when so many certainties are vanishing, technology is changing things at an ever more rapid pace,  social structures are evolving, the path of our weather and landscape seems unsure. Will the strong heart of Croft flex, or break? As shown  in the events and decisions and actions evident here in this book, the people of Croft can make their own path in response to and across the tide of  a bigger history.

# Appendix A: Croft Voices

**This is a list of people interviewed for the book. Full recordings of the interviews are available in most cases. List sorted alphabetically by christian name.**

| | |
|---|---|
| **Alan Kirk** | Alan was born at Bullmire Farm in 1948 and was the farmer there all of his life. |
| **Alison Kennedy** | Born Alison Matthews in Croft in 1974 Alison lived away from Croft after she graduated. And returned in the noughties to care for her mother Tessa. She still lives in the village. |
| **Ann Carnelly** | Ann Reed came to Croft during the war having been born in York in 1940. She was about 1 when she came to Croft and she moved to Darlington on her marriage in the sixties. |
| **Bert and Jean Walker** | Bert (Albert) Walker was born in 1928. His family moved to Birch Springs, Halnaby in 1942 and he was later the farmer there. Bert died in 2023. Jean married Bert in 1952, and is from Darlington. |
| **Bill Chaytor** | Bill was born William Drewett Chaytor in 1937 at Leases Hall near Bedale and spent his childhood in Coverdale. He came to Croft in 1965 to manage the Croft Estate. He lived in Croft from then until his death in 2023. |
| **Bob Middleton** | Bob was born in 1923 in Toronto. He joined the RCAF in 1943 and became a Navigator. In September 1944 he was posted, with the rest of his bomber crew, to Croft Aerodrome and flew 33 missions from there until he returned home in June 1945. Bob was interviewed a few months before his death in October 2021. |
| **Cath Wood** | Cath was born in North Shields, maiden name Marshall. She married Mike in the fifties and still lives in Croft. |
| **Charlie Headon** | Charlie was born in number 2 South Parade in 1932. He was the third son of Lawrence and Ada Headon, younger brother of Jack and Jim, and older brother of Margaret. He bought The Moorings in 1974 and lived there with his widowed mother until 1982 after which he moved to Hurworth Place. Charlie died in 2021. |
| **Dave Headon** | Dave was born in Croft in 1950, the son of Jim Headon, and still lives in the village. |

*Crofts Crossing*

| | |
|---|---|
| **David Coates** | Born in Croft and the son of Herbert (Bert) Coates, David lived with his family in The Terrace. He left Croft to go to university and has not returned to live there. |
| **David Kellie-Smith** | David was born in 1940, at Croft Hall. He lived with his mother at Woodbine Cottage until he went to boarding school aged 7. After that he came home for school holidays and lived in London after leaving university. |
| **David Walker** | David Walker was born in 1954 and is the son of Lawrie Walker and Elizabeth Pearson and was born at Vince Moor East. He has moved around with his work and now lives in Norfolk. |
| **Doris Cameron** | Doris was born in 1928 at Vince Moor West and lived there all of her life until she died in 2022, in the same house where she was born. |
| **Ian Calvert** | Ian's grandparents lived at 8 South Parade. His parents moved to Banks Terrace in Hurworth Place which is where he was born and brought up. |
| **Ian Dougill** | Ian was born at number 5 South Parade in 1933. He left Croft when he went to university in 1951 and did not return to live there. His parents lived at number 5 until the early 1970s when they moved into Darlington. |
| **Jane Parlour** | Jane was born at Townend Farm in Dalton-on-Tees and has lived in Dalton almost all of her life. |
| **Janet McKenzie** | Janet was born Janet Pearson in London in 1946, but belongs to the Pearson family from Vince Moor East. Her parents got a house in Carroll Place that same year, when her father was demobbed from the army. She lived away from Croft between 1968 and 2002. |
| **John Green** | John Green was 7 when he came to Croft with his parents in 1946. He was brought up at Monkend Hall where his parents worked and is Sandra Veerman's brother. He has lived in Croft for the rest of his life. |
| **John Hennessy** | John was born in Catterick in 1962 but came to live in South Parade when he was just one, when his father left the army. He now lives in Darlington. |
| **Julie Clacher** | Julie Clacher was born in Croft in 1970 and has lived in the village all her life. |
| **Katherine Banner** | Katherine Banner was born in 1962 at Home Farm, Halnaby, daughter of Lawrie and Eva Banner, and now lives near Stapleton. |
| **Margaret Chapman** | Margaret was born Margaret Headon at number 2 South Parade, Croft in 1934 and attending Croft School until the age of 14. She married George Chapman in 1956. Margaret moved with her family to Hampshire because George got a job there, but they returned to Hurworth Place on his retirement. |
| **Margaret Horseman** | Margaret was born in the house she has always lived in, on Tees View, Hurworth Place. |

## Appendix A: Croft Voices

| | |
|---|---|
| **Mary Andrew** | Born at Waterloo Farm in 1936, Mary's maiden name was Turnbull. She lived her whole life on what would have been the Halnaby Estate, mostly as a farmer. Mary died in 2023. |
| **Mary Bossinger** | Mary's father was Reverend Charlesworth and she was born in Darlington a little before he took up his post in Croft. She left Croft in 1959 with the rest of her family who later went to South Africa. I interviewed her in 2022 on one of her return visits to Croft. |
| **Mike Wood** | Mike Wood was born in Bishop Auckland in 1930 but his family moved to Cullercoats, on the Northumberland coast, soon afterwards. Work brought him to the Croft area. Mike died in January 2023. |
| **Molly Ingham** | Molly was born 1922, in Hurworth Place. She moved over the bridge to Croft in the 1960s |
| **Nick Kirkwood** | Nick was born in Hurworth. His association with Croft came when his parents bought Croft Mill in the 1970s. Having lived in various places during his life, Nick has recently come to live in Croft |
| **Paul Fletcher** | Paul Fletcher was born at Croft in 1952, the son of Ron Fletcher who makes several appearances in this book. At the time of his birth the Fletchers lived at Spa Cottages and later moved to Newtown |
| **Peter Metcalfe** | Born in 1930, Peter's young life was spent at Pepperfield Farm. As an adult he moved to North Cowton, which is where he died, still working, in 2022. |
| **Peter Percival** | Peter was born at Cockleberry in 1951 and left there in 1962 when his family were re-housed in Barton. He still lives in Barton |
| **Reg Harrison** | Reg Harrison was born in Canada in 1922 and was in the RCAF during WW2 including a spell at Croft. He was a month away from 100th birthday when I interviewed him over the phone. |
| **Sally Lilley** | Sally Lilley is the granddaughter of Jack Headon and was brought up in Carroll Place where she still lives. |
| **Sally Still** | Sally Still is the daughter of Lawrence and Dorothy Arnett and was brought up in Pond House at Hurworth. She lived at Monkend Hall from the mid 1970s until the 2010s when she moved to Piercebridge. |
| **Sandra Veerman** | Sandra's maiden name was Green and she was born in 1950 at the Northallerton maternity home. She is the sister of John (also interviewed) and grew up at Monkend Hall where her parents worked for the Parlours. She lived in Holland with her husband Ari until 1998 when they returned to Croft, and she still lives there. |
| **Sue and Martyn Coates** | Sue and Martyn came to Croft in 1986 and quickly established themselves as mainstays of village life. They lived I South Parade and brought up their family there. They still live in Croft. |

# Appendix B: Maps & Aerial Photographs

| Page # | Title | Description |
|---|---|---|
| 220 | 1722 Estate Map for Henry Chaytor | A map of the Croft Estate, the earliest known map showing the village centre |
| 221 | Map of Croft Rural District Council Area | This map dates from a handbook dated around 1960, but boundaries would not have changed since 1894 when the RDC was set up. |
| 222 | Croft in 1930 | A hand-drawn map with key, showing the state of the village in 1930. |
| 224 | The village centre in 1951 | An RAF aerial picture of Croft, with a key, gives a view of the village centre post war |
| 226 | Pre-war farms and proposed aerodrome | Map showing the position of the aerodrome amongst local farms |
| 227 | Croft Aerodrome | Map of the completed aerodrome. The numbered circles are bomber stands. |
| 228 | Halnaby Estate 1950 | A map and sale schedule produce for the 1950 sale of the Halnaby Estate |
| 230 | Croft Estate farms in 1964 | A map of the Croft Estate's farms at the time of Bill Chaytor's arrival as head of the estate (1964) |

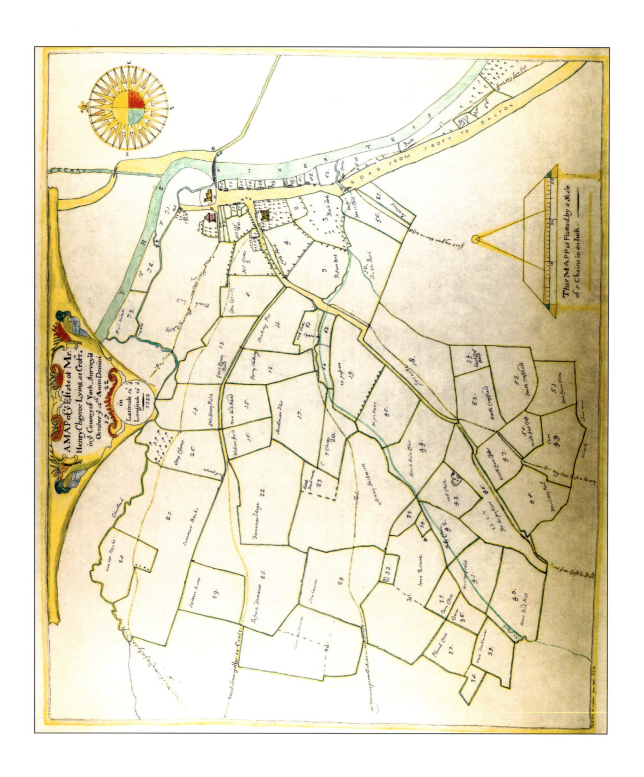

*Appendix B: Maps & Aerial Photographs*

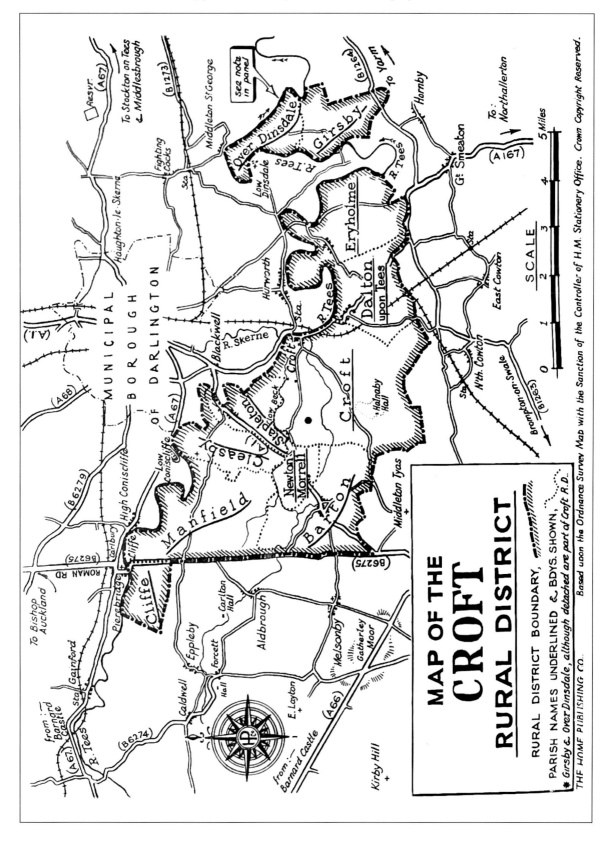

## Crofts Crossing

This map has been devised specifically for this publication by Colin Williams in order to get round a specific mapping problem.

The Ordnance Survey surveyed Croft in 1912 for their map published in 1914. However they did not return to do a full resurvey until the 1970s for their Landranger series. This leaves a bit of a gap in terms of trying to chart the development of Croft from 1930! Colin has drawn the map and I have provided a key that describes what Croft looked like in 1930, based on my research on the development of the village. Buildings erected after 1912 are numbered on the map and the table gives notes on names and dates.

In addition to this map there is an annotated aerial view of Croft in 1951 on page 224

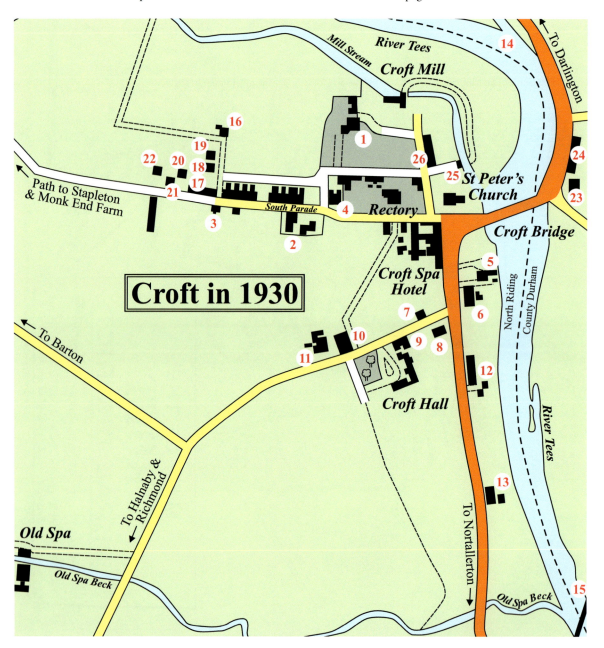

## Appendix B: Maps & Aerial Photographs

1. **Monk End Hall**
Probably a house here from the 1600s but the bulk of the current house is early to mid 18th century. Next to the hall is the old stables.

2. **School**
These two buildings comprise the School House (where school was) and the Schoolmaster's House on the left, both built ca 1845 from the original bequest for a National School.

3. **Monkend Gardens**
House built ca 1895, but 'Monkend Gardens' was also used to name all of the market garden area to the west South Parade.

4. **The Gable/The Moorings**
Built for Joseph Chambers Summer 1911. "The Moorings" not the name until 1970s. "The Gable" originally "Rose Villa".

5. **Bridge House**
Probably built by Sir William Chaytor, first baronet. Early to mid nineteenth century. Listed.

6. **The Limes/Woodbine Cottage**
Eighteenth century. The Limes probably early century, Woodbine Cottage later. Both listed.

7. **Pear Tree Cottage**
Unsure of date.

8. **Ashgrove**
Built by Sir Wm Chaytor. Mid nineteenth century. Listed.

9. **Richmond Terrace**
Victorian – unsure of date.

10. **The Terrace**
Built as lodging houses for the New Spa by Sir Wm Chaytor early 19th century. Listed.

11. **South Terrace**
Mid 19th Century. Listed.

12. **Cottages on Northallerton Road**
The long row of cottages are referenced in the 1840 census. One was the home of Benjamin Raisbeck, the last toll keeper on Croft Bridge. The other detached cottage I believe was Strawberry Cottage, a small farm.

13. **Stairmand's Cottage/Park View**
I believe this is Stairmand's house, sometimes known as Park View. Around here (but not marked on the map) was also Waterside, built by William Parlour in 1912.

14. **Skerne/Tees conjunction**
This is the point where the River Skerne, which flows through Darlington, joins the River Tees.

15. **Tees Railway Bridge**
Railway viaduct built 1838 for Great North of England Railway

16. **Rose Cottage**
Unsure of date but is on earliest OS map of 1850.

17. **Terrace on corner of South Parade and Monk End**
The four-house terrace that existed in 1930 comprised, in the middle, two adjoining terrace-type houses built ca. 1912 (now nos 20 and 21), and two end terrace houses built later. Thorneycroft was built in 1926 and the other house in 1927.

18. **St Kitts/Durley**
A pair of semis built before 1927: they appear on the site plan for #19 but have not found a specific plan for them.

19. **Brentwood**
Built October 1927 for a Miss Boagey, original name Trebor.

20. **Shirley Cottage**
The first detached house at the west end of South Parade built before November 1926.

21. **Pair semis**
Built 1927.

22. **The Anchorage**
Built for a Miss Mathewson in 1928.

23. **The Comet Hotel**
Built around 1840 I believe. In Hurworth Place.

24. **Tees View**
In Hurworth Place.

25. **Stepping Stones**
Built for Mr and Mrs Dingle, who ran the Croft Spa Hotel. They bought the land in March 1925 and Stepping Stones was definitely built before October 1927.

26. **Monkend Terrace**
Built 1865 to 1870 by several different builders.

## Crofts Crossing

*Appendix B: Maps & Aerial Photographs*

1  Croft Bridge
2  St Peters Church
3  Croft Rectory. The Rectory itself is on the right partly obscured by trees, but everything left of that, up to the next house (Which would be The Gable) was the Rectory garden.
4  Monkend Hall. To the right is the hall, with separate stable block just above it. On the left you can see the extensive back field.
5  Croft Mill. Note the extent of the mill field, which swept right round from the cluster of mill buildings to the bridge. The line of the mill head-race can followed by the line of trees on the left, across the top of the market gardens, from Clow Beck.
6  Croft School. With school gardens to the right.
7  Carroll Place. Newly built and occupied from 1949.
8  Croft Spa Hotel. Note extensive buildings behind and the expanse of the swimming pool on the bottom edge of the hotel plot (this used to be a vegetable garden.)
9  Stairmand‚Äôs Market Garden, bottom, and Strawberry Cottage, above, before The Limes and Woodbine Cottage which are parallel to the Northallerton Road Legend for Croft Village Centre 1951 (2)
10 The New Spa. The building running left to right is the three Spa Cottages. The building at right angles to it is the New Spa Bath-house. The tennis court can be seen to the right before the road.
11 Oakwood. Oakwood House, the largest building, is still occupied Sunderland Borough Council at this point. There was also Oakwood Lodge.
12 Gerry Andrew‚Äôs Market Garden. Mr Andrew lived at Rose Cottage and had a market stall in Darlington, supplied by his extensive market garden seen here. He also had piggeries – the building parallel to the Stapleton briadle way which runs right to left here.
13 Old Spa. The farm house and Old Spa Villa can be clearly seen at the middle and bottom of the group of buildings. But there is a building at the top of this group which I believe could be the remains of the Old Spa Bath-house. The Spa Beck can be seen running parallel to the bath down the bridge on the Middleton Tyas Road.

# Crofts Crossing

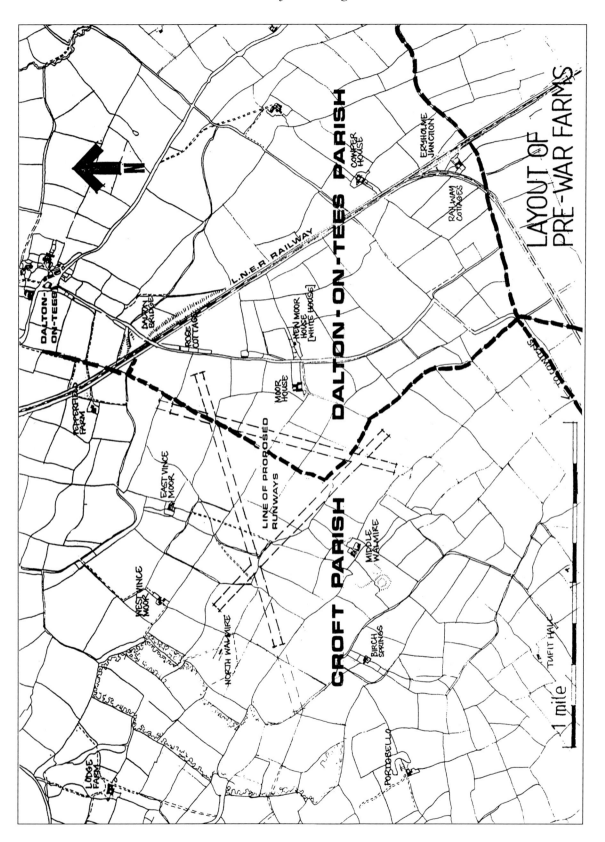

## Appendix B: Maps & Aerial Photographs

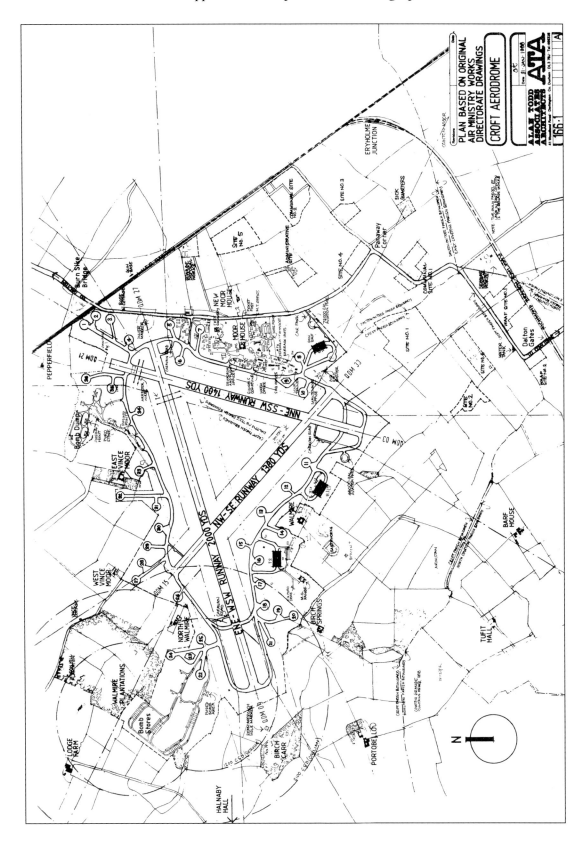

# Crofts Crossing

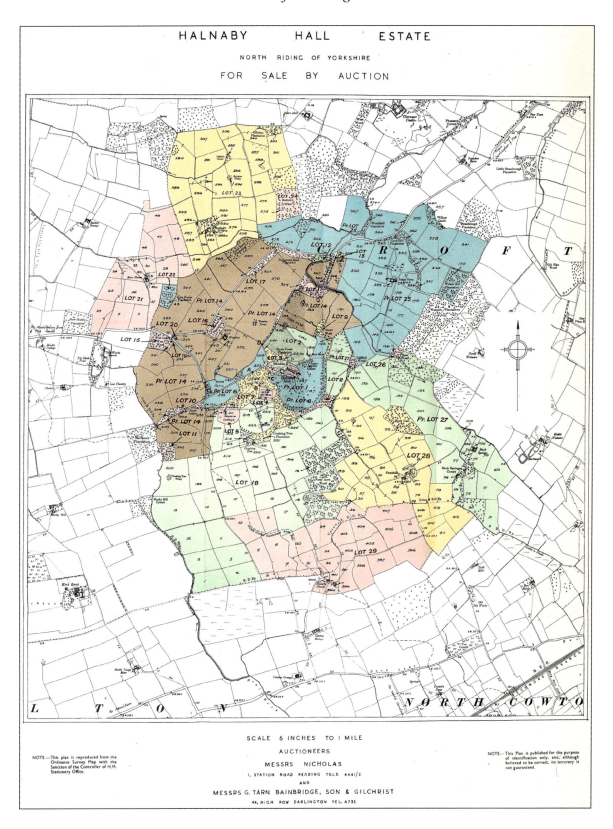

# Schedule of Lots.

| Lot No. | Description. | Area. | | |
|---|---|---|---|---|
| | | A. | R. | P. |
| 1 | Halnaby Hall... | 15 | 2 | 7 |
| 2 | Stables, part Park and Lake | 24 | 0 | 29 |
| 3 | North Front Plantation | 2 | 2 | 39 |
| 4 | Kitchen Garden | 3 | 0 | 23 |
| 5 | Keeper's Cottage and Land | 6 | 2 | 10 |
| 6 | Home Farm | 56 | 3 | 2 |
| 7 | Long Wood, Church Wood, Creaking Tree Plantation | 26 | 2 | 32 |
| 8 | Ha-Ha Plantation and Calfold Wood | 6 | 0 | 5 |
| 9 | Short Walk Plantation | 3 | 1 | 0 |
| 10 | Mrs. Flowers' Cottage | 0 | 0 | 16 |
| 11 | Two of South Lodges, South Wood and The Rush Plantation | 9 | 1 | 20 |
| 12 | North Lodge (West) and Plantation | 1 | 2 | 16 |
| 13 | North Lodge (East) and Plantation | 0 | 2 | 17 |
| 14 | Waterloo Farm | 337 | 2 | 5 |
| 15 | West Wood | 6 | 0 | 4 |
| 16 | Waterloo Plantation... | 4 | 0 | 24 |
| 17 | Richmond Road Plantation | 6 | 2 | 8 |
| 18 | Creaking Tree Farm with Forty Acre Wood | 344 | 2 | 20 |
| 19 | West Lodge (West) | 0 | 0 | 32 |
| 20 | West Lodge (East) | 0 | 0 | 36 |
| 21 | Moor House Farm | 114 | 1 | 6 |
| 22 | Moor House Plantation | 5 | 1 | 17 |
| 23 | Bullmire Farm | 210 | 0 | 15 |
| 24 | Bullmire Whin | 11 | 0 | 15 |
| 25 | Lodge Farm | 270 | 1 | 5 |
| 26 | Rear Wood | 1 | 2 | 33 |
| 27 | Birch Springs Farm | 184 | 2 | 34 |
| 28 | Portobello Farm | 177 | 3 | 11 |
| 29 | Halnaby Grange Farm | 187 | 1 | 33 |
| | **TOTAL AREA** | **A. 2,018** | **2** | **34** |

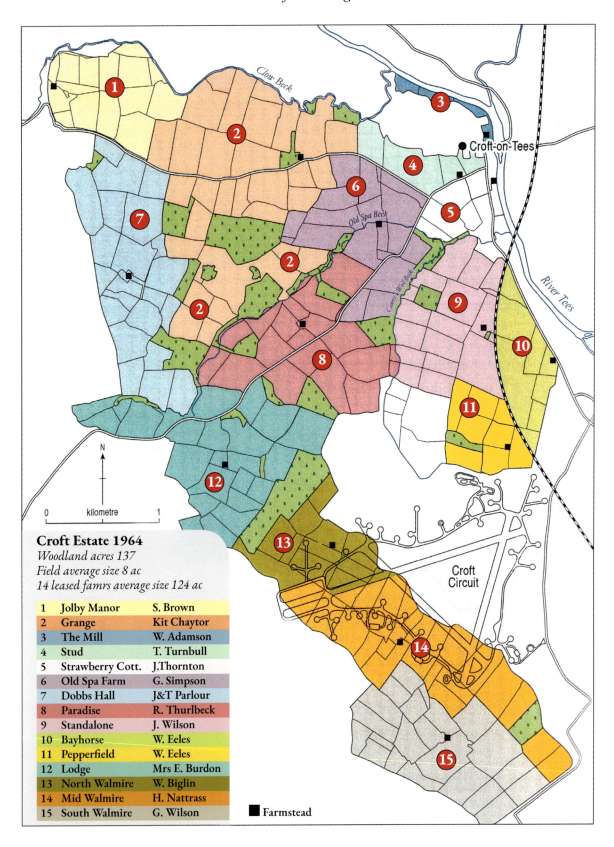

# BIBLIOGRAPHY

By far the largest number of references in this work are to archival records or newspaper stories. The list below is of books that are also cited or which formed my appreciation of the context of Croft's history in the period.

**[Authors Unknown]**
*The official guide to Darlington and Croft Rural Districts* (Darlington, 1952)

**Madeleine Beard**
*English landed society in the twentieth century* (London, 1989)

**Ronald Blythe**
*Akenfield: portrait of an English village* (London, 1969)

**David Brown**
*Aerodromes in North Yorkshire and wartime memories* (Stockton-on-Tees, 1996)

**Paul Bradley, David Harvey, Matt Lobley and Michael Winter (editors)**
*The real agricultural revolution: the transformation of English farming 1939-1985* (Woodbridge, 2021)

**Alfred Henry Chaytor**
*Essays sporting and serious* (London, 1930)

**Alfred Henry Chaytor**
*Letters to a salmon fisher's sons* (London, 1910)

**William Drewett Chaytor**
*Coverdale to Croft: A Yorkshire landowner's memoirs, his family story, farming and fears for the earth* (Durham, 2020)

**Croft Parish Council**
*The Croft-on-Tees millennium book* (Croft-on-Tees, 2000)

**Jonathan Falconer**
*RAF bomber airfields of World War 2* (Shepperton, 1992)

**James J Halley**
*Broken Wings: Post-war Royal Airforce accidents* (Tunbridge Wells, 1992)

**C Jane Hatcher**
*Richmondshire Architecture* (Richmond, 1990)

**R W Hoyle (editor)**
*Our hunting fathers: field sports in England after 1850* (Lancaster, 2007)

**Sophie Jackson**
*Churchill's Unexpected Guests: Prisoners of War in Britain in World War II* (Cheltenham, 2010)

**Lois Louden**
*Distinctive and inclusive: The National Society and Church of England schools 1811-2011* (London, 2012)

**W W Lowther**
*Wish you were here: an account of Sunderland's wartime evacuation* (Sunderland, 1989)

**Andrew Marr**
*A history of modern Britain* (London, 2008)

**Robert J Middleton and Daniel R Middleton**
*Luck is 33 eggs: memories and photographs of an RCAF navigator* (Self-published, 2021)

**Simon W Parry**
*Intruders over Britain: the story of the Luftwaffe's night intruder force 1940-45* (London, 1987)

**Chapman Pincher**
*Pastoral Symphony: A bumpkin's tribute to country joys* (Shrewsbury, 1993)

**A J Pollard**
*A Perfect Paradise: Eryholme from 1066 to the Present* (Eryholme, 2019)

**A J Pollard**
"Richard Clervaux of Croft: A North Country Squire in the Fifteenth Century"
*The Yorkshire Archaeological Journal*, Vol 50 (1978) pp. 151-169

**John Martin Robinson**
*The English country estate* (London, 1988)

**Brian Short, Charles Watkins and John Martin (editors)**
*The front line of freedom: British farming in the Second World War*,
The Agricultural History Review Supplement Series 4 (Exeter, 2006)

**Roy Strong, Marcus Binney and John Harris**
*The destruction of the country house 1875-1975* (London, 1974)

**J A Tannahill**
*European Volunteer Workers in Britain* (Manchester, 1958)

**Roger Taylor and Edward Wakening**
*Lewis Carroll, photographer: The Princeton University albums* (Princeton and Oxford, 2002)

**Alan A B Todd**
*Pilgrimages of Grace: A history of Croft aerodrome* (Darlington, 1993)

**Martin Wainwright**
*The English village: history and traditions* (London, 2011)

**Derek Wood**
*Attack warning red: the Royal Observer Corps and the defence of Britain 1925-1975* (London 1976)

**Victoria County History**
*A history of the County of York North Riding*, Volume 1 (London, 1914)

*Picture Permissions*

# PERMISSIONS

A good number of the pictures in this publication have been scanned from sources owned by the author (eg non-copyright postcards) and some pictures are the author's own photographs.

A small number are unattributable and likely to be out of copyright due to their age.

For those which aren't in the above categories the following permissions have been given in writing.

**Interviewee permissions (by page number):**

| | |
|---|---|
| Margaret Chapman | 13, 50, 63, 69 |
| Charlie Headon | 141, 210, 211 |
| Brian Walker | 82, 153, 159, 161, 167 |
| David Walker | 82, 88, 89, 100, 155 |
| Peter Percival | 111, 114, 115 |
| Sara Campling (for Doris Cameron) | 151, 154, 175 |
| Sandra Veerman | 165, 189, 191 |
| Bill Chaytor/Kate Chaytor-Norris | 171, 174, 230 |
| David Coates | 34, 179 |
| Sally Still | 70, 72 |
| Dave Headon | 69, 76 |
| Dan Middleton | 90, 95 |
| With kind permission from Alan Todd | 226, 227 |

**Other permissions (by page number):**

| | |
|---|---|
| Picture courtesy of the Darlington & Stockton Times: | 31, 35, 113, 154, 156, 190, 201 |
| Picture courtesy of The Northern Echo: | 129 |
| Picture courtesy of the Northern Despatch: | 103 |
| Picture courtesy of The Evening Chronicle: | 197 |
| With permission from Thames & Hudson: | 129 |
| With permission from Historic England: | 121, 130, 143, 224 |
| With permission from the North Yorkshire County Record Office: | 117, 118a, 220 |
| With permission from Darlington Local Studies Centre: | 17, 122, 143 |
| With permission from The Story, Durham: | 118b, 187, 228, 229 |
| Licensed by Alamy Limited: | 196 |
| With permission from The National Archives: | 58 |

The certificate reproduced in page 104 is Crown Copyright and reproduced under the terms of the General Register Office for England and Wales.

# INDEX

Note: page references in *italics* are illustrations; those in **bold** are tables

Abbot's buses 39, 102, 113
Abon, Alex 108, 109
Abon, Henry **68**
Acts of Parliament
    Administration of Estates Act (1925) 170
    Agricultural Development Act (1939) 158
    Conservation of Wild Creatures and Wild Plants Act (1975) 185
    Defence (General) Regulations (1939) 87
    Education Act (1870) 38
    Education Act (1918) 38
    Education Act (1944) 37, 38, 58
    Education Act (1988) 60n17
    Housing Act (1923) 117, 119
    Housing Act (1924) 119
    Housing Act (1936) 108
    Housing Act (1947) 119
    Local Government Act (1894) 21, 24
    Local Government Act (1974) 21, 23, 145
    Tithe Act (1936) 124
Adamson, Florence Muriel ('Muriel') 94, 122
Adamson, Selina 94, 95, 122
Adamson, Stephen 122
Adamson, Thomas Vasey 122
Adamson, William **68**, 80, 94, 95, 121, 122, 163, 164, *165*
aerodrome 6, 30, 78, 86–105, *88*, *99*, *130*, 152, 159–60, *227*
Air Ministry 87, 88, 104, 159, 169
Air Raid Precautions (ARP) 67, **67**, **68**, 70, 73–4, 86
Alderson, Percy 25

Alice House 128, 143, 144
Allen, Edith 42, 44–5, 46–7, 48, 177, 208
Allison, George 21
Allison, John 162
allotments 80, 127, 162
The Anchorage, South Parade 36, **65**, **67**, 119, 223
Andrew, Gerry 80, 83, 162, 200, 225
Andrew, Mary (*née* Turnbull) 28, 30, 48–9, 81, 82, 136–7, 146, 159, 163, 167–8, 169, 193, 217
Andrew, Richard 146, 165–6, 169
Anne, Princess 193
Appleton Cottage (*aka* Monkend Bungalow) *63*, 105n6, 124
Army Service Corps 69, 71, 73
Arnett, Dorothy (*née* Parlour) 71, *72*, 73
Arnett, Lawrence Wilfred ('Lawrie') 30, **68**, 70, *72*, 73, 74–7, 196, 206
Arnotdale, Falkirk 131
Ashgrove 223
Atkinson, Mr and Mrs 127
Australia 81, 85, 91
Auxiliary Fire Service 67, **67**, **68**, 74, 77, 79
Auxiliary Territorial Service (ATS) 79
Aykley Heads estate 53

Backhouse, Elizabeth Barclay 200
Bagshaw, Dr Ian 28
Baker, Maurice 145
Bamlett, Robert 21
Banks Terrace, Hurworth Place 18, 21, 84, 92, 103, 140, 216
Banner family 49, 81, 136, 167, **168**, 169, 216
Barker, Joyce and Kenneth 103
Barnard Castle 49

# Index

Barningham, Tom **66**
Barron, Connie and Betty *63*, 66
Barton 21, 22, 26, 28, 37, 41, 109, 192
    Barton School 37, 48–9, 67
    housing 49, 108, 113, 115–16, 217
    World War 2 75
Bay Horse Farm 120, 171, 175, *230*
Beadon, Captain Frederick Scarth 13–15, 133, 157, 167
Bedale 25, 132, 193, 215
Berry, Miss 39, 40
Beswick, Robert 12, 162
Bevan, Aneurin 111
Biglin family 15n11, 29, 96, 153, *155*, **158**
Binks, Joseph **68**
Birch Springs Farm 83, 93, 94, 116, 153, 155, 157, 161, *229*
    *see also* Walker family
Blackwell 23, 176, 192
Blackwell Pumping Station 182
Blythe, Ronald 150
Blyton, Enid 27, 59
Boagey, Miss 119
boarding schools 36, 48, 49, 51, 72, 216
Bolton Castle 20
Bonomi, Ignatius 137
Booth, Jack 108–9
Bossinger, Mary (*née* Charlesworth) 125–6, 217
Bowes family 21
Bowes, Richard 73, 117, 119
Bradley, Alice 91
Bramley, Ada 28
Bramley, Lilian 59n1
Brentwood 119, 223
brewing 9, 91, 195–6, *197*, 198–9
Bridge House (*aka* The Poplars) **66**, **68**, 120, *178*, 201, 223
British Legion 75
Brittain, Miss 39
Brook House 82
Brown family 83, *230*
brownies 35, 36

Bullmire Farm 28, 37, 48, 80, **158**, 166, **168**, 192, 215, *229*
Burdon family 166, **168**, 169, 207
buses 9, 10, 38, 39, 48, 49, 76, 87, 102, 108, 113, 140, *204*
Byron, Lord 129, *129*, 134

'C' Company, 12th North Riding (Gilling) Battalion *70*, 75, *76*, 77
Calder, Francis 201
Calvert, Ian 18, 33, 84, 92, 103, 210, 211–12, 216
Cameron family 30, 154–5, *154*
Cameron, Doris (*née* Hobson) 129, 139, 151–2, *151*, 153, 154–5, 172, 200, 216
    childhood 27, 29–30, 38, 93, 139, 156
    on hunting 193–4
    World War 2 62, 87, 93, 139
Canada 81, 85, 86, 91, 94–5, *95*, 100, 122, 217
    *see also* Royal Canadian Air Force (RCAF)
Canny Well 13, 20
Carnelly, Ann (*née* Reed) 29, 31, 36, 78–9, 83, 96, 97, 193, 215
Carroll, Lewis (Charles Lutwidge Dodgson) 18, 53, 124, 126
Carroll Place 40, 48, 103, 108–9, 115, 216, 217, 225
cars 9, 10, 11, 24, 60n14, 76, 204, 205
Carter, Robbie 80
Cassel, Sir Ernst 54
Catterick 92, 154, 216
Cayley, Charles 184
CB Inn, Arkengarthdale 176, 177
Chalfont St Giles 110
Chambers, Joseph 5, 13, 223
Chapman, Barry and Diana 59
Chapman, George *179*, 216
Chapman, Margaret (*née* Headon) 19, 27–8, 36, 52, 80, 205, 216
    schooling 39, 41, 42
    World War 2 *63*, 66, *69*, 75, 79, 81, 83, 96
Charlesworth, Reverend Gerald Edward 35, 45, 46, 49, 114, 124–5, 126, *156*, 202–4
Chatwin House, Hurworth 10, 28

235

Chaytor family 31, 213

Chaytor, Alfred Drewett 169

Chaytor, Alfred Henry 10, 138–9, 169, 170–1, 183, 185–6

Chaytor, Anthony 20

Chaytor, Catherine Beatrice ('Betty') 36, 51, **68**, 177

Chaytor, Christopher William Drewett ('Kit') 10, 58, 164, 171, *171*, 174, 196
    churchwarden 126, 188
    Clervaux Castle, demolishes 139
    country sports *171*, 183, 186, 188
    Croft Estate succession 169–70
    and Croft School 46
    farmers, concern for 167, 172
    George V's Silver Jubilee 206
    gifts land for housing 108
    loans temporary Rectory 203
    public office 108, 135, 172, 180, 188
    weir, opposes 180, 182
    woodland 173
    World War 2 51, 69, 87

Chaytor, D'Arcy 170

Chaytor, Dorothy 10, **66**, **68**, 79, 139

Chaytor, Sir Edmund, 6th Baronet of Croft and Witton Castle 9, 71, 138, 169, 173

Chaytor, Sir Edward Walter Clervaux 139, 170

Chaytor, Sir Henry 121, *220*

Chaytor, Isabella 138

Chaytor, Margaret Clare 36, 60n34, 201

Chaytor-Norris, Trevor 175

Chaytor, Rachel (*née* Pease) 193

Chaytor, Sir Walter, 5th Baronet of Croft and Witton Castle 71

Chaytor, Sir William, 1st Baronet of Croft and Witton Castle 20–1, 137, 138, 141, 150

Chaytor, Sir William, 2nd Baronet of Croft and Witton Castle 137–8

Chaytor, Sir William, 3rd Baronet of Croft and Witton Castle 53, 138

Chaytor, William Drewett ('Bill') 33–4, 80, 142–4, 169–70, 183, 186–7, 199, 208, 209, 215
    Croft Estate, sells parts 59, 109, 122, 143–4, 175, 185
    Croft Estate, succeeds to 169–75
    environmental concerns 171, 174, 175, 191
    farming concerns 109, 120, 172–5
    housing concerns 109, 120, 122, 142
    public office 24, 172
    Village Hall 35, 199, 201

Chequers Inn, Dalton 86

Chilton, George **68**

Christadelphian Hall, Hurworth Place 22–3, 200

church *see* St Peter's Church

Church Commissioners 47, 124, 126–7, 128

Church of England 21, 37–8, 124
    *see also* Croft Church of England Primary School

Churchill, Winston 70

civil parishes 21

Clacher, Julie 28, 33, 42, 45, 216

Cleasby 21, 108, 176

Cleasby Grange 192

Clervaux Castle 10, 29–30, 78, 137–40, *137*, 146, 166, 188, 192

Clervaux family 20

Clervaux Trust 175

Cleveland 24, 25

Clow Beck spring 13, 15, 32, 33, 164, 179, 186, 187, *187*, 192

Coach House 124

Coates, Carol 103

Coates, David 76, *179*, 216

Coates, Herbert ('Bert') 23, 46, 48, 64, 75, 76, 177, 179, *179*, 180, 182, 207–8

Coates, Sue and Martyn 212, 217

Cockerton 162, 205

Cockleberry 49, 110–16, *111*, *113*, *114*, *115*, 203, 207, 214, 217

The Comet Hotel *22*, 91, 92, 183, 195, *204*, 223

conservation 145–7

Conyers, D'arcy 134

Conyers Falchion *17*, 18

Cooper, Jack 108

Cooper, Richard 127, 204

Cornwall 71–3

# Index

Coronation celebrations 195, 196, 206–8, *207, 208*
Corrie, Monkend **67**, 119
Cottam, Annie 59n4
council housing 107–9, 116, 118, 119
*Country Life* magazine 134–5, 136, 185
country sports 138, 150, 183–94
County Durham 9, 17, *17*, 18, 21, 24–5, 53, 59, 80, 87, 97, 168, 176, 188, 199
    *see also individual towns and villages*
County War Agricultural Executive Committees (CWAECs) 158–9
Creaking Tree Farm 82, **168**, *229*
Crisp, Mabel 40
Croft Aerodrome 6, 30, 78, 86–105, *88, 99, 130*, 152, 159–60, 192–3, *227*
Croft Beagles 183–5
Croft Bridge *8*, 15, 17–18, *17*, 19, 20, 21, *22*, 23, 37, *178*, 213, 225
    flooding 60n12, 177–9
    World War 2 75
Croft Church of England Primary School 37–48, 225
Croft Estate 20, 58, 87, 142, 169–75, 179, *220*
    buys Monkend 162, 164
    country sports 185, 187–8
    farms on 166–7, 169, 171, 172–3, 174–5, *230*
    land leases 35, 53, 201
    land sales 47, 53, 59, 109, 120, 122, 143–4, 162, 175, 185
    Sir Edmund sells Estate to Alfred Henry Chaytor 138, 169, 171
Croft Hall 28, **66**, **68**, 120, 137, 139, 150, 170, 173
Croft House, Hurworth Place 54
Croft Mill 21, **68**, 94, 121–3, *121, 122*, 163–4, 194n6, 198, 225, *230*
    flooding 177, 179, *181*
Croft Millennium Book 5, 80
Croft Parish 21–2, 26, 37, 87, 146–7, 157–8, 202
    *see also* Parish Council
Croft Residents Association 47–8, 145
Croft Rural District Council (RDC) *see* Rural District Council (RDC)
Croft School 37–48, 49, 127–8, *127*, 139, 140, 156–7, 216
    corporal punishment 42, 43, 44–5
    evacuees 62, 65, **65**, 66, 67
    School Management Committee 13, 37, 42, 45, 46
'Croft Spa' as name of village 19, 21–3, 140–4
Croft Spa Hotel 9–11, 20, 21, 43, *72*, 106n26, 133, 141, *178*, 195–9, *196*, 211, 225
    advertisements for 24, *197*
    country sports 192, 199
    garage business 15n8, 31, 49
    royal celebrations 195, 196, 206, *207*, 208, 209
    swimming pool *72, 197*, 198, *198*
    World War 2 74, 79, 91, 92
Croft Spa railway station 20, 140, 156
Croft Village Development Plan 145–6
Crossman, Richard 182
Crown and Anchor pub, Dalton 86
cubs 33–4, 35
Cumbria 24
Curle, Alexander Ormiston 133
Curle, Eliza 131

Dalton 19–20, 21, 33, 88, 200, 206, 209, *226*
    Croft School 37, 39, 43, 49
    housing 113
    pub 30–1, 86
    residents 43, 71, 187, 216
    World War 2 62, 87–8, *98*, 101
    *see also* Townend Farm (*later* Village Farm)
Dalton Beck 86
Dalton Hall 187
Dalton, Reverend James 124
Darlington *17*, 46, 91, 133, 136, 168, 176, 182, 210, 215, 216, 217
    brewing 9, 195
    country sports 184, 185, 186, 192
    day trips to New Spa 141
    employment 115, 145, 151, 210
    hospitals 30, 74
    housing 115, 118, 139, 145–6, 147n6
    market 11, 151, 152, 162, 205, 225
    pollution 186

postal system 21, 22, 23
schools 39, 49–50, 57, 60n15
shopping 152, 205
social life for Croft residents 24, 92, 155–6
transport to 9, 24, 38, 92, 113, 140, 155–6, 205
World War 2 62, 74, 77, 80, 81, 92, 96
*Darlington & Stockton Times (D&S)* 11, 23, 25, 54, 62–4, 65, 73, 77, 135
Darlington Aero Club 102
Darlington Borough Council 25, 113, 147n6
Darlington Equitable Building Society 119, 167
Darlington Road *22*, 84, 140, 176, 177
Darlington Rural District Council 24, 25
Davison, John 187
Davison, Thomas 86
Day, Mrs E.M. 48
Death Duties 170
Dent, Sue 35, 36
Deuchars brewery 91, 195–6, *197*, 198–9
Dimmock, Harry 133, 168, 187, *188*
Dingle, Loris and Mary 9, 195, 223
Dinsdale 53, 54
Dishforth airfield 88
Dixon-Johnson family 53–4, 55, 56
Dobbs Hall Farm **158**, 167, 171, *230*
Dobson, Mr W 61–2, 67
Dodgson, Reverend Charles 18, 37, 53, 124
Dodgson, Charles Lutwidge (Lewis Carroll) 18, 53, 124, 126
Dodgson Trust 46
Domesday Book 19
Dorman, Sir Bedford 65
Dougill, Elizabeth ('Betty') 49, *50*, **68**
Dougill, Ian 19, 24, 28, 49–51, *50*, 52, 94–5, 102, 110, 164–5, 202, 216
World War 2 80, 83, 91, 94–5
Du Gay, Michael Joseph ('Captain Du Gay') 9, 195–6, 206
Duberley, George 53
Dugdale, Captain Thomas (MP) 11
Dundas Castle 131

Durham, Bishop of 17–18, *17*
Durham County Council 53, 180, 192–3
Durham Home Guard 75
Durley 119, 223

ecclesiastical parish of Croft 19–20
Eden, Stan 184, 185
Edinburgh 14, 54, 131, 132, 133
Edwards, Lionel 185
Eeles, Walter **65**, 67
electricity 30–1, 46, 64, 117, 122, 123, 150, *154*, 157, 173, 174
Elizabeth II, Queen 207–9, *207*, 210
Ellerton Abbey 64
Elvington airfield 97
English Heritage 122, 123
Environment Agency 179
Eryholme 21, 33, 37, 39, 49, 62, 93, 101, 108, 179, 209
estate management 166–75
European Community 161
evacuees 54, 55, 61–7, *63*, **65–6**

Falshaw, Tom **66**
The Farmers' Rights Association 159
farming 10, 60n17, 149–61, *151*, *153*, *155*, *156*, *159*, **160**, *161*, *175*
evacuees 62, 64
farm size 157, 160–1, 172–3, 174, *230*
housing for agricultural workers 14, 30–1, 107, 108, 109, *154*
National Farm Survey (1941) 60n21, 122, 150, 157, 160, 163
schooling 13, 48–9
wages 10–11, 150
World War 2 62, 64, 69, 76, 80–4, *82*, 87, 90, 157–9, **158**
Young Farmers' Club 30, *31*, 65
*see also* market gardens
Fell, George 12, 13, 38–9, 40, 41, 42, 43–4, *43*, 45, 51, 64
World War 2 62, **65**, 67

Fell, Jean 12, 40, *43*
Fell, John 43
Fell, Sarah **67**
field sports 138, 150, 183–94
fishing 32, 33, 183, 184, 185–7, *187*
Fletcher, Doreen 199–200
Fletcher, Paul 35, 173, 217
Fletcher, Ronald ('Skip') 33–4, *35*, 173, 174, 177, 199, 208, 209
flooding 9, 15, 47, 60n12, 164, 176–9, *181*, 185, 187
Flowers, Arthur 48
Food Control Committee 79–80
footpaths 33, 137, 179
forestry 153
fox hunting 183, 184, 185, 192 4
Framwellgate 53
Fraserburgh 110
Fyfe, David 13, 124
Fyfe, Louise 66

The Gable (*previously* Rose Villa), South Parade 5, 13, *13*, 15n9, 28, 128, 177, 210, 215, 223
gamekeepers 133, 139, 168, 187–8
Garrington, Henry **68**
Gateshead 57, 61, 62, 64, 65, 66, 67, 105n6
Geldard, Ralph 56, 58, **65**
Geneva Convention 81, 85
George V, King 195, 196, 206
George VI, King 196, 206
George Wimpey & Co 88
Gibbon, Barbara 35
Gibbon's garage 49
Gilling 59n4, *70*, 75–7, 81
Girsby 37, 39, 62, 94
Godfrey family 145, 179
Goosepool Farm 87, 102
Gotto family 71–3
Grainger, Edith 55
Grammar Schools 38, 49, 50
Grange Farm 171, 174, 175, *230*
The Grange (Hurworth Grange) 18, 19, 103, 200

Great North Road (now A167) 11, 17–18, 20, 141, 192
Great Smeaton Parish 21
Green family 35, 37
Green, Gladys 37, *165*, 191
Green, John Jnr 29, 40, 142, 163–4, *165*, 176–7, *191*, 216
Green, John Snr 37, *165*, 177, *191*
Green, Trevor 32, 44, 142, 191
Gregory, George Norris *129*, 134, 135–6
grouse 80, 183, 188–9, 191
guides 14, 35–6

Hall, William **65**, 67
Halnaby Estate 12–14, 22, 30, 48, 87, 131–7, 146, 166–9, 175, 196, *228*
 country sports 154, 183, 187, *188*
 sale of 133–4, 146, 154, 155, 157–8, 166–9, *167*, **168**, *228*, *229*
 *see also individual farms*
Halnaby Grange Farm 129, **168**, *229*
Halnaby Hall 10, *14*, 21, 81, 129, *129*, *130*, 132–7, 146, 150, 167, 169, 193
Halnaby township 19–20, 21, 38, **68**, 87, 156
Hardy, Stan 43
Harrison, Flight Lieutenant Reg 90, 91, 100, 217
Harrison, W. A 135
Harrogate 21, 102
Hartforth Grange 81
Hartlepool 9, 67, 141
Hatcher, Jane 123
Hauxwell, Wilfred and Elsie 120, 162
Hawthorn Towers, Seaham 55
Haynes, William **66**
Headon, Ada 11, *50*, 91, 210, 215
Headon, Charlie 5, 40, 109, *179*, 208, 209–12, *210*, *211*, 215
 childhood 27–8, 39, 43, 59n2, *63*, *69*
 World War 2 62, *63*, 66, *69*, 76–7, 91
Headon, Dave 76–7, 215
Headon, Jack 11, 28, 69, *69*, 108, 109, 217
Headon, Jim 11, *13*, 28, *69*, 76–7, 80, 215

Headon, Lawrence 11, **68**
Headon, Mary 177, 209
Hennessy, John 29, 32, 33–4, 36, 44, 216
Heseltine, Michael 123
Hesp, Tom **68**
High Schools 38, 39, 140
High Thorn **65**, **67**, 102, 119–20, 162
hind houses 150
Hinde, Ernest 9, 10–11, 195
hirings day 151
Hobsbawm, Eric 5
Hobson family 27, 28, 87, *151*, 154, *154*, **158**
Hodgson, Ernie 75
Hodgson, William 154
Holiday, Thomas **68**
Home Farm 81, 136, 146, 166, 167, 168, **168**, 169, 216, *229*
Home Guard 67, 68, 69, *69*, 70, *70*, 74, 75–7, *76*
Hooker, Joseph Dalton 124
Horne, Daisy and William **68**
Horseman, Margaret 19, 23, 32, 35, 36, 37, 92, 95, 142, 200, 216
Horton, Nicholas 127, 204
housing 21, 107–20, *117*, *118*, 127, 139, 145–6, 162
    council housing 107–9, 116, 118, 119
    Darlington 115, 118, 139, 145–6, 147n6
Hull 67, 91
Hume, George (*later* Cardinal Basil Hume) *188*
Hume, Madeline *188*
Hume, Sir William Errington 133, *188*
hunting 154, 183–5, 192–4
Hurworth Grange (The Grange) 18, 19, 103, 200
Hurworth House 137
Hurworth Hunt 192, 193
Hurworth parish 18, 37
Hurworth Place 18–19, 20, 21–3, *22*, 26, 28, 204, 206, 209
    churches 22–3, 37, 91
    flooding 176
    residents 18, 19, 54, 59n1, 71, 73, 75, 122, 215, 216, 217

    schools 37
    shopping *22*, 140, 205
    social life for Croft residents 200, 204
    World War 2 91, 92
Hurworth Road *22*, 140, 200, 205
Hurworth village 19, 23, 24, 27, 36, 37, 73, 109, 113, 122, *176*, 186, 217
    flooding 60n1, 176, 177
    medical services for Croft 10, 23, 28
    schools 37, 103
    weir 179, 180
    World War 2 84
Hutchinson, Mr 199

Ibbotson, Eric 39
Imperial Chemical Industries (ICI) 179–82
independent schools 37, 48, 49, 50, 67
Ingham, Molly 18, 44, 52, 57, 217
Ingham, Ralph 59
Inness family 12, **65**, **67**, 80, 118, *118*, 119–20, 162, 184
Ireland 131, 132
Iron Well 13

*Jabberwocky* (Carroll) 18
James Russel Trust 131
Jenkins, David *17*
Joad, Reverend SC 62, 64
John Laing & Son 88
Johnson, Agnes Harrison 53
Johnson, Cuthbert Greenwood (*later* Dixon-Johnson) 53
Joicey Road School, Gateshead 57
Jolby Farm 35, 83, 192
Jolby Lane 165, 192
Jolby Manor 192, *230*
Jolby Mill 121
Jolby township 19–20, 21
Jones, Inigo 134

Keeper's Cottage 187
Kellie-Smith, David 28, 51, 191, 201, 216

Kennedy, Alison (*née* Matthews) 29, 32–3, 36, 44–5, 209, 215

Kirk family 28, 48, 80, **158**, 166, 167, **168**, 215

Kirkbank POW Camp 81, 82

Kirknewton, Northumberland 54

Kirkwood, Gerald 122, 123, 179, *181*

Kirkwood, Nick 34, 122, 123, 198, 217

Kitson, Timothy (MP) 15n7, 24, 25

Laing, Rodney **68**

Land Army 67, 81, 158

Larcombe, Hugh 145

Law, Reverend Frederick Henry 124, 186

Lawn Cottage (The Stables) 73

Lazenby, Charles **66**, **68**

Le Roy, George Densel ('Ben') 94

Leases Hall, Bedale 132, 193, 215

Lee, Alice 56

Lewis Close 42, 109, 146

Lewis, Fred *101*

Lilley, Sally 32, 36, 44, 217

The Limes (*later* Woodbine Cottage) 11, 20, 38, **68**, 120, 156, 216, 223, 225

Lindboe, Johan 14, **68**, 133

Linden Court, Hurworth Place 122, 164

Linton-on-Ouse airfield 88

Lithuania 83, 85

Littleton, Reverend Arthur 126–7, 128, 200, 209

Liverton Mines 126

Lloyd, Chris 81, 205

Lodge Farm **158**, 166, 167, 168, **168**, 169, 175, *229*, *230*

London 20, 51, 72, 108, 110, 140, 216

Lough, William 86

Low Middleton 51

Luftwaffe 95, 97–8

Macmillan, Harold 86

Mahaddie, Hamish 101–2

Manfield civil parish 21, 108

market gardens 11, 21, 80, 109, 150, 157, 162–3

Andrew's 83, 162

Inness's 12, *118*, 162, 184

Stairmand's 29, 120, 162, 225

Titchmarsh's 102, 162

Marrett, Edward **66**

Marske, Swaledale 34

Mathewson, Janetta Fraser 60n14, 119

Matthews family 44–5, **67**, 128, 215

 *see also* Kennedy, Alison (*née* Matthews)

May, George 138

McKenzie, Janet (*née* Pearson) 20, 28, 36, 45, 103, 108–9, 204, 205, 216

McKernan, Arthur A 104, *104*

McQueen, Captain George Bliss 131

meadows 164–5

measles 56–7, 64, 157

medieval period 17–18, 27n2, 121, 177, 202

Metcalfe family 152, **158**

Metcalfe, Peter 28, 30–1, 39, 40, 42, 43–4, 87, 96, 152, 217

Meteor aircraft 102–5

Methodist Chapel, Hurworth Place 91

Middle Walmire Farm *155*, 174–5, *174*, *175*, *230*

Middlemiss, John *154*, 209

Middlemiss, T.W. 196

Middlesbrough 67, 73, 91, 110, 140, 176

Middleton, Bob 6, 86, 89–90, 95–6, *95*, 98–9, 100–1, 215

Middleton St George 24, 87, 89, 94, 96, *101*, 102–4

Middleton Tyas Road 33, 48, 137, 225

Middleton Tyas village 22, 24–5, 48, 81, 127, 166

midwives 28

Milbank family 14, 129, 132

Mill Race development 128, 146, 177, 191

Miller, Mr W 62

mills *see* Croft Mill; Jolby Mill; Riding Mill

mining 126, 138, 151

Ministry of Agriculture (MAF) 122, 150, 153, 157, 159

Ministry of Food 79, 80, 81, 158

Ministry of Health (MOH) 55, 61, 64, 66, 107–8, 110–11, 112

Minns, Mrs 38, 39, 156
Minns, Percy **68**
Minsteracres 55
mixed farming 153, 160
Monkend Bungalow (*aka* Appleton Cottage) *63*, 105n6, 124
Monkend Estate (not built) *117*, *118*
Monkend Farm 60n9, **65**, **67**, **158**, 162, 179, 200
Monkend Gardens (*now* Monkend House) **65**, *118*, 119, 120, 162, 223
Monkend Hall 21, 32, 37, 51, 73, 117, 119, 124, *163*, 207, 208, 217, 223, 225
    Church fete 204
    country sports 80, 190, *191*
    Croft School 46, 48
    dog breeding 190
    Green family 29, 32, 37, *165*, 190, *191*, 216, 217
    listed building 122, 123
    royal celebrations 206
    Women's Institute 77
    World War 2 **68**, *70*, 76, *76*
    Young Farmers' Club 30, 31
Monkend Stables **68**
Monkend Terrace 15, 20–1, **66**, **68**, 119, 128, 141, 146, 176, 179, 223
Monkend township 19–20, 21
Moor House Farm 166, **168**, *229*
The Moorings, South Parade 5, *13*, 15n9, 28, 177, 210, 215, 223
Mosley, George **66**
Mosley, Richard **68**
motor racing 102, 116, *230*
Musard, Enisan 19, 20
Myers family **168**
Mynarski, Pilot Officer Andrew *101*

NAAFI (Navy, Army and Air Force Institutes) 83, 94, 154
National Archives 77, 104, 110, 150
National Fire Service (NFS) 74, 79
National Health Service (NHS) 28, 111, 112
National Insurance 28
'National Savings' events 206–7
National Schools 37–8
The National Society for Promoting Religious Education 37–8
National Union of Agricultural Workers (NUAW) 107, 108
Nattress family *155*, *175*
Neasham village 24, 39, 179, 180, 186
Nettlefriend, Bob 19
New Spa bath-house *10*, 15n2, 20, 36, **66**, 141–4, *143*, *144*, 225
New Zealand 91, 170
Newbus Grange 137, 185
Newcastle 25, 61–2, 80, 87, 110, 120
Newtown 60n13, **68**, 166, 173, 187–8, 217
Newtown-Taylor, Colonel 157
Noelle, Captain 97
Normanhurst 119
North Cowton 48, 49, 75, 217
North Ferriby 132
North Lodge, Halnaby Hall 14, 15n11, **68**, 137, 147n19, *229*
North Riding 19, 24–5, 62, 64, 66–7, 105n5, 193
North Riding County Council 21, 23, 25, 65
North Riding County War Agricultural Executive Committee (CWAEC) 158–9
North Riding Division, Yorkshire County Council (NRCC) 64–5, 66, 74, 135, 145, 179–80
North Riding Education Committee 37, 46, 47, 49, 66, 157
North Walmire Farm 29, 59n6, 96, *130*, *155*, **158**, 175, *230*
North Yorkshire County Council 48, 172
Northallerton 24, 29, 135, 182
Northallerton Road 9, 11, 15n2, 36, 59n4, 60n8, 120, 162, 171, 173, 199, 205, 223
*Northern Echo* 58, 135, 145, 164, 180–2, 212n3
Northumberland 54, 80, 188, 217
Northumbrian River Authority (NRA) 177–8
Notton, Thomas **65**
nurses 28, 36, 49, 52, 56, 60n14, **68**, 210

Oakwood 18, 48, 53–4, **66**, 96, 225
    Oakwood House 52, 57, 58, 59, 225
    Oakwood Lodge 56, 58, 59, 225
Oakwood School 48, 52, 55–9, *58*, 207, 214
Oates, Albert Edward 119
Observer Corps 67, **67**, **68**, 77–9, *78*, 97
Old Spa bath-house 20, 141–3, *141*, 225
Old Spa Beck (*previously* Sunnebeck) 13
Old Spa Farm 10, 20, 108, 109, 141, 166, 225, *230*
Open Air School movement 56, 57, 59
otter hunting 183, 184–5, 192
Over Dinsdale 21, 54, 62
Oxneyfield Farm 84

Paradise Farm *31*, 38, **158**, 166, *230*
Parish Council 5, 41, 80, 128, 191
    Croft name change 23
    Croft School 47, 48
    flood schemes 177, 179
    housing 109
    royal celebrations 196, 206, 207, 208
    stalwart members 172, 211, 212
    Village Hall 200–1
    the weir 179–80
Park View (*aka* Stairmand's Cottage) 59n4, 120, 223
Parlour family 213, 217
    of Dobbs Hall Farm **158**
    of Monkend Hall 21
    of Village Farm 84
Parlour, Gladys (*née* Gotto) **68**, 71–2, *72*, 73, 74–5, 77, *189*, *206*
Parlour, Jane 81, 84, 216
Parlour, John 35, *230*
Parlour, Mary Elizabeth (*née* Nesom) 71
Parlour, Peter 30, 76, 84–5
Parlour, Tom 35, *230*
Parlour, Captain William ('Captain' or 'Will') 10, 24, 35, 36, 71–4, *72*, 128, 180, *189*, *190*, 191
    Air Raid Precautions 70, 73–4
    churchwarden 12, 126, 188
    District Councillor 73–4
    dogs *189*, 190, *190*, 191
    grouse moors 80, 103, 188
    Rural District Council 12, 108
    schools 46, 55, 188
    World War 1 71
    World War 2 55, 62, **68**, 70, 73–4, 79, 80–1
    Young Farmers' Club 30
Parlour, William (Captain William's father) 71, 73–4, 185, 223
Parochial Church Council 127, 147n17, 172
Parrington, Mr W.F. 56
Payne, Ernest **65**
Pear Tree Cottage **66**, 223
Pearson family *89*, 90, *93*, *100*, 108
Pearson, Albert and Alan 43, 44
Pearson, Bill 109
Pearson, Elizabeth 216
Pearson, Mr 173, 177, 209
Pease, Maurice **68**
Peat, Charles (MP) 184
Pelham-Burn, Charles Maitland 131, 133
Pelham-Burn, Kathleen (*later* Kathleen Moore, Countess of Drogheda) 131, 133
Pepperfield Farm 28, 30–1, 78, 79, 87, 96, 120, 152, **158**, 175, 217, *230*
Percival, Edgar 113
Percival, Nellie 113, 115
Percival, Peter 48, 49, 113, 114, *114*, 115, 217
pheasant shooting 183, 187, 188
Philip, Prince, Duke of Edinburgh 182
Phoney War 64
Picton 122, 163
Pilmore Cottages 84
Pincher, Chapman 92, 166, 180, 183–4, 186
Pinedell 120
Place family of Halnaby 20, 21
Plumtree Cottage/Plum Tree House 53, **68**
Polam Hall (school in Darlington) 36
pollution 33, 86, 179, 186
Pond House, Hurworth 73, 217
The Poplars (*aka* Bridge House) **66**, **68**, 120, *178*, 201, 223

Portobello Farm 30, *155*, **168**, *229*
postal system 19, 23
postcards 19, 22, *22*, 141, *144*
Prisoners of War (POWs) 81–6, *82*, 158
prostitution 91, 94

railway 9, 20, 92, 93, 108, 140, 156, 163, 199, 223
Raine, Annie 55, **66**
Raisbeck family 200, 223
Raper family **158**
rationing 61, 62, 74, 79–80, 107, 134, 158, 159
Raw, Richard 22, 205
Reading 168, **168**
Reason, Arthur **168**, 169
The Rectory 12–13, *12*, 48, 80, 121, 124–8, *127*, 146, 225
Rectory Cottages 13, **68**, 124
Red Cross 67, **68**, 93
Renton, David 112
requisitions 55, 87, 90, 159
Reynolds, Heather 36, 60n14
Reynolds, Reginald 60n14, **65**, **67**
Richmond 10, 15n7, 20, 24–5, 35, 44, 93, 140, 147n7, 177
    County Modern school 45, 47, 140
    Grammar School 50, 140
    High School 39, 48, 140
Richmond Road Plantation 169, *229*
Richmond Rural District Council 25, 86
Richmond Terrace 22, 97, 103, 125, 202, 223
Richmondshire District Council 41, 109, 128, 143, 145, 191
Riding Mill 55, 139, 183, 186
Riseborough, Arthur 10, 141
Riseborough, Mary 24, **66**, 141, 142
Robson, Drs Mark and Eva 28
Robson, Robert 86
Rockcliffe Farm 18, 97
Rose Cottage 223, 225
Rose Villa Farm 116

Rose Villa (*later* The Gable), South Parade 5, 13, *13*, 15n9, 28, 128, 177, 210, 215, 223
'Rosedale,' South Parade 119
Rotherham 46
Roxburgh Hotel, Edinburgh 132
Royal Air Force (RAF) 69, *69*, 77, 86–105, *103*, *104*, *130*
Royal Canadian Air Force (RCAF) 86–102, *88*, *89*, *90*, *95*, *98*, *99*, *100*, *101*, 215, 217
Rufus, Alan, Count of Brittany 19, 20
Rural District Council (RDC) 12, 21, 71, 102, 145, 171, 198, *220*
    abolished 145
    Halnaby Hall demolition 134, 135
    housing 107–8, 110–11, 112, 115, 116, 117, *117*, 119, 120, 139, 145
    local boundaries 24–5
    Oakwood School 55, 56, 58
    weir 179–80
    World War 2 54, 61, 64, 67, 68–9, 74, 77, 80, 81, 86
Russel, James 131, 154

Saunders, George **68**
Schmidt, Feldwebel Gunter 98
Schoolhouse 12, 39, 43, 45, 46, **65**, **67**, 223
Schoolmaster's House 11–12, 223
schools
    Barton School 37, 48–9, 67
    Darlington 39, 49–50, 57, 60n15
    Oakwood School 48, 52, 55–9, *58*, 207, 214
    old school 11–13, *13*, 37–8, 46–8, 127–8, *127*, 177, 200
    Richmond 39, 45, 47, 48, 50, 140
    school leaving age 28, 38, 45, 47
    *see also* Croft Church of England Primary School
Schools Gardening Movement 40
Scott-Harden, Anthony and Daphne (*née* Arnett) 73
Scout Hut 35, 145, 199, 200, 201
scouts 33–5, *34*, *35*, 199–200, 202
Seaham 55, 110
Secondary Moderns 38, 103
sewerage 117, 122, 186

# Index

Sharnberry English Setters 190, *190*
Sharp, Ernest 136, **168**, 169
Sharp, Miss G 41
Sheffield 46, 140
Shirley Cottage 119, 223
shooting 14, 51, 154, *171*, 183–4, 185, 187–91, *188*, *191*
shopping 22, 80, 113, 152, 204–5, *204*
Silvertop family 55
Simpson family 108
Simpson, Samuel George 10, *230*
Skeeby 24–5
Skerne, River 15, 32, 176, 179, 186, 223
Smith family 12
Smith, Bill 145, 199
Smith, Cliff 206
Smith, Reverend John W 53
Smith, Margarete 15n11
Smith, Maria Grey 53–4
Smith, Mary C **68**
Smith, Walter **68**
Smythe, Patrick Cecil 133
Sockburn Worm 18
South Africa 126, 204, 217
South Parade (SP) 15, 20–1, 36, 37, 47–8, *118*, 119, 141, 162, 216
    The Anchorage 36, **65**, **67**, 119, 223
    flooding 176, *176*, 177, 179
    The Gable (*previously* Rose Villa) 5, 13, *13*, 15n9, 28, 128, 177, 210, 215, 223
    The Moorings 5, *13*, 15n9, 28, 177, 210, 215, 223
    number 1 12, **68**, *118*, 217
    number 2 11, 19, 27–8, *50*, **68**, *69*, 76, 209, 215, 216
    number 4 47–8
    number 5 28, 51, **68**, 216
    number 7 **66**, 179
    number 8 29, 32, 216
    number 9 **65**
    number 10 48
    number 12 **65**
    number 13 **66**
    number 17 73
    Sunnybrae **68**, 119
    Tarlogie **68**
    World War 2 **65**–**6**, **68**, 75, 76
South Shields 119, 138
South Terrace 20, 21, 165, 223
Soviet Union 79, 84–6
Spa Beck 9, 20, 184, 225
Spa Cottages 97, 143–4, *144*, 173, 217, 225
Spa Hotel *see* Croft Spa Hotel
Spa Road Cottage 173
spa trade 10, 20, 21, 141, 150
    *see also* New Spa bath-house; Old Spa bath-house
Spa Woods 21, 57, 173
Special Constables 67, **67**, **68**
Spennithorne Hall 137–8
squatters' camp 102, 110–16
St Kitts **65**, 119, 223
St Mary's Abbey, York 20, 21
St Peter's Church 14, *16*, 36, 37, 46, 73, 102, 126, 128, 129, 139, 176, 202–4, *211*, 213, *218*, 225
    churchwardens 12, 126, 127, 188
    community celebrations *34*, *156*, 157, 202–4, 206, 207, 209
    early history 18, 20, 21, 201
    Rogation Sunday *156*, 157
    and the school 36, 37–8, 47, 48, 200
    Sunday School 36, 202
    *see also* Parochial Church Council; The Rectory
St Peter's Churchyard 122, 124, 132, 133, 187, 213–14
St Thomas's Church, Cockleberry 114, 203
stables 11, **68**, 121, 124, 127, 169, 190, 223, *229*
The Stables (Lawn Cottage) 73
Stairmand family 59n4, 120, 162
Stairmand's Cottage (*aka* Park View) 59n4, 120, 223
Stairmand's market garden 29, 120, 162, 225
Standalone Farm 57, **158**, 166
Stapleton 19–21, 62, 75, 108, 119, 192, 200, 216, 225
Steggall, Edward **68**
Steggall, Frederick **66**
The Stell 13, 29

Stepping Stones 223
Stevenson, family 152
Still, Sally (*née* Arnett) 32, 36–7, 71, 73, 74, 217
Stockton 53, 60n14, 141, 176
Stoddard, John 188, 191
Stokesley 25
Strawberry Cottage 11, 59n4, 120, 223, 225, *230*
Strong, Roy *129*
Sunderland 9, 87, 91, 141, 151, 225
    Oakwood School 52, 55–9, *58*
    wartime evacuees from 61, 62, 64, 65, 66, 67
Sundern 29
Sunnybrae, South Parade **68**, 119
Swaledale 34, 64, 188
Sweet Well 13, 20
swimming 11, 32, 33
swimming pool 15n8, *72*, *197*, 198, *198*

Tarlogie, South Parade **68**
Taylor, James R **68**, 108
TB 57, 71
Tees, River 17, 19, 25, *178*, 209
    Croft Mill 33, 121, 123
    fishing 183, 185–7, *187*
    flooding 9, 15, 164, 176–82, *181*
    re-routed 33, 123, 186
    World War 2 75
Tees View, Hurworth Place 19, 27, 71, 96, *204*, 205, 216, 223
television 35, *43*, 208, 211
tennis 36, 72, 129, 134, 141, 142, *179*, 211, 225
The Terrace 15, 20, 21, 46, **68**, 103, *103*, 141, 146, *156*, 216, 223
Thew, George 86
Thompson, Henry **168**
Thompson, Mr W 56, 57
Thorneycroft 24, 119, 223
Thornton family 11, 59n4, 120, 173, 205
Thurlbeck family *31*, 38, **158**, 177
timber 86, 108, 134, 168, 173
Tindall, Dr and Mrs 5, 10, 28

Titchmarsh, John and Lilian 102, 120, 162
Todd, Alan 6, 83, 86, 87–8, 96, 97, 98
Todd, Jane Marian Rutherford 132
Todd, John (MP) 132
Tomalin-Reeves, Mrs A J 47–8
Tompkins, Reverend Harry 12, 13, 36, 93, 124, 202
Town, Betty (*née* Knight) *189*, 190, *190*, 191
Townend Farm (*later* Village Farm) 76, 84, 216
Turnbull & James bus garage 9
Turnbull family 39, 60n21, **158**, 166, 168, **168**, 169, 193
Turnbull, Isabella and Joe **65**

Ukraine/Ukrainians 84–6
United States of America (USA) 40, 56, 81, 85, 90

Valente, Natalie and Marcello 53, 59
Vaux, Angela 193–4
Veerman, Sandra (*née* Green) 29, 32, 35, 37, 44, 142, 165, *165*, 176–7, 190, 191, 217
Verne-Jones, Harold **65**, 67
Victorian period 12–13, 47, 146, 186
Village Farm (*previously* Townend Farm) 76, 84, 216
Village Hall 22–3, 35, 51, 145, 162, 195, 200–1, *201*, 211, 212
Vince Moor East Farm *88*, 93, 108, 216
Vince Moor West Farm 27, 62, 87, 90, 93, 154–5, *154*, **158**, 193, 216

Walker family 24, 25, *82*, 94, 153, *153*, 155–6, 166, **168**, 215
Walker, (Albert) Bert 81, *82*, 93–4, 96, 152–3, 155–6, *155*, *159*, 163, 167, 215
Walker, Brian 28, 30, 49, *161*
Walker, David 101–2, *101*, 216
Walmire 19–20, 87
Wardle, Leslie 59
Warnegate Products Ltd 136
water supplies 30, 31, 64, 86, 88, 90, 114, 122–3, 150, *154*, 157, 174, 180
Waterloo Farm 28, 30, 37, 48, *82*, **158**, 163, 166, 167, 168, **168**, 217, *229*

## Index

Waterside **68**, 71, 120, 171, 185, 223
Watson, Tom 184
Weardale 188, *189*, 190
Wearside 52
Weigh House **68**
weir, proposed 179–82, 186
West Lodges, Halnaby 48, *148*, 169, *229*
White-Samson, Mr & Mrs 199
Whitworth, Richard C. **67**
Whitworth, Robert 46
Wigley, Harold 45–6
Williamson family 53, 54
Wilshaw, Dr 64
Wilson family 15, 121, 163
Wilson, Colonel Joshua 132
Wilson, Thomas 46
Wilson-Todd family 10, 14–15, 87, 129, 131–3, 154, 168, 187, *188*, 193, 206
Winston (village) 14
Witton Castle 137, 138
Women's Institute (WI) 65, 74–5, 77, *206*
Women's Royal Army Corps (WRAC) 79
Women's Voluntary Service (WVS, *later* WRVS) 62, 67, 77, 113
Wood, Lisa 33
Wood, Mike and Cath 128, 140, 143–4, 199–200, 205, 209, 215, 217
Woodbine Cottage (*earlier* The Limes) 11, 20, 38, **68**, 120, 156, 216, 223, 225
woodland 13, 134, 166, 168, 173, 174, *230*
World War 1 14, 54, 69, 71, 72, 73, 81, 139, 174
World War 2 29, 43, 51, 54, 55, 60n7, 61–106, *107*, 146, 198, 206–7
 *see also* aerodrome; evacuees
Worsley, Colonel Sir William *70*, *76*
Worth, Frank 134
Wright family **168**
Wrightson, Mr 208, 209
Wrightson, Tom 172, 174
Wyvill, Marmaduke 133

Yeolmbridge House, near Launceston, Cornwall 72–3
York 20, 21, 29, 135, 215
York, Archbishop of 17
York Minster 17, 102
Yorkshire 24, 80, 102, 168
 boundaries 17, 24–5
 World War 2 88
Young Farmers' Club 30, *31*, 65
Young, Peter 5
Young Wives Club 202, *203*

Zelasko, Mrs 13
Zetland Hunt 192–3

# Croft's Crossing

A North Yorkshire parish
in the mid-twentieth century